AFRO AMERICANA: A COMPREHENSIVE BIBLIOGRAPHY OF RESOURCE MATERIALS IN THE OHIO STATE UNIVERSITY LIBRARIES BY OR ABOUT BLACK AMERICANS

Mary Dawson Walters

compiler

Office of Educational Services
The Ohio State University Libraries
Columbus, Ohio
1969

FOREWORD

This timely bibliography of resource materials by or about Black Americans held in the collections of The Ohio State University Libraries was in demand even before it was published. In the spring of this year the compiler of the current bibliography, Professor Mary D. Walters of the Acquisition Department of the University Libraries, edited a shorter bibliography in connection with "Black History Week" which contained something over 400 titles and was restricted to black history. This greatly enlarged work contains over 3,000 titles, including those in the first work, and covers the entire range of human endeavor.

The scope of the collection can be further illustrated by the inclusion in the bibliography of quite early materials such as Samuel Stanhope Smith's **An Essay on the Causes of the Variety of Complexion and Figure in the Human Race,** 1788 and William Cooper Nell's **The Colored Patriots of the American Revolution ...,** 1885 as contrasted to very recent publications such as Sonny Decker's **The Empty Spoon,** 1969 and Merton Coulter's **Negro Legislators in Georgia During the Reconstruction,** 1968.

Ohio State has a good representative collection of Black materials, many in first editions, of the slavery and reconstruction periods which were acquired as published over the years. For some unexplained reason, Ohio State did not acquire Black literature systematically from 1955 to 1960 and is now trying to obtain it before it becomes critically scarce. The really big boom in the publication of Black materials began shortly after the 1954 Supreme Court school decision and the beginning in 1960 of the Civil Rights protest movement.

The stock of the previous compilation dealing only with black history was quickly exhausted. Hopefully the present work will meet the need for a reasonable period of time. Writers, publishers, people in academia and others are slowly beginning to recognize the contribution of Black Americans to literature and to all phases of American life. Librarians have a heavy responsibility to acquire as rapidly as possible library materials which relate to these contributions, and writers and historians have an even greater responsibility to write about and chronicle Negro contributions. In this way we can begin to present a clearer and more accurate picture of the history of this country and the great contributions which all Americans have made to its progress. In time the artificial distinctions between white, brown, black and yellow will disappear as meaningless.

Based upon the number of courses in Black Studies now available at Ohio State and with others in the offing, and the demands for this bibliography even before it is published, I have every reason to believe that it will fill an urgent need at The Ohio State University among students, faculty, and administration and hopefully will be of value in other institutions.

The items in the bibliography are available under the usual inter-library loan conditions and by photocopy.

Lewis C. Branscomb
Director of Libraries
The Ohio State University

August 1969

CONTENTS

DEDICATED

To my son Bob, and
to my grandchild Candace
who are my inspiration

INTRODUCTION

It was not until this research was begun was it realized how difficult it must be for the scholar, unfamiliar with many of the technical aspects of library records, to find useful resource materials on the study of Black Americans. Although there are many bibliographies available which list the author and title of helpful materials, there are times when the item needed cannot be found. Those sources which were useful in the compilation of this work are found in the bibliographic section. It is hoped that the use of this bibliography of resource materials by or about Black Americans saves the researcher time which may be used in his quest for the knowledge he seeks.

The titles included are not restricted to literature written by Black authors but include materials which relate to the study of Black Americans, if the author has involved them in a significant manner. Some examples of inclusions are: Gunnar Myrdal, a Swedish economist and sociologist, has written extensively on the problems of Black Americans; and Phillis Wheatley, though born in Africa and was brought to America as a slave, has likewise made outstanding contributions to the literary field. Pertinent resource literature which treats the problem of jobs, housing, discrimination, education, history, etc. is found here. Restrictions have, however, been placed on the scope of materials in that they relate only to Black Americans — Black Africans are excluded. Some may disagree with many of the authors here, but nevertheless their presentation represent various points of view and cast light on several aspects of problems peculiar to the American culture. No attempts have been made to correct any inconsistencies which exist in capitalization of words in titles, particularly in the use of "Negro"; all have been listed as they appear in the records of The Ohio State University Libraries, to show the views prevalent at the time of publication.

Each title, except the section on "Recently Acquired," shows the classification, location and various editions. If the title is only in The Ohio State University Main Library, the location has been omitted; however, if simultaneously the title is in any other campus library, both locations are given. Unpublished theses are not included.

Arriving too late to be included but deserving note is the "Afro-American Laboratory" in the Education Library at Ohio State. These resources include books, films, filmstrips, portraits, records, and artifacts relating to the Afro-American in North America.

"The purpose of this Laboratory is to illustrate and correct the historical distortions, omissions, and myths giving rise to pervasive racism in American society .... It helps develop selectivity and sensitivity toward choice of direction in the values that should be." The grade level ranges from elementary to adult and serves primarily the teacher education program of the College of Education but is available to any interested scholar.

Finally, appreciations are expressed to the following Elsetta Williams, Baiba Vilums, Anita Chris Lingard, Nancy Randall, Susan B. Lummanick and Sallie Lemczik, who worked tirelessly in the compilation of the work. I am likewise indebted to the library administration for granting research time to assemble these materials. I accept full responsibility for any omissions.

M. D. W.

PSYCHOLOGY

Allport, Gordon Willard
The nature of prejudice. Cambridge, Massachusetts: Addison-Wesley, 1954
BF575 P9 A5 (Main, Social Work, Education)

Another edition.
BF575 P9 1954a (Undergraduate)

Pattern and growth in personality. New York: Holt (1965, c1961)
BF698 A437 (Undergraduate, Social Work, Education, Main)

Bettelheim, Bruno
Overcoming prejudice. . . . Chicago: Science Research Associates, c1953
BF575 P9 B4 (Education)

Bloom, Benjamin Samuel
Stability and change in human characteristics. New York: Wiley (1965), c1964)
BF831 B64 (Main, Home Economics, Health Center, Education)

Bruce, Myrtle Heisen
Factors affecting intelligence test performance of whites and Negroes in the rural South. New York, 1940
BF21 A6 no. 252

Chicago Urban League
A staff report on "A scientist's report on race differences," by Frank C. J. McGurk. Chicago Urban League, Research Department, Chicago, 1956
BF432 N5 M318 C5 (Social Work)

Clark, Kenneth Bancroft
Prejudice and your child. Boston: Beacon Press (c1955)
BF723 R3 C5 (Social Work)

Crane, Albert Loyal
Race differences in inhibition. New York, 1923
BF21 A6 no. 63 (Education)

Criswell, Mrs. Juan (Henning)
A sociometric study of race cleavage in the classroom. New York, 1939
BF21 A6 no. 235 (Education)

Ferguson, George Oscar
The psychology of the Negro. New York: The Science Press (1916)
BF21 A6 vol. 36 (Education)

Goodlett, Carlton Benjamin
The mental abilities of twenty-nine deaf and partially deaf Negro children. (Charleston, West Virginia: Jarrett, 1940)
BF432 N5 G6

Goodman, Mary Ellen
Race awareness in young children. Cambridge, Massachusetts: Addison-Wesley, 1952
BF723 R3 G6 (Education, Social Work, Main)

Hirsh, Selma G
Fear and prejudice. (1st edition New York: Public Affairs Committee, 1957)
BF575 P9 H49 (Main, Social Work, Education)

The fears men live by. (1st edition)
New York: Harper (c1955)
BF575 P9 H5 (Browsing Room)

Hunt, Joseph McVicker
Intelligence and experience. New York: Ronald (1961)
BF431 H93 (Education)

Another edition
BF431 H93 1961a (Health Center)

Jahoda, Marie
Race relations and mental health. (Paris) UNESCO (1960)
BF575 P9 J3 (Main, Social Work, Education)

Kahn, Lessing Anthony
The organization of attitudes toward the Negro as a function of education. Washington: American Psychological Association. (1952)
BF1 P99 vol. 65 no. 13 (Education)

Keith, Sir Arthur
The place of prejudice in modern civilization . . . . London: Williams & Norgate ltd., 1931
BF575 P9 K4

Kennedy, Wallace A
A follow-up normative study of Negro intelligence and achievement. Tallahassee: Florida State University, 1965
BF432 N5 K4 (Education)

Klineberg, Otto
Negro intelligence and selective
migration. New York: Columbia
University Press, 1935
BF432 N5 K64 (Education)

Race and psychology. Paris: UNESCO
(c1951)
BF731 K64

Another edition
BF731 K64 1951a (Social Work)

Race differences. New York and
London: Harper & Brothers, 1935
BF731 K65

Kluckhohn, Clyde, editor
Personality in nature, society and
culture. (1st edition) New York: Knopf,
1948
BF698 K56 (Main, Education, Social
Work)

Krech, David
Elements of psychology. (1st edition)
New York: Knopf, 1958
BF121 K77 (Education)

Littig, Lawrence William
A pilot study of personality factors re-
lated to occupational aspirations of
Negro college students. (Washington)
Howard University (1966?)
BF698 L77 (Education)

Lott, Albert J
Negro and white youth; a psychological
study in a border state community.
New York: Holt, Rinehart and Winston
(1963)
BF731 L6 (Social Work)

Mayo, Marion Jacob
The mental capacity of the American
Negro. New York: The Science Press
(1913)
BF21 A6 no. 28 (Education)

Osborne, Robert Travis
Racial difference in school achievement. Edinburgh: Mankind Quarterly,
1962
BF432 N5 O8

Pompilo, Peter T
The relationship between projection
and prejudice . . . . Catholic University of America Press, 1957
BF575 P9 P6 (Education)

Postman, Leo Joseph, editor
Psychology in the making; histories of
selected research problems. New York:
Knopf, 1962
BF81 P6 (Education)

Price, Joseph Saint Clair
The measurement of the intelligence of
the Negro. Institute, West Virginia:
West Virginia State College (1930)
BF432 N5 P7 (Education)

Saenger, Gerhart
The social psychology of prejudice ....
(1st edition) New York: Harper (1953)
BF575 P9 S3 (Education, Main)

Shuey, Audrey Mary
The testing of Negro intelligence.
Lynchburg, Virginia: J. P. Bell
Company (1958)
BF432 N5 S4 (Main, Education)

Another edition
BF432 N554 1966 (Education, Social
Work)

Society for the Psychological Study of
Social Issues
Readings in social psychology. 3rd
edition. New York: Holt, 1947
HM251 S72 (Main, Education, Social
Work)

Tyler, Leona Elizabeth
The psychology of human differences.
New York: Appleton-Century (1947)
BF697 T8 (Education)

Another edition
BF697 T8 1956 (Education, Health
Center)

Another edition
BF697 T8 1965 (Education, Undergraduate)

Willis, Larry Jordon
A comparative study of the reading
achievement of white and Negro chil-
dren. Nashville, Tennessee: George
Peabody College for Teachers, 1939
BF456 R2 W73 (Main, Education)

Wilner, Daniel M
Human relations in interracial housing. Minneapolis: University of Minneapolis Press (c1955)
BF636 W69 (Main, Education, Architecture)

RELIGION and RELIGIOUS SECTS

Abbott, Lyman
Henry Ward Beecher. Hartford, Connecticut: American Publishing Company (etc.) 1887
BX7260 B4 A42 1887

Bailey, Kenneth Kyle
Southern white Protestantism in the twentieth century. (1st edition) New York: Harper & Row (1964)
BR535 B3

Blyden, Edward Wilmot
Christianity, Islam and the Negro race. Edinburgh: University Press, 1967. (Reprint of 1887 edition)
DT4 B5 1887a

Brownlee, Fred Leslie
New day ascending. Boston: Pilgrim (1946)
BV2360 A52 B7

Campbell, Ernest Queener
Christians in racial crisis. Washington: Public Affairs Press (c1959)
BR560 L5 C3

Clark, Elmer Talmage
The small sects in America. Nashville, Tennessee: Cokesbury Press (c1937)
BR516 C59

Congar, Yves Marie Joseph
The Catholic Church and the race question. Paris: UNESCO (1953)
BR115 R12 C6

Cone, James H
Black theology and black power. New York: Seabury, 1969
BT734.2 C6

Coulter, Ellis Merton
When John Wesley preached in Georgia .... Savannah: Georgia Historical Society, 1925
BR555 G3 C8

Culver, Dwight W
Negro segregation in the Methodist Church. New Haven: Yale University Press, 1953
BX8382 A17 C8 1953

Daniel, William Andrew
The education of Negro ministers. New York: George H. Doran Company (c1925)
BV4080 D18

Davies, Alfred T., editor
The pulpit speaks on race. New York: Abingdon Press (1965)
BT734.2 D3

Dubois, William Edward Burghardt
The Negro church. Atlanta, Georgia: The Atlanta University Press, 1903
HT1521 A1 A8 no. 8

Fauset, Arthur Huff
. . . Black gods of the metropolis. Philadelphia, 1944
BR563 N4 F3 1944a

Another edition
BR563 N4 F3 1944b (Undergraduate)

Fichter, Joseph H
Social relations in the urban parish. (Chicago) University of Chicago Press (1956, c1954)
BV637 F5 (Main, Undergraduate)

Foley, Albert Sidney
God's men of color. New York: Farrar, Straus (c1955)
BX4670 F6

Frazier, Edward Franklin
The Negro church in America. New York: Schocken Books (1964, c1963)
BR563 N4 F7 (Main, History Graduate)

Fromm, Eric
Man for himself. New York: Holt (1964, c1947)
BJ45 F7 1947a (Main, Education)

Gillard, Rev. John Thomas
The Catholic Church and the American Negro. Baltimore: Saint Joseph's Society Press, 1929
BX1407 N4 G47

The Negro American. 4th edition (Cincinnati) Catholic Students' Mission Crusade (1948)
BX1407 N4 G5 1948 (Social Work)

Haynes, Leonard L
The Negro community within American
Protestantism, 1619-1844. Boston:
Christopher Publishing House (c1953)
BR563 N4 H3

Heard, William H
From slavery to the bishopric in the
A. M. E. Church. (Philadelphia, Pa.:
The A. M. E. Book Concern) 1924
BX8449 H4 A3

Herberg, Will
Protestant, Catholic, Jew; an essay in
American religious sociology. Garden
City, N. Y.: Doubleday (c1955)
BR525 H46 (Main, Education, Under-
graduate)

Hoshor, John
God in a Rolls Royce; the rise of
Father Divine, madman, menace or
Messiah. New York: Hillman-Curl, 1936
BX7350 H82

Hough, Joseph C
Black power and white Protestants.
New York: Oxford University Press,
1968
BT734.2 H6

Johnston, Ruby Funchess
The development of Negro religion.
New York: Philosophical Library
(c1954)
BR563 N4 J6

The religion of Negro Protestants....
New York: Philosophical Library
(c1956)
BR563 N4 J62

Lawton, Samuel Miller
The religious life of South Carolina
coastal and sea island Negroes. Nash-
ville, Tennessee: George Peabody
College for Teachers, 1939
BR563 N4 L42 1939 (Main, Education)

Lee, Robert, editor
Cities and churches: readings on the
urban church. Philadelphia:
Westminster (1962)
BV637 L4

Lenski, Gerhard
The religious factor; a sociological
study of religion's impact on politics,
economics, and family life. (1st
edition) Garden City, N. Y.: Doubleday, 1961
BL60 L4 (Social Work)

Another edition
BL60 L4 1963 (Undergraduate)

Loescher, Frank Samuel
The Protestant church and the Negro...
Philadelphia (University of Pennsyl-
vania Press) 1948
BR563 N4 L6 1948a

Lomax, Louis E
When the word is given. (1st edition)
Cleveland: World Publishing Co. (1963)
BP222 L6 (Main, Undergraduate)

Love, Emanuel King
History of the First African Baptist
church .... Savannah, Georgia: The
Morning news printing, 1888
BX6480 S45 F5

McNeill, Robert B
God wills us free: the ordeal of a
Southern minister. New York: Hill &
Wang (1965)
BX9225 M287 A3 (Browsing Room)

Mays, Benjamin Elijah
The Negro's church. New York:
Institute of Social and Religious
Research (c1933)
BR563 N4 M4

Another edition
BR563 N4 M4 1933a (Undergraduate)

Merton, Thomas
Seeds of destruction. New York:
Farrar, Straus and Giroux (1965,
c1964)
BT734.2 M4

Moellering, Ralph Luther
Christian conscience and Negro
emancipation. Philadelphia: Fortress
Press (1965)
BT734.2 M6

Myers, Gustavus
History of bigotry in the United States.
New York: Random (1943)
BR516 M99 (Main, Undergraduate)

Nelson, William Stuart, editor
The Christian way in race relations.
New York: Harper (1948)
BR115 R12 N4

Niebuhr, Helmut Richard
The social sources of denomination-
alism. New York: H. Holt & Co. (c1929)
BR115 S6 N6 (History Graduate)

Another edition
BR115 S6 N6 1929a

Another edition
BR115 S6 N6 1957a (Undergraduate)

Oldham, Joseph Houldsworth
Christianity and the race problem. New
York: George H. Doran Co. (c1921)
BR115 R12 O4

Another edition
BR115 R12 O4 1933 (Education)

Osborne, William Audley
The segregated covenant; race rela-
tions and American Catholics.
(New York) Herder and Herder (1967)
BT734.2 O8

Parker, Robert Allerton
The incredible messiah. Boston: Little,
Brown, 1937
BX7350 P24

Patrick, James Ruey
A study of ideals, intelligence and
achievements of negroes and whites.
(Athens, Georgia, 1926)
BF731 P31

Payne, Daniel Alexander
Recollections of seventy years. New
York: Arno Press, 1968
BX8449 P3 A3 1888a (Main, Under-
graduate)

Persons, Stow
American minds: a history of ideas.
New York: Holt (c1958)
B851 P4 (Main, History Graduate,
Education, Undergraduate, Mershon)

Powell, Adam Clayton
Against the tide; an autobiography ....
New York: R. R. Smith, 1938
BX6455 P63 A3

Keep the faith, baby! New York:
Trident Press, 1967
BX6452 P6

Ramsey, Paul
Christian ethics and the sit-in. New
York: Association Press (1961)
BT734.3 R3 (Browsing Room)

Reed, William J
Rome and the Negro .... (Louisville,
Ky.) Press of the Louisville anzeiger,
1907 (c1906)
BX4694 R4

Root, Robert
Progress against prejudice; the church
confronts the race problem. New York:
Friendship Press (c1957)
BR115 R12 R6

Russell, Jean
God's lost cause; a study of the
Church and the racial problem.
(London) S. C. M. Press (1968)
BT734.2 R8

Visser't Hooft, Willem Adolph
The ecumenical movement and the
radical problem. Paris: UNESCO (1954)
BR115 R12 V5

Washington, Booker T
Character building. New York: Double-
day, Page & Company, 1902
BJ1581 W3

Washington, Joseph R
Black religion; the Negro and Chris-
tianity in the United States. Boston:
Beacon Press (1964)
BR563 N4 W3

The politics of God. Boston: Beacon
Press (1967)
BR563 N4 W33

Wesley, Charles Harris
Richard Allen, apostle of freedom.
Washington, D. C.: The Associated
Publishers, Inc. (c1935)
BX8473 A4 W5

Williams, Ethel L
Biographical directory of Negro minis-
ters. New York: Scarecrow Press, 1965
BR563 N4 W5 (Reference)

Woodson, Carter Godwin
  The history of the Negro church.
  Washington, D. C.: The Associated
  Publishers (c1921)
  BR563 N4 W8

Year book of Negro churches, with
  statistics and records of achievements
  of Negroes in the United States...
  1935/36–1939/40. Wilberforce, Ohio:
  Printed at Wilberforce University
  (1940?)
  E185.7 Y39

HISTORY – GENERAL

Africa seen by American Negroes.
  (Paris) Présence africaine (1958)
  DT14 A35

American Sociological Society.
  Race and culture contacts. 1st edition.
  New York and London: McGraw-Hill
  Book Co., Inc., 1934
  CB197 R44

American Society of African Culture
  Pan-Africanism reconsidered.
  Berkeley: University of California
  Press, 1962
  DT30 A5

Davidson, Basil
  Black mother; the years of the African
  slave trade. Boston: Little, Brown
  (1961)
  DT352 D3 (Main, Undergraduate)

Banton, Michael P
  White and coloured .... New Brunswick,
  N. J.: Rutgers University Press, 1960
  (c1959)
  DA125 N4 B3

Bosworth, Allan R.
  America's concentration camps. New
  York: Norton (1967)
  D805 U5 B6 (Main, Undergraduate)

Braithwaite, William Stanky Beaumont,
  comp.
  Victory! celebrated by thirty-eight
  American poets .... Boston: Small,
  Maynard & Company (c1919)
  D526.2 B7 1919

Dowd, Jerome
  The Negro in American life. Student's
  edition. New York & London: Century
  Company (c1926)
  AH439 D74 (Main, Commerce)

DuBois, William Edward Burghardt
  Color and democracy: colonies and
  peace. New York: Harcourt, Brace and
  Company (1945)
  D816 D8

The world of Africa; an inquiry into
  the part which Africa has played in
  world history. New York: The Viking
  Press, 1947
  DT21 D8

Another edition
  DT21 D8 1965

Dykeman, Wilma
  Prophet of plenty; the first ninety
  years of W. D. Weatherford. (1st
  edition) Knoxville: University of
  Tennessee Press (1966)
  CT275 W38 D9

Fleming, Beatrice Jackson
  Distinguished Negroes abroad. Washington, D. C.: The Associated Publishers (1946)
  CT2750 A1 F5

Florida. State University, Tallahassee.
  Research Council.
  The Negro in American society. Talla-
  hassee: Florida State University,
  1958
  AS36 F57 no. 28

Hall, Leland
  Salah and his American. New York:
  A. A. Knopf, 1934
  DT310 H17

Hankins, Frank Hamilton
  The racial basis of civilization ....
  New York: Knopf, 1926
  CB195 H24 (Main, Social Work)

Johnson, James Weldon
  Along this way. New York: The Viking
  Press, 1933
  CT2750 J67 A2

Lejan, Francis
  Carolina chronicle, 1706-1717. Berkeley: University of California Press,
  1956
  D1 C2 vol. 53

Lomax, Louis E
  The reluctant African. (1st edition)
  New York: Harper (c1960)
  DT15 L6

Mes, G M
  Mr. white man, what now? Johannes-
  berg: Afrikaanse Pers-Boekhandel,
  1965
  CB427 M4

Mooney, Chase Curran
  Civil rights: retrospect and prospects.
  New York: Macmillan (c1961)
  D6 S52 no. 37 (Education)

Moton, Robert Russa
  Finding a way out: an autobiography.
  Garden City, N.Y.: Doubleday Page &
  Company, 1921
  CT275 M9 A2

Olbrich, Emil
  **The development of sentiment on
  Negro suffrage to 1860.** (Madison,
  Wisconsin) The University of Wis-
  consin, 1912
  D1 W81 vol. 3

Quinn, Edward G
  The sense of the sixties. New York:
  Free Press (1968)
  CB427 Q5

Radin, Paul
  The radical myth. New York: McGraw-
  Hill, 1934
  CB195 R12

**Remarks on the colonization of the
  western coast of Africa, by the free
  Negroes of the United States, and the
  subsequent civilization of Africa and
  suppression of the slave trade.** New
  York: W. L. Burroughs' Steam Power
  Press, 1850
  DT631 R38

Robinson, Wilhelmena S
  Historical Negro biographies. (1st
  edition) New York: Publishers Company (1967)
  DT18 R6 (Reference)

Rogers, Joel Augustus
  World's great men of color. (3rd edi-
  tion) New York (c1947-
  DT18 R63 1947 (Reference)

Scott, Emmett Jay
  **Scott's official history of the Ameri-
  can negro in the world war.** (Chicago:
  Homewood Press, c1919)
  D639 N4 S4

**This is our war, selected stories of six
  war correspondents who were sent over-
  seas by the Afro-American newspapers.**
  (Baltimore) The Afro-American Company, 1945
  D810 N4 T4

Wedlock, Lunabelle
  **The reaction of Negro publications and
  organizations to German anti-Semitism.**
  Washington, D. C.: The Graduate
  School, Howard University, 1942
  DS145 W39 (Main, Education)

White, Walter Francis
  A rising wind. Garden City, N. Y.:
  Doubleday, Doran & Company, Inc.,
  1945
  D810 N4 W5

Williams, Charles Halston
  Sidelights on negro soldiers. Boston:
  B. J. Brimmer Co., 1923
  D639 N4 W7

Wilson, Ruth (Danenhower)
  Jim Crow joins up. New York: Press of
  W. S. Clark (1944)
  D810 N4 W7

  Another edition
  D810 N4 W7 1945 (Social Work)

Wirth, Louis
  The ghetto. Chicago: University of
  Chicago Press (1928)
  DS123 W79 1956 (Main, Social Work)

  Another edition
  DS123 W79 1956a (Undergraduate)

Woodson, Carter Godwin
  The African background outlined, or
  Handbook for the study of the Negro.
  Washington, D. C.: the Association for
  the study of Negro life and history,
  inc. (c1936)
  DT3 W89

Wright, Richard
  Black power .... New York: Harper
  (c1954)
  DT511 W7 (Main, History Graduate)

HISTORY – ELEMENTS OF POPULATION RACE RELATIONS

American Assembly
  The population dilemma. Englewood
  Cliffs, N.J.: Prentice-Hall (1963)
  HB851 A4 (Main, Agriculture,
  Commerce)

  Another edition
  HB851 A4 1963a (Commerce, Social
  Work)

Adamic, Louis
  A nation of nations. New York and
  London: Harper & Brothers (1945)
  E184 A1 A17 (Main, Education)

Alland, Alexander
  American counterpoint. New York: The
  John Day Company (1943)
  E184 A1 A4

Anti-defamation League
  The treatment of minorities in second-
  ary school textbooks, by Lloyd Marcus.
  (New York, 1963, c1961)
  E184 A1 A55 (Education)

Barron, Milton Leon
  American minorities; a textbook of
  readings in intergroup relations. (1st
  edition) New York: Knopf, 1957
  E184 A1 B26 (Social Work, Main)

  Minorities in a changing world. New
  York: Knopf, 1967
  E184 A1 B27 (Main, Undergraduate)

Baruch, Dorothy (Walter)
  ... Glass house of prejudice. New
  York: W. Morrow & Company, 1946
  E184 A1 B29 (Main, Education, Social
  Work)

Berry, Brewton
  Almost white. New York: Macmillan
  (1963)
  E184 A1 B4 (Main, Browsing Room,
  Social Work)

Bogue, Donald Joseph
  Components of population change,
  1940-50:.... (Oxford, Ohio) Scripps
  Foundation for Research in Popula-
  tion Problems. (1957)
  HB3505 B58 (Agriculture)

  The population of the United States.
  Glencoe, Illinois: Free Press (c1959)
  HB3505 B6 (Commerce, Architecture,
  Social Work, Agriculture, Reference,
  Main, Physical Education - Women)

  Another edition
  HB915 A1 S3 no. 12

  Another edition
  HB915 A1 S3 no. 14

Brown, Francis James, editor
  One America, the history, contribu-
  tions, and present problems of our
  racial and national minorities ....
  Revised edition. New York: Prentice-
  Hall, Inc., 1945
  E184 A1 B79 1945 (Main, Education)

  Another edition
  E184 A1 B79 1952 (Reference, Main)

  Our racial and national minorities;
  their history, contributions, and pres-
  ent problems. New York: Prentice-Hall,
  Inc., 1937
  E184 A1 B8 (Main, History Graduate,
  Social Work)

Buck, Pearl (Sydenstricker)
American argument. New York: J. Day
Company (1949)
E169.1 B92

Bureau for Intercultural Education,
New York.
**Problems of race and culture in Ameri-
can education.** no. 1-10, 1943-1954
(New York & London; Harper &
Brothers
E184 A1 S4 (Main, Education, Home
Economics)

Cheney, John Vance
Memorable American speeches.
Chicago: Lakeside Press, R. R.
Donnelley & Sons, 1907-1910 4 vols.
E173 C5

Race and nationality in American life.
(1st edition) Boston: Little, Brown
(c1957)
E184 A1 H28 (History Graduate, Social
Work)

Cole, Stewart Grant
Minorities and the American promise.
New York: Harper (1954)
E184 A1 S4 no. 10 (Education)

Conference on Discrimination and the
Law, University of Chicago, 1963.
Discrimination and the law. Chicago:
University of Chicago Press (1965)
E184 A1 C58 1963 (Social Work)

Cook, James Graham
The segregationists. (1st edition) New
York: Appleton-Century-Crofts (1962)
E184 A1 C6

Cooke, Jacob Ernest
Frederick Bancroft, historian. (1st edi-
tion) Norman: University of Oklahoma
Press (c1957)
E175.5 B18 C6

Degler, Carl N
Out of our past .... New York: Harper
(c1959)
E178 D4

Dexter, Harriet Harmon
What's right with race relations. (1st
edition) New York: Harper (1958)
E184 A1 D4

Du Bois, Rachel
**Build together Americans; adventures
in intercultural education for the secondary school.** New York, Philadelphia:
Hind, Hayden & Eldredge & Eldredge,
inc. (1945)
E184 A1 D8 (Education)

Eaton, Clement
The growth of Southern civilization.
New York: Harper (1961)
E173 N4 E3 (Main, History Graduate,
Undergraduate)

Eisenstadt, Murray
The Negro in American life. New York:
Oxford Book Co. (1968)
E184.6 E4

Eleazer, Robert Burns
Reason, religion, and race. New York:
Abingdon-Cokesbury (c1950)
E184 A1 E38 (Education)

**School books and racial antagonism, a
study of omissions and inclusions that
make for misunderstanding.** Atlanta,
Ga.: Executive Committee, Conference
on Education and Race Relations (1937)
E185.61 E38

**Understanding our neighbors, an edu-
cational approach to America's major
race problem.** Atlanta, Ga.: Conference
on Education and Race Relations
(1942)
E185.61 E384

Elliot, John H.
**Building bridges between groups that
differ in faith, race, culture.** (4th edi-
tion) New York: American Brotherhood
Commission on Religious Organiza-
tions, The National Conference of
Christians and Jews, 1948
E184 A1 E4 1948 (Social Work)

Epstein, Benjamin R
"Some of my best friends ...." New
York: Farrar, Straus & Cudahy (1962)
E184 J5 E6 (Main, Social Work,
Mershon, Undergraduate)

Fairchild, Henry Pratt
**Race and nationality as factors in
American life.** New York: Ronald Press
Company (1947)
E184 A1 F3 (Education, Main)

Forster, Arnold
The trouble-makers, an Anti-defamation League report. (1st edition) Garden City, N. Y.: Doubleday, 1952
E184 A1 F6 (Main, Journalism)

Race; the history of an idea in America. Dallas: Southern Methodist University Press, 1963
E184 A1 G6 (Main, Undergraduate)

Foster, Laurence
Negro-Indian relationships in the Southeast .... Philadelphia, 1935
E99 S28 F7

Gossett, Thomas F
Race; the history of an idea in America. Dallas: Southern Methodist University Press, 1963
E184 A1 G5 (Main, Undergraduate)

Habe, Hans
Der Tod in Texas; eine amerikanische Tragödie.... München: K. Desch (1964)
E169.02 H28

Handlin, Oscar
Children of the uprooted.... New York: G. Braziller (1966)
E184 A1 H22 (Main, Undergraduate)

Another edition
E184 A1 H28 1957a

Another edition
E184 A1 H28 1957b (Undergraduate)

The uprooted; the epic story of the great migrations that made the American people. (1st edition) Boston: Little, Brown, 1951
E184 A1 H3 (Browsing Room, Undergraduate, Social Work)

Harlan, Louis R
The Negro in American history. Washington, D. C.: American History Association (1965)
E175.1 H3 (History Graduate, Education)

Another edition
D6 S52 no. 61 (Education)

Hauser, Philip Morris
Population perspectives. New Brunswick: Rutgers University Press (1961, c1960)
HB3505 H3 (Main, Reference, Architecture)

Hawkins, Hugh, editor
Booker T. Washington and his critics: the problem of Negro leadership. Boston: Heath (1967, c1962)
E169.1 P72 H3 (Education)

Higham, John
Strangers in the land; patterns of American nativism 1860-1925. New Brunswick, N. J.: Rutgers University Press, 1955
E184 A1 H5 (History Graduate)

Another edition
E184 A1 H5 1963 (Undergraduate)

Institute for Religious and Social Studies, Jewish Theological Seminary of America
Discrimination and national welfare.... New York: Harper (1949)
E184 A1 I5 (Main, Social Work)

Unity and difference in American life, a series of addresses .... New York and London, published by Institute for Religious and Social Studies, Harper & Brothers (1947)
E184 A1 I6 (Main, Education, Social Work)

Julius Rosenwald fund
Directory of agencies in race relations, national, state, and local. Chicago, Illinois:Julius Rosenwald Fund, 1945
E184 A1 J9

Karelsen, Frank E
Human relations, a challenge to our public schools .... New York, 1947
E184 A1 K3 (Education)

Lee, Alfred McClung
Race riots aren't necessary. (New York) The Public Affairs Committee, Inc., c1945.
E184 A1 L4 (Main, Education, Social Work)

Lerner, Adolf R
The challenge of hate. (New York: F. F. F. Publishing, Inc., c1946)
E184 A1 L6

Locke, Alain LeRoy, editor
When peoples meet; a study in race and culture contracts. New York; Committee on workshops, Progressive education association (c1942)
CB5 L8 (Main, Education)

Mabley, Jack
Who's on first? Fair play for all Americans. (1st edition) New York: Public Affairs Committee, 1956
E184 A1 M12 (Main, Education, Social Work)

MacIver, Robert Morrison
The more perfect union; a program for the control of inter-group discrimination in the U.S. New York: Macmillan Co., 1948
E184 A1 M15 (Main, Social Work)

Mack, Raymond W
Patterns of minority relations. (New York: Anti-defamation League of B'nai B'rith, 1964)
E184 A1 M16 (Education)

McWilliams, Carey
Brothers under the skin. Boston: Little Brown & Co., 1943
E184 A1 M2 (Social Work)

Another edition
E184 A1 M2 1951

Race discrimination and the law. (New York) National Federation for Constitutional Liberties (1945)
E184 A1 M23 (Social Work)

Maningault, G
The United States unmasked. London: E. Stanford, 1879
E168 M27

Marcus, Lloyd
The treatment of minorities in secondary textbooks. New York: Anti-defamation League (1963, c1961)
E184 A1 A55

Marden, Charles Frederick
Minorities in American society. New York: American Book Co., (c1952)
E184 A1 M33 (Main, Undergraduate)

Another edition
E184 A1 M33 1962 (Undergraduate)

Mazyck, Walter H
George Washington and the Negro. Washington, D. C.: The Associated Publishers (c1932)
E312.17 M47

A monthly summary of events and trends in race relations. (Nashville) 1943-(No more published after vol. 5, no. 7/8, Apr./May, 1948)
E184 A1 M6

National Council of Women of the United States. Human Relations Committee
Intergroup relations in the United States. New York: (National Council of Women in the United States) 1959
E184 A1 N3 (Reference)

Odum, Howard Washington
American regionalism; a cultural-historical approach to national integration. New York: H. Holt & Company (c1938)
E179.5 O26

Pipkin, James Jefferson
The Negro in revelation, in history, and in citizenship. St. Louis, New York: N. D. Thompson Publishing Company (c1902)
E183.6 P5

Powdermaker, Hortense
Probing our prejudices. New York: Harper (c1944)
E184 A1 P6 (Agriculture)

Raab, Earl, ed.
American race relations today. New York: Doubleday, 1962
E184 A1 R28

Prejudice and society. (New York: Anti-Defamation League of B'nai B'rith, c1959)
E184 A1 R3

Roche, John Pearson
The quest for the dream; the development of civil rights and human relations in modern America. New York: Macmillan (1964, c1963)
E184 A1 R55 (Browsing Room, Main)

Rose, Arnold Marshall
America divided, minority group relations in the United States. (1st edition) New York: A. A. Knopf, 1948
E184 A1 R6

Race prejudice and discrimination.... (1st edition) New York: Knopf, 1951
E184 A1 R7 (Main, Education)

Rozwenc, Eugene C., ed.
Slavery as a cause of the Civil War.
Boston: Heath (c1949)
E169.1 P72 R66 (Undergraduate)

Another edition
E169.1 P7 vol. 5 (Commerce, Main)

Another edition
E169.1 P72 R66 1963 (Main, Undergraduate)

Schrieke, Bertram Johannes Otto
**Alien Americans; a study of race rela-
tions.** New York: The Viking Press,
1936
E184 A1 S3 (Main, Social Work)

Thompson, Edgar Tristram
**Race relations and the race problem, a
definition and an analysis.** Durham,
North Carolina: Duke University Press,
1939
E184 A1 T4 (Main, Social Work)

Thorpe, Earl Endris
Negro historians in the United States.
Baton Rouge, La.: Fraternal Press
(c1958)
E175 T5 (History Graduate)

U. S. Community Relations Service
Report. 1964/65- Washington: Govern-
ment Printing Office
E184 A1 U517 (Reference)

Vander Zanden, James Wilfrid
**American minority relations; the
sociology of race and ethnic groups.**
New York: Ronald Press Company
(1963)
E184 A1 V3 (Main, Education, Social
Work, Health Center)

Wagley, Charles
Minorities in the new world. New York:
Columbia University Press, 1958
E29 A1 W3 (Main, Mershon, Under-
graduate)

Williams, Robin Murphy
**Strangers next door; ethnic relations
in American communities.** Englewood
Cliffs, N. J.: Prentice-Hall (1964)
E184 A1 W47 (Agriculture, Social Work,
Main, Education)

The origins of segregation. Boston:
D. C. Heath (1968)
E169.1 P72 W5 (Main, Education)

Woodward, Comer Vann
Reunion and reaction. Boston: Little,
Brown (1951)
E681 W6 (History Graduate)

Another edition
E681 W6 1966 (Undergraduate)

Woofter, Thomas Jackson
**Races and ethnic groups in American
life.** New York and London: McGraw-
Hill Book Company, Inc., 1933
E184 A1 W6 (Main, History Graduate,
Education)

Young, Donald Ramsey
**American minority peoples; a study in
racial and cultural conflicts in the
U. S.** New York and London: Harper &
Brothers, 1932
E184 A1 Y68

Ziegler, Benjamin Munn, ed.
Desegregation and the Supreme Court.
Boston: Heath (c1958)
E169.1 P72 Z5 (Education)

HISTORY — SINCE EMANCIPATION

Adams, Julius J
**The challenge, a study in Negro lead-
ership.** New York: Mallet, 1949
E185.61 A3

Adams, Russell L
Great Negroes, past and present.
Chicago: Afro-American Publishing
Company (c1964)
E185.96 A4 1964 (Reference)

Adoff, Arnold, comp.
Black on black: commentaries by Negro Americans. New York: Macmillan (1968)
E185.5 A3 (Browsing Room)

Ahmann, Matthew H., ed.
The new Negro. Notre Dame, Indiana: Fides Publishing (1961)
E185.6 A35 1961a

Akademii Nauk SSSR. Institut etnografii Protiv rasizma. Moskva: Nauka, 1966
E185.61 A43

Allen, James Steward
The Negro question in the United States. New York: International Publishing (c1936)
E185.6 A42

Alvord, John Watson
Letters from the South, relating to the condition of freedmen, addressed to Major General O. O. Howard, commissioner Bureau of R., F., and A. L. Washington, D. C.: Howard University Press, 1870
E185.2 A4

American Academy of Political and Social Science, Philadelphia
The Negro protest. Special editor Arnold Rose. Philadelphia, 1965
E185.61 A45

American Association of University Women, Wilberforce (Ohio) Branch
Despite discrimination; some aspects of Negro life in the United States of America. (Wilberforce) 1949
E185.6 A45

Der Amerikanische Neger uber sich selbst.
Wien: Verlag neue Welt, 1952
D185.5 A5

Andrews, Robert McCants
John Merrick, a biographical sketch. (Durham, North Carolina: Press of the Seeman printery, c1920)
E185.97 M56 A5 (Commerce)

The Anglo-African magazine....
vol. 1-2, no. 1-3; Jan. 1859-Mar. 1860. (New York: T. Hamilton, 1859-60) New York: Arno Press & The New York Times, 1968
E185.5 A58 (Main, Undergraduate)

Aptheker, Herbert, ed.
A documentary of the Negro people in the United States. (1st edition) New York: Citadel Press (1951) 2 vols.
E185 A58 (History Graduate)

Another edition
E185 A58 1951b (Reference)

Another edition
E185.A58 1951c (Education)

Essays in the history of the American Negro. New York: International Publishing (1945)
E185 A6

To be free; studies in American Negro history. New York: International Publishing (1948)
E185 A63 (History Graduate)

Archer, William
Through Afro-America, an English reading of the race problem. New York and London: Chapman and Hall, Ltd., 1910
E185.61 A67

Armstrong, Nancy
The study of an attempt made in 1943 to abolish segregation of the races on common carriers in the state of Virginia. (Charlottesville) University of Virginia, 1950
E185.93 V8 A8

Association for the Study of Negro Life and History, Inc.
Annual report... Washington, D. C. (19—
E185.5 A8

Attwell, Ernest T
Public recreation and the colored neighborhood facilities. (n.p., 1938)
E185.93 O2 C7

Atwood, Jesse Howell
Thus be their destiny: the personality of the Negro youth in three communities. Washington, D. C.: American Commission on Education, 1941
E185.6 A88

Bailey, Harry A., ed
Negro politics in America. Columbus, Ohio: C. E. Merrill Books (1967)
E185.6 B3

Bailey, Thomas Pearce
Race orthodoxy in the South, and other aspects of the Negro question. New York: The Neale Publishing Company, 1914
E185.61 B14

Baker, Roy Stannard
Following the color line: American Negro citizenship in the progressive era. New York: Harper & Row (1964)
E185.61 B16 1964

Baldwin, James
The fire next time. New York: Dial Press, 1963
E185.61 B28 (Browsing Room, Undergraduate)

Nobody knows my name; more notes of a native son. New York: Dial Press, 1961
E185.61 B3 (Browsing Room, Social Work)

Notes of a native son. New York: Dial Press, 1963 (c1955)
E185.61 B33 1955 (Browsing Room, Social Work)

Barbour, Floyd B., comp.
The black power revolt; a collection of essays. Boston: P. Sargent (1968)
E185.615 B3 (Main, Education, Social Work)

Barton, Rebecca Chalmers
Witnesses for freedom. (1st edition) New York: Harper (1948)
E185.96 B3

Beam, Lura
He called them by the lightning: a teacher's odyssey in the Negro South, 1908-1919. Indianapolis: Bobbs-Merrill (1967)
E185.93 S8 B4

Becker, John Leonard
The Negro in American life.... Sponsored by the Council Against Intolerance in America.... New York: Messner, Inc. (1944)
E185.6* B39 (Main, Education)

Belfrage, Sally
Freedom summer. New York: Viking Press (1965)
E185.93 M6 B4 (Browsing Room, Undergraduate)

Bell, Juliet Ober
Interracial practices in community Y. W. C. A.'s; a study under the auspices of the commission to gather interracial experience.... New York: National Board, Y.W.C.A., 1944
E185.61 B4

Benners, Alfred H
Slavery and its results.... (Macon, Georgia: The J. W. Burke Company, c1923)
E185.6 B42

Bennett, Lerone
Before the Mayflower; a history of the Negro in America, 1619-1964. Revised edition, Chicago: Johnson Publishing Company, 1964
E185 B4 1964 (Browsing Room)

Another edition
E185 B4 1966 (Main, Undergraduate)

Black power, U. S. A., the human side of Reconstruction, 1867-1877. (1st edition) Chicago: Johnson Publishing Company, 1967
E185.2 B38

Confrontation: black and white.... Chicago: Johnson Publishing Company, 1965
E185 B42

The Negro mood, and other essays. Chicago: Johnson Publishing Company, 1964
E185.61 B43

Pioneers in protest. (1st edition) Chicago: Johnson Publishing Company, 1968
E185.96 B4

What manner of man; a biography of Martin Luther King, Jr. Chicago: Johnson Publishing Company, 1964
E185.97 K5 B4 (Browsing Room)

Bentley, George R
A history of the Freedmen's Bureau. Philadelphia: University of Pennsylvania, 1955
E185.2 B4 1955a (History Graduate)

Bernard, Jessie Shirley
Marriage and family among Negroes.
Englewood Cliffs, New Jersey:
Prentice-Hall (c1966)
E185.86 B4 (Main, Social Work)

Bicknell, Marguerite Elizabeth
**Guide to information about the Negro
and Negro-white adjustments....**
(Memphis: Brunner Printing Company)
1943
E185.61 B5

Billingsley, Andrew
Black families in white America.
Englewood Cliffs, New Jersey:
Prentice-Hall (1968)
E185.86 B5 (Social Work)

The Black American and the press.
(by) Armistead S. Pride (and others)
Edited by Jack Lyle. New York: L. A.
W. Richie Press (1968)
E185.615 B5 (Journalism, Under-
graduate)

Blair, Lewis H
**The prosperity of the south dependent
upon the elevation of the Negro.** Richmond, Virginia: Waddey, 1889
E185.61 B63

Bolte, Charles Guy
Our Negro veterans .... (New York:
Public Affairs Commission, Inc., 1947)
E185.6 B6 (Main, Education)

Bontemps, Arna Wendell
Anyplace but here .... New York: Hill
and Wang (1966)
E185.6 B72 1966

100 years of Negro freedom. New York:
Dodd, Mead, 1963 (c1961)
E185.6 B7 (Main, Undergraduate)

Story of the Negro. New York: A. A.
Knopf (1st edition) 1948
E29 N3 B6

Another edition
E29 N3 B6 1958

They seek a city. Garden City, New
York: Doran & Company, 1945
E185.6 B72

We have tomorrow. Boston: Houghton,
Mifflin Company, 1945
E185.96 B7 (Main, Education)

Booker, Simeon
Black man's America. Englewood
Cliffs, New Jersey: Prentice-Hall
(1964)
E185.6 B76 (Main, Undergraduate)

Botume, Elizabeth Hyde
First days amongst the contrabands.
New York: Arno Press, 1965
E185.93 S7 B6 1893a (Undergraduate,
Social Work)

Bowen, Joshua David
**The struggle within: race relations in
the United States.** (1st edition) New
York: Norton (1965)
E185.61 B64

Boyd, Malcolm
You can't kill the dream .... Richmond:
John Knox Press (1968)
E185.61 B65

Boyle, Sarah Patton
**The desegregated heart; a Virginian's
stand in time of transition.** New York:
Morrow, 1962 (i.e. 1963, c1962)
E185.61 B66 (Browsing Room)

Bratz, Howard, ed.
**Negro social and political thought,
1850-1920; representative texts.** New
York: Basic Books (1966)
E185 B735

Brawley, Benjamin Griffith
Negro builders and heroes. Chapel Hill:
The University of North Carolina
Press, 1937
E185.96 B82

The Negro genius. New York: Dodd,
Mead & Company, 1937
E185.82 B819

**The Negro in literature and art in the
United States.** New York: Duffield &
Company, 1918
E185.82 B82

A short history of the American Negro.
New York: Macmillan Company, 1913
E185 B7

Another edition
E185 B7 1919

**A social history of the American Negro
problem in the United States....** New
York: Macmillan Company, 1921
E185.61 B74

Breitman, George
Anti Negro prejudice; when it began,
when it will end. (New York) Pioneer
Publishing (1960)
E185 B72

The last year of Malcolm X. New York:
Merit Publishers (1967)
E185.97 L5 B7 (Main, Undergraduate)

Brink, William J
Black and white; a study of United
States racial attitudes today. New
York: Simon & Schuster (1967)
E185.615 B7 (Social Work)

The Negro revolution in America; what
Negroes want, why and how they are
fighting, whom they support, what
whites think of them and their demon-
strations .... New York: Simon &
Schuster, 1964 (c1963)
E185.61 B79

Broderick, Francis L
Negro protest thought in the twentieth
century. Indianapolis: Bobbs-Merrill
Company (c1965)
E185 B73 1965 (History Graduate,
Reference)

Another edition
E185 B73 1965a (Education)

W. E. B. DuBois, Negro leader in a
time of crisis. Stanford, California:
Stanford University Press, 1959
E185.97 D8 B7 (Main, Social Work)

Broom, Leonard
Transformation of the Negro American.
(1st edition) New York: Harper & Row
(1965)
E185.6 B8

Brotz, Howard, ed.
Negro social and political thought:
1850-1920. New York: Basic Books
(1966)
E185 B735

Brovchenkov, Anatolii E
Pochemu ne spalos' prezidentu?
Moskva: Gos. Izd-vo polit lit-ry, 1963
E185.61 B85

Brown, Claude
Manchild in the promised land. New
York: Macmillan (1967, c1965)
E185.97 B86 A3 (Main, Browsing Room,
Education, Social Work, Undergraduate)

Brown, Earl Louis
... The Negro and the war. (New York:
Public Affairs Committee, Inc.) 1942
E185.61 B87

Brown, H. Rap
Die nigger die; a political auto-
biography. New York: Dial Press (1969)
E185.97 B78 A3 (Browsing Room)

Brown, Ina Corinne
Race relations in a democracy. (1st
edition) New York: Harper (1949)
E185.61 B88 (Social Work)

The story of the American Negro ....
New York: Friendship Press (c1936)
E185.6 B87

Brown, William Montgomery
The crucial race question; or, Where
and how shall the color line be drawn..
2nd edition Little Rock, Arkansas:
The Arkansas Churchman's Publishing
Company, 1907
E185.61 B9 1907

Brown, William Wells
The Black man. 2nd edition. New York:
Johnson Reprint, 1969 (c1863)
E185.96 B84 1863a

My southern home: or The south and
its people. 3rd edition. Boston: A. G.
Brown & Company, 1882 (c1880)
E185 B74 1882

Buckmaster, Henrietta, psued.
Freedom bound. New York: Macmillan
(c1966, c1965)
E185.2 B9

Bulloch, Ralph W
In spite of handicaps; brief biographical sketches with discussion outlines
of outstanding Negroes now living who
are achieving distinction in various
lines of endeavor .... Freeport, N. Y.:
Books for Libraries Press (1968)
E185.96 B86 1927a

Bunche, Ralph J
... A world view of race .... Washington, D. C.: The Associates in Negro Folk Education, 1936
E185.61 B94

Buni, Andrew
The Negro in Virginia politics, 1902-1965. Charlottesville: University of Virginia Press (1967)
E185.93 V8 B86

Burgess, Margaret Elaine
Negro leadership in a southern city Chapel Hill: University of North Carolina Press (1962)
E185.61 B95

Burns, W. Haywood
The voices of Negro protest in America.... New York, London: Oxford University Press (c1963)
E185.61 B96

Butcher, Margaret Just
The Negro in American culture. (1st edition) Based on materials left by Alan Locke. New York: Knopf, 1956
E185.82 B89

Cable, George Washington
The Negro question; a selection of writings on civil rights in the South. Garden City, N.Y.: Doubleday, 1958
E185.61 C14

Another edition
E185.61 C14 1958 (Undergraduate)

The silent South, together with the freedman's case in equity and the convict lease system .... New York: C. Scribner's Sons, 1885
E185.61 C15

Another edition
E185.61 C15 1889 (Undergraduate)

Caldwell, Erskine
In search of Bisco. New York: Farrar, Straus & Giroux (1965)
E185.61 C155 (Main, Undergraduate, Browsing Room)

California. Department of Education.
The Negro in American history textbooks; a report. Sacramento, 1964
E185 C26 1964

California. University.
The Negro in American history textbooks .... Sacramento: California State Department of Education, 1964
E185.61 C157 1964

Calvin, Ira
The lost white race .... Brookline, Massachusetts: Countway-White Publishing (1945)
E185.61 C16

Cannon, Poppy
A gentle knight; my husband, Walter White. New York: Rinehart (1956)
E185.97 W6 C3

Canzoneri, Robert
"I do so politely," a voice for the South. Boston: Houghton Mifflin, 1965
E185.61 C2

Carawan, Guy
Ain't you got a right to the tree of life? New York: Simon and Schuster (c1966)
E185.93 S7 C3

Carmichael, Stokley
Black power; the politics of liberation in America. New York: Random House (1967)
E185.615 C3 (Browsing Room, Main, Social Work)

Carpenter, Marie Elizabeth (Ruffin)
The treatment of the Negro in American history school textbooks; a comparison of changing textbook content, 1826 to 1939.... (Menasha, Wis: George Banta Publishing Company, c1941)
E185 C29 1941a

Carter, Robert L
Equality. New York: Pantheon Books (1965)
E185.61 E6

Cayton, Horace
Black workers and the new unions. Chapel Hill: University of North Carolina Press, 1939
E185.8 C38 (Main, Commerce)

Center for Research in Marketing, Peekskill, N.Y.
The Negro population: 1965 estimate and 1970 projections. Peekskill, New York, 1966
E185 C4 (Reference)

Center for the Study of Democratic
Institutions.
Lyndon B. Johnson, Robert C. Weaver,
Joseph P. Lyford and John Cogley on
the Negro as an American. (Santa
Barbara, California, 1963)
E185.61 C4

Cherry, Gwendolyn
Portraits in color: the lives of colorful
Negro women. (1st edition) Patterson,
N. J.: Pageant (1962)
E185.96 C5

Chamberlain, Bernard Peyton
The Negro and crime in Virginia.
(Charlottesville) University of
Virginia, 1936
E185.93 V8 C44

Chambers, Bradford, comp.
Chronicles of Negro protest ....
New York: Parents' Magazine Press
(1968)
E185.61 C5 (Social Work)

Child, Lydia Maria
The freedmen's book. Boston: Ticknor
and Fields, 1865
E185.86 C47

Another edition
E185.86 C47 1865a (Undergraduate)

Clark, Kenneth Bancroft
The Negro protest; James Baldwin,
Malcolm X, Martin Luther King talk
with Kenneth B. Clark. Boston: Beacon
Press (1963)
E185.61 C55 (Main, Social Work, Under-
graduate)

The Negro student at integrated
colleges .... (New York) National
Scholarship Service & Fund for Negro
Students, 1963
E185.82 C5 (Education)

Clark, Mary T
Discrimination today; guidelines for
civil action.... New York: Hobbs,
Dorman (1966)
E185.61 C56

Clark, Septima (Poinsette)
Echo in my soul. (1st edition) New
York: Dutton, 1962
E185.97 C59 A3

Clarke, Jacquelyn Mary (Johnson)
These rights they seek; a comparison
of the goals and techniques of local
civil rights organizations. Washington,
D.C.: Public Affairs Press (1962)
E185.93 A3 C5

Clayton, Edward T
The Negro politician, his success and
failure. Chicago: Johnson Publishing
Company, 1964
E185.6 C6

Cleaver, Eldridge
Soul on ice. New York: McGraw-Hill
(c1968)
E185.87 C6 (Browsing Room, Main)

Cohn, David Lewis
God shakes creation. New York, Lon-
don: Harper & Brothers, 1935
E185.93 M6 C58

Where I was born and raised. Boston:
Houghton, Mifflin Company, 1948
E185.93 M6 C6 (Main, Undergraduate)

Coleman, Charles C
Patterns of race relations in the South.
New York: Exposition Press (1949)
E185.61 C6

Coles, Robert
Children of crisis: a study of courage
and fear. (1st edition) Boston: Little,
Brown (1967)
E185.61 C624 (Social Work, Under-
graduate)

The Color line series. no. 1- New York,
National Urban League (1933-
E185.8 A1 C6 (Commerce)

Another edition
E185.6 C7 1944

Commission on Interracial Cooperation.
America's tenth man; a brief summary
of the Negro's part in American history. (17th edition) Atlanta: Conference
on Education and Race Relations (1939)
E185.6 C7 1939

Conference in southern communities....
Atlanta, Georgia (c1921)
E185.61 C629

Conference on Education and Race Relations
Education for southern citizenship....
Atlanta, Georgia (1939)
E185.61 C7 1938

Southern opinion and race relations.
Atlanta, Georgia (1938)
E185.61 C63 1938

Population problems in the South, a brief supplement to the study of civics and American problems. Atlanta (1939)
E185.6 C75

2nd, Nashville, 1932
Education and racial adjustment....
Atlanta, Georgia: Executive Committee of the Conference (1932)
E185.61 C73 1932

Communism and the Negro revolution.
Richmond, Virginia: Patrick Henry Group (1964)
E185.61 C64

The Communist position on the Negro question.... (New York, 1935?)
E185.61 C65

Conference on Negro-Jewish Relations in the United States, New York, 1964
Negro-Jewish relations in the United States, papers and proceedings....
New York: Citadel Press, 1966
E185.61 C734 1964

Conference on Negro Land-Grant Colleges for Co-ordinating a Program of Cooperative Studies, Atlanta University
Report. 1st-2nd; 1943-44. Atlanta, Ga.
E185.6 C74 (Education)

Conference on the participation of the Negro in national defense. Normal and Agricultural Institute, Hampton, Va., 1940
Findings and principal addresses ...
November 25-26, 1940. (Hampton? 1940)
E185.5 C74

Conrad, Earl
The invention of the Negro. New York: P. S. Eriksson (c1966)
E185 C77 (Main, Social Work)

Jim Crow America. New York: Duell, Sloan & Pearce (1947)
E185.6 C76 (Main, Social Work)

Council for Democracy
The Negro in America; how we treat him and how we should. (New York, c1945)
E185.61 C737 (Social Work)

Council on Social Work Education
Racial tensions in a northern city; an evaluation of a community organization case record .... New York (1959, 1956)
E185.61 C74 (Social Work)

Cox, Oliver Cromwell
Sex ratio and marital status among Negroes. (Menasha, Wis., 1940)
E185.86 C87

Crawford, George Williamson
The Talladega manual of vocational guidance (The red book). (Talladege, Alabama) Published under the auspices and official censorship of the Board of Trustees of Talladega College (c1937)
E185.8 C7 (Education)

The Crisis: a record of the darker races.
New York: National Association for the Advancement of Colored People, 1912-
E185.5 C8

Cromwell, John W
The Negro in American history. New York: Johnson Reprint (c1914) 1968
E185 C87 1914a

Cronon, Edmund David
Black Moses .... Madison: University of Wisconsin Press, 1955
E185.97 G3 C7

Crow, John E
Discrimination, poverty, and the Negro.
Tucson: University of Arizona Press (1968)
E185.93 A6 C7

Crum, Mason
Gullah; Negro life in the Carolina Sea islands. Durham, North Carolina, Duke University Press, 1940
E185.93 S7 C9

Cruse, Harold
The crisis of the Negro intellectual.
New York: William Morrow & Company, 1967
E185.82 C7 (Browsing Room)

Cruse, Harold
Rebellion or revolution? New York: Morrow, 1968
E185 C9 (Social Work, Browsing Room, Undergraduate)

Dabbs, James McBride
The southern heritage. New York: Knopf, 1959 (c1958)
E185.61 D3

Dabney, Wendell P.
Maggie L. Walker ... the woman of her work. Cincinnati: The Dabney Publishers (1927)
E185.97 W28 D3

Daedalus. (Cambridge, Massachusetts)
The Negro American. Edited and with introductions by Talcott Parsons and Kenneth B. Clark, and with a foreword by Lyndon B. Johnson.... Boston: Houghton Mifflin, 1966
E185.6 D24

Dalflume, Richard M.
Desegregation of the United States Armed Forces.... (Columbia) University of Missouri Press, 1969
E185.63 D3

Dancy, John Campbell
Sand against the wind: the memoirs of J. C. Dancy. Detroit: Wayne State University Press, 1966
E185.97 D3 A3 (Browsing Room, Social Work)

Daniel, Bradford, ed.
Black, White and gray; twenty-one points of view on the race question. New York: Sheed & Ward (1964)
E185.61 D32 (Browsing Room)

Daridan, Jean
De Lincoln à Johnson, nois et blancs. Paris: Calmann-Levy (1965)
E185.6 D28

David, Jay, comp.
Growing up black. New York: Morrow, 1968
E185.96 D3 (Browsing Room)

Davie, Maurice Rea
Negroes in American society. New York: McGraw-Hill, 1949
E185.6 D3 (Main, Commerce)

Davis, Allison
Children of bondage; the personality development of Negro youth in the urban South. Washington, D. C.: American Council on Education, 1940 (Ann Arbor, Michigan: Edwards Brothers, 1950)
E185.86 D26 1950 (Education)

Davis, Edwin Adams
The barber of Natchez. Baton Rouge: Louisiana State University Press (c1954)
E185.97 J7 D3

Davis, John A
How management can integrate Negroes in war industries. (Albany?) New York State War Council, Committee on Discrimination in Employment, 1942
E185.8 D26 (Main, Commerce)

Davis, John Preston, ed
The American Negro reference book.... Englewood Cliffs, New Jersey: Prentice-Hall (1966)
E185 D3 (Reference, Undergraduate, Social Work)

Davis, Robert E
The American Negro's dilemma; the Negro's self-imposed predicament. New York: Philosophical Library (c1954)
E185.6 D35

Delany, Martin Robison
The condition, elevation, emigration, and destiny of the colored people of the United States. New York: Arno Press, 1968
E185.D4 1852a (Main, Undergraduate)

Dexter, Henry Martyn
What ought to be done with the freedmen and with the rebels? Boston: Nichols & Noyes, 1865
E185 2 D4

Dies, Jesse Walter
Jim Crow. Ann Arbor: Ann Arbor Publishing (1951)
E185.61 D4

Donald, Henderson Hamilton
The Negro freedman; life conditions of the American Negro in the early years after emancipation. New York: H. Schuman, 1952
E185.2 D6 (History Graduate)

Doyle, Bertram Wilbur
The etiquette of race relations in the
South.... Chicago: University of
Chicago Press (c1937)
E185.61 D75

Another edition
E185.61 D75 1934

A study of business and employment
among Negroes in Louisville. By
associates of Louisville Municipal
College, University of Louisville,
Louisville Urban League, Central
Colored High School. (Louisville, Ky.,
1944)
E185.93 K2 D6 (Main, Commerce)

Drake, St. Clair
Race relation in a time of rapid social
change; a report of a survey. New
York: National Federation of Settle-
ment and Neighborhood Centers (1966)
E185.615 D7 (Social Work)

Drimmer, Melvin, comp.
Black history; a reappraisal.... (1st
edition) Garden City, New Jersey:
Doubleday, 1968
E185 D7

Drotning, Phillip T.
Black heroes in our Nation's history; a
tribute to those who helped shaped
America. (1st edition) New York:
Crowles Book Co. (1969)
E185 D719 (Browsing Room)

A guide to Negro history in America.
Garden City, New York: Doubleday,
1968
E185 D72 (History Graduate)

Dubois, William Edward Burghardt
The autobiography of W. E. B. Dubois;
a soliloquy on viewing my life from the
last decades of its first century. (1st
edition. New York) International Publishers (1968)
E185.97 D8 A3

Dusk of dawn; an essay toward an autobiography of a race concept .... New
York: Harcourt, Brace & Company
(c1940)
E185.97 D8

The gift of black folk. New York: Johnson Reprint, 1968 (c1924)
E185 D8 1924a

The Philadelphia Negro .... Philadel-
phia, Pennsylvania: Published for the
University, 1899
E185.9 N3 D8

The soul of black folk; essays and
sketches .... 3rd edition Chicago: A.C.
McClurg & Company, 1903
E185.5 D8 1903b

Another edition
E185.5 D8 1911

Another edition
E185.5 D8 1920

Another edition
E185.5 D8 1953

Dunbar, Ernest
The black expatriates; a study of
American Negroes in exile. (1st
edition) New York: Dutton, 1968
E185.94 D8 (Main, Journalism, Brows-
ing Room)

Dunbar, Leslie W
A republic of equals. Ann Arbor: Uni-
versity of Michigan Press (1966)
E185.615 D8

Duncan, Hannibal Gerald
...The changing race relationship in
the border and northern states....
Philadelphia, 1922
E185.61 D8

Dykeman, Wilma
Neither black nor white.... New York:
Rinehart (1959, c1957)
E185.61 D9

Ebony.
vol. 1- Chicago: Negro Digest Publishing Company, Inc., 1945-
E185.5* E18

The Negro handbook. Chicago: Johnson Publishing Company, 1966
E185 E2 (Reference, Undergraduate)

White on black; the views of twenty-
two white Americans on the Negro.
Chicago: Johnson Publishing Co., 1963
E185.6 E2 (Browsing Room)

The white problem in America. Chicago: Johnson Publishing Company, 1966
E185.615 E2

Eckstein, Otto
Education, employment and Negro equality. (Washington) United States Department of Labor, Manpower Administration (1968)
E185.61 E34 (Main, Education)

Edmonds, Helen Grey
The Negro and fusion politics in North Carolina, 1894-1901. Chapel Hill: University of North Carolina Press (1951)
E185.93 N6 E4 (Main, History Graduate)

Edwards, Gilbert Franklin
The Negro professional class. Glencoe, Ill.: Free Press (c1959)
E185.82 E3 1959 (Main, Social Work)

Edwards, Paul Kenneth
The southern urban Negro as a consumer. New York: Prentice-Hall, Inc., 1932
E185.6 E26

Edwards, William James
Twenty-five years in the Black belt. Boston: The Cornhill Company (c1918)
E185.82 E32

Ehrmann, Bess Virginia (Hicks)
"Thenceforward and forever free." New York: Horizon House (c1945)
E185.96 E35

Eleazer, Robert Burns
Twelve million Negro Americans, their background progress and present day problems. (2nd edition) Atlanta, Ga.: Conference on Education and Race Relations (1942)
E185.6 E4 1942 (Social Work)

Ellison, Earl Jerome
These rights are ours to keep. (1st edition, New York: Public Affairs Committee, 1948)
E185.61 E47 (Education, Social Work)

Embree, Edwin Rogers
American Negroes, a handbook. New York: The John Day Company (1942)
E185.6 E53

Brown America; the story of a new race. New York: The Viking Press, 1931
E185.6 E54 (Main, Social Work)

Brown America, the story of a tenth of the nation. New York: The Viking Press, 1943
E185.6 E55

13 against the odds. New York: The Viking Press, 1944
E185.96 E53

Eppse, Merl R
A guide to the study of the Negro in American history.... Nashville, Tennessee: National Educational Publishing Company, Inc. (c1937)
E185 E63

Another edition
E185 E63 1943 (Reference)

The Negro, too, in American history. Nashville, Tennessee: National Educational Publishing Company, Inc., 1943
E185 E64

Equality (by) Robert Carter .... New York: Pantheon Books (1965)
E185.61 E6

Essien-Udom, Essien Udosen
Black nationalism; a search for identity in America. Chicago: University of Chicago Press (1962)
E185.61 E75 (Main, Social Work, Undergraduate)

Ethridge, Mark Foster
America' obligation to its Negro citizens.... Atlanta, Georgia: Conference on Education and Race Relations (1937)
E185.61 E84

Evans, Maurice Smethurst
Black and white in the Southern states, a study of the race problem in the United States from a South African point of view.... New York, London: Longmans, Green & Company, 1915
E185.61 E9

Evers, Mrs. Medgar
For us, the living. Garden City, New York: Doubleday (1967)
E185.97 E94 E9 (Browsing Room)

Facts on File, Inc., New York.
Civil rights, 1960-63; the Negro campaign to win equal rights and opportunities in the United States.... New York
(1964)
E185.61 F3 (Reference)

Fager, Charles E
White reflections on black power.
Grand Rapids: W. B. Eerdmans Pub-
lishing Company (1967)
E185.615 F3

Farmer, James
Freedom, when? New York: Random
House (c1965)
E185.61 F53

Fauset, Arthur
For freedom. Philadelphia: Franklin
Publishing & Supply Company (1934)
E185.96 F3 1934 (Main, Education)

Ferman, Louis A., ed.
Negroes and jobs; a book of readings...
Ann Arbor: University of Michigan
Press (1968)
E185.8 F4 (Commerce, Main, Social
Work)

Fishel, Leslie H
The Negro American; a documentary
history.... (Glenview, Illinois) Scott,
Foresman (1967)
E185 F5 (Education, Main)

Another edition
E185 F5 1967a

Flipper, Henry Ossian
Negro frontiersman. El Paso, Texas:
Texas Western College Press, 1963
E185.97 F5 A3 1963

Fontaine, William Thomas
Reflections on segregation, desegrega-
tion, power and morals. Springfield,
Illinois: Thomas (1967)
E185.615 F6

Ford, James W
The Negro and the democratic front.
New York: International Publishing
(c1938)
E185.6 F68

Fortune, Timothy Thomas
Black and white; land labor, and poli-
tics in the South. New York: Arno
Press, 1968
E185.61 F6 1884a (Undergraduate)

Foster, William Zebulon
The Negro people in American history.
New York: International Publishing
(c1954)
E185 F6

Another edition
E185 F6145

Franklin, John Hope
The free Negro in North Carolina.
Chapel Hill: University of North Car-
olina Press, 1943
E185.93 N6 F8 (Main, History
Graduate)

From slavery to freedom; a history of
American Negroes. (1st edition) New
York: A. A. Knopf, 1947
E185 F83 (Main, Social Work)

Another edition
E185 F83 1956 (History Graduate,
Undergraduate)

Another edition
E185 F83 1967 (History Graduate,
Education)

The Negro in twentieth century America; a reader on the struggle for civil
rights. New York: Vintage Books
(1967)
E185.61 F68 (Social Work)

Another edition
E185.61 F68 1967a

Negro youth at the crossways. Wash-
ington, D.C.: American Council of
Education, 1940
E185.6 F84 (Education, Main, Social
Work)

Another edition
E185.6 F84 1967 (Education)

Frazier, Edward Franklin
Black bourgeoisie. Glencoe, Illinois:
Free Press (c1957)
E185.61 F7 (Main, Social Work)

Another edition
E185.61 F7 1957a (Undergraduate)

The free Negro family .... Nashville,
Tennessee: Fisk University Press,
1932
E185 F85

Another edition
E185.86 F83 1932a (Main, Undergraduate)

The Negro family in the United States.
Chicago: University of Chicago Press
(1939)
E185.86 F84

Another edition
E185.86 F84 1948 (Main, Social Work)

Another edition
E185.86 F84 1966 (Main, Social Work)

Another edition
E185 F86 1957 (Social Work, Main,
Undergraduate)

The Negro in the United States. New
York: Macmillan Company 1949
E185 F86

**Negro youth at the crossways, their
personality development in the middle
states....** Washington, D.C.: American
Council on Education, 1940
E185.6 F84 (Main, Education)

Another edition
E185.6 F84 1967

On race relations: selected writings.
Chicago: University of Chicago Press,
1968
E185 F87

Freedom of Information Conference, 8th,
University of Missouri, 1965.
Race and the news media.... (New
York) Anti-Defamation League of B'nai
B'rith (c1967)
E185.61 F73 1965

Another edition
E185.61 F73 1965a (Main, Journalism)

Freedomways. A quarterly review of the
Negro freedom movement. vol. 1-
Spring 1961-   (New York)
E185.5 F7

Friedman, Leon, comp.
**The civil rights reader; basic docu-
ments of the civil rights movement.**
New York: Walker (1967)
E185.61 F75 (History Graduate, Jour-
nalism, Undergraduate)

Friends, Society of American Friends
Service Committee.
**Race and conscience in America; a re-
view prepared for American Friends
Service Committee** (by an authorized
working party. 1st edition) Norman:
University of Oklahoma Press (c1959)
E185.61 F8

Gallagher, Buell Gordon
American caste and the Negro college.
New York: Columbia University Press,
1938
E185.82 G16

Another edition
1966
E185.82 G16 1938a

**Color and conscience; the irresponsi-
ble conflict....** New York, London:
Harper & Brothers (1946)
E185.61 G16

Gannett, Henry
**Statistics of the Negroes in the United
States.** Baltimore: The Trustees, 1894
E185.89 S8 G3

Garfinkel, Herbert
**When Negroes march; the March on
Washington Movement in the organi-
zational politics for FEPC.** Glencoe,
Illinois: Free Press (c1959)
E185.61 G23 (Main, Social Work)

Garvey, Amy Jacques
Garvey and Garveyism. (Kingston,
Jamaica, c1963)
E185.97 G3 G3

Garvey, Marcus
**Philosophy and opinions of Marcus
Garvey.** New York: Arno Press, 1968
E185.97 G3 A3 1968 (Undergraduate)

George, Wesley Critz
The biology of the race problem.
(Richmond) Distributed by the National
Putnam Letters Committee, 1962
E185.61 G4

**Race, heredity, and civilization; human
progress and the race problem.** London:
Britons Publishing Society, 1964
E185 G44 1964

Gibbs, Mifflin Wistar
Shadow and light. New York: Arno
Press, 1968
E185.97 G5 1920a (Main, Under-
graduate)

Gibson, John William, ed.
**Progress of a race; or The remarkable
advancement of the American Negro,
from the bondage of slavery, ignorance
and poverty to the freedom of citizenship, intelligence, affluence, honor and
trust.** Revised and enlarged by J. L.
Nichols.... Naperville, Illinois: J. L.
Nichols & Company (c1920)
E185 G47 1920

Gilligan, Francis James
**The morality of the color line; an
examination of the right and wrong of
the discriminations against the Negro
in the United States.** Washington,
D. C.: Catholic University of America,
1928
E185.61 G5

Ginzberg, Eli
**The middle-class Negro in the white
man's world.** New York: Columbia
University Press, 1967
E185.82 G5

**The Negro challenge to the business
community.** New York: McGraw-Hill
(1964)
E185.8 G48 (Main, Commerce)

The Negro potential. New York:
Columbia University Press, 1956
E185.8 G5

Another edition
E185.8 G5 1956a (Education, Social
Work)

**The troublesome presence: American
democracy and the Negro.** (New York)
Free Press of Glencoe (1964)
E185 G5

Goff, Kenneth
Reds promote racial war. (Englewood,
Colorado, c1958)
E185.61 G55

Golden, Harry Lewis
Mr. Kennedy and the Negroes. (1st
edition) Cleveland: World Publishing
Company (1964)
E185.61 G58 (Rare Book Collection,
Browsing Room)

Goldstein, Naomi
**The roots of prejudice against the
Negro in the United States.** Boston:
Boston University Press, 1948
E185.61 G6 (Main, Education)

Goldston, Robert C
The Negro revolution.... New York:
Macmillan (1963)
E185 G6 (Browsing Room)

Goldwin, Robert Allen, ed.
100 years of emancipation.... Chicago:
Rand McNally (1964)
E185.61 G62 1964

Gordon, Asa H
**Sketches of Negro life and history in
South Carolina.** (n.p., W. B. Conkey
Company, c1929)
E185.93 S7 G6

Graham, Hugh Davis
**Crisis in print; desegregation and the
press in Tennessee.** (Nashville) Vanderbilt University Press (1967)
E185.93 T3 G7 (Journalism)

Grant, Joanne, comp.
**Black protest, history, documents, and
analyses, 1619 to the present ....**
(New York: Fawcett World Library,
1968)
E185 G7 (Journalism)

Green, Constance (McLaughlin)
**The secret city; a history of race re-
lations in the Nation's Capital.** Prince-
ton, New Jersey: Princeton University
Press, 1967
E185.93 D6 G7 (Main, Undergraduate)

Greene, Harry Washington
**Negro leaders; a study of educational
and social background factors of prominent Negroes whose life sketches are
carried in national directories.** Institute, West Virginia: West Virginia State
College (1936)
E185.82 G79

Greene, Lorenzo Johnston
The Negro wage earner. The Associa-
tion for the Study of Negro Life and
History, Inc. (c1930)
E185.8 G8

Gregory, Dick
The shadow that scares me. (1st edition) Garden City, New York: Doubleday, 1968
E185.615 G7 (Browsing Room)

Grier, Eunice
**Negroes in five New York cities: a
study of problems, achievement, and
trends.** (New York) New York State
Commission against Discrimination,
1958
E185.93 N56 N46 1959 (Social Work)

**Privately developed interracial hous-
ing; an analysis of experience.** Berkeley: University of California Press,
1960
E185.89 H6 G7 (Main, Architecture)

Grier, William H
Black rage. New York: Basic Books
(1968)
E185.625 G7 (Browsing Room)

Griffin, John Howard
Black like me. Boston: Houghton
Mifflin, 1961
E185.61 G7 (Main, Undergraduate)

Gross, Bella
**Clarion call; the history and develop-
ment of the Negro people's convention
movement in the United States from
1817 to 1840.** New York, 1947
E185 C79 G7 (Social Work)

Grossack, Martin M
**Mental health and segregation; a se-
lection of papers and some book chap-
ters by David P. Ausubel (and others).**
New York: Springer Publishing Com-
pany (c1963)
E185.625 G7 (Education, Social Work,
Main)

Guild, Mrs. June (Purcell)
Black laws of Virginia. Richmond,
Virginia: Whittet & Shepperson, 1936
E185.93 V8 G9 (Main, History
Graduate)

**Think on these things; some black-
white problems as seen by a group of
Negro southerners.** Santa Barbara,
California: Schauer Publishing Com-
pany (c1947)
E185.61 G8

Guzman, Jessie Parkhurst
**Some achievements of the Negro
through education.** (2nd revised edition) Tuskegee Institute, Alabama:
Department of Records and Research,
1951
E185.96 G8 1951

Haley, James T., comp.
**Afro-American encyclopedia; or, The
thoughts, doings, and sayings of the
race....** Nashville, Tennessee: Haley
& Florida, 1896
E185.6 H25

Halsey, Margaret
**Color blind; a white woman looks at
the Negro....** New York: Simon &
Schuster, 1946
E185.61 H19

Another edition
E185.61 H19 1946a

Hampton Negro Conference.
(Annual report) Hampton, Virginia:
Press of the Hampton Normal and
Agriculture Institute, 1898-1900. 3 vols.
E185.5 H23

Handlin, Oscar
**Fire-bell in the night; the crisis in
civil rights.** (1st edition) Boston:
Little, Brown (1964)
E185.61 H23 (Main, Social Work,
Undergraduate)

Harkey, Ira Brown
**The smell of burning crosses; an auto-
biography of a missing newspaper-
woman....** Jacksonville, Illinois:
Harris-Wolfe (1967)
E185.61 H26 (Journalism, Main)

Harlan, Howard Harper
John Jasper — a case in leadership.
(Charlottesville) University of
Virginia, 1936
E185.97 J39 H2

Harlem quarterly.
vol. 1, no. 1; winter 1949/50.... (New
York)
E185.5 H3

Harris, Abram Lincoln
**The Negro as capitalist; a study of
banking and business among American
Negroes.** Philadelphia: American Acad-
emy of Political & Social Science, 1936
E185.8 H3

Harris, Edward E
Some social effects of race relations.
New York: The American Press, 1968
E185.8 H34

Hayes, Laurence John Wesley
The Negro federal government worker;
a study of his classification status in
the District of Columbia, 1883-1938.
Washington, D. C.: The Graduate
School, Howard University, 1941
E185.8 H4 (Commerce, Main)

Haygood, Atticus Greene
Our brother in black; his freedom and
his future.... New York: Phillips &
Hart, Cincinnati: Walden & Stowe
(etc.) 1881
E185.6 H4

Haygood, Harry
Negro liberation. New York: Inter-
national Publishing (1948)
E185.6 H42

Haynes, George Edmund
The Negro at work in New York City.
New York: Arno Press 1968
E185.93 N56 H3 1912a (Undergraduate)

The trend of the races. New York:
Council of Women for Home Missions
and Missionary Education Movement
of the U.S. & Canada (c1922)
E185.61 H29

Hays, Brooks
A southern moderate speaks. Chapel
Hill: University of North Carolina
Press (c1959)
E185.61 H3

Hedgeman, Anna (Arnold)
The trumpet sounds. (1st edition) New
York: Holt Rinehart and Winston (1964)
E185.97 H4 (Browsing Room)

Hentoff, Nat
The new equality. New York: The
Viking Press (c1965)
E185.61 H4 (Main, Undergraduate)

Hercules, Eric E L
Democracy limited.... Cleveland, Ohio:
Central Publishing House (1945)
E185.6 H45

Herndon, Angelo
Let me live. New York: Random
House (c1937)
E185.97 H55

Hernton, Calvin C
Sex and racism in America. New York:
Grove Press (1966? c1965)
E185.62 H4 1965a

White papers for white Americans. (1st
edition) Garden City, New York:
Doubleday, 1966
E185.61 H43

Hill, Roy L
Rhetoric of racial revolt. Denver:
Golden Bell Press, 1964
E185.6 H5

Hodges, Carl G
Illinois Negro historymakers. Chicago:
Illinois Emancipation Centennial
Commission, 1964
E185.93 I2 H6

Holmes, Samuel Jackson
The Negro's struggle for survival, a
study in human ecology. Berkeley,
California: University of California
Press, 1937
E185.88 H6

Another edition
E185.88 H6 1965

Holt, Lee
The summer that didn't end. New York
Morrow, 1965
E185.61 H6

Holt, Rackham
George Washington Carver. Garden
City, N.Y.: Doubleday, Doran & Com-
pany, Inc., 1943
E185.97 C33 H7 (Chemistry, Main,
Education, Undergraduate)

George Washington Carver, une bibliographie americaine. New York: Over-
seas Editions, Inc. (c1943)
E185.97 C33 H72

Mary McLeod Bethune; a biography.
New York City: Doubleday, 1964
E185.97 B4 H6

Holtzclaw, William Henry
The Black man's burden. New York:
Neale Publishing Company, 1915
E185.97 H75

Houser, George M
We challenged Jim Crow! (New York:
Fellowship of Reconciliation Congress
of Racial Equality, 1947?)
E185.61 H67

Hughes, Langston
Fight for freedom; the story of the
National Association for the Advance-
ment of Colored People. New York:
Norton (1962)
E185.5 M276 H8 (Reference, Under-
graduate)

A pictorial history of the Negro in
America. New York: Crown (c1956)
E185 H8

Another edition
E185 H8 1968 (Browsing Room,
Journalism)

Hullinger, Edwin Ware
Plowing through; the story of the
Negro in agriculture. New York: W.
Morrow & Company, 1940
E185.8 H9 (Commerce, Main)

Hunton, George K
All of which I saw, part of which I
was; the autobiography of George K.
Hunton as told to Gary MacEoin. (1st
edition) Garden City, N.Y.: Doubleday,
1967
E185.61 H85

Huszar, George Bernard de, comp.
Equality in America, the issue of
minority rights. New York: H. W.
Wilson Company, 1949
E185.61 H88

Ianniello, Lynne, ed.
Milestones along the march; twelve
historic Civil Rights documents from
World War II to Selma.... New York:
F. A. Praeger (1966, c1965)
E185.61 I2 (Undergraduate, Reference)

Another edition
E185.61 I2 1965a

Imbert, Dennis I
The Negro after the war. 1st edition
New Orleans, Louisiana: Williams
Printing Service, 1943
E185.61 I32

Isaacs, Harold Robert
The new world of Negro Americans.
New York: John Day Co. (1963)
E185.61 I75 (Social Work)

Ivanov, Robert Fedorovich
Bor'ba negrov za zemliu i svobodu na
IUge SShA. 1865-1877gg. Moskva: Izd-
vo Akademii nauk SSSR, 1958
E185.2 I8

Jack, Robert L
History of the National Association for
the Advancement of Colored People.
Boston: Meador Publishing Company,
1943
E185.5 N276 J2

Jackson, Luther Porter
Free Negro labor and property holding
in Virginia, 1830-1860. New York,
London: D. Appleton-Century Company,
Inc. (1942)
E185.93 V8 J14 (Main, Commerce)

Negro office-holders in Virginia 1865-
1895. Norfolk, Va.: Guide Quality
Press, 1945
E185.93 V8 J13

The Virginia free Negro farmer and
property owner, 1830-1860. (Washington, D. C., 1939)
E185.93 V8 J2

Jacob, Joseph Simeon
A comparative study of the incidence
of insanity among Negroes and whites.
Athens, Georgia, 1938
E185.88 J15

Jacobs, Paul
Prelude to a riot; a view of urban
America from the bottom. New York:
Random House (1968, c1967)
E185.615 J3 (Social Work)

Jacobson, Julius
The Negro and the American labor
movement. Edited by J. Jacobson (1st
edition) Garden City, N.Y.: Anchor
Books, 1968
E185.8 J3 (Commerce, History
Graduate)

Jarrette, Alfred Q
Politics and the Negro. Boston:
Vinjano Educational Publishers, 1964
E185.96 J3

Jefferson, Thomas Le Roy
The old Negro and the new Negro.
Boston: Meador Publishing Company,
1937
E185.86 J45

Jervey, Theodore Dehon
The slave trade; slavery and color....
Columbia, S. C.: The State Company,
1925
E185.61 J4

Johnsen, Julia Emily, comp.
...Selected articles on the Negro problem.... New York: H. W. Wilson Company, 1921
E185.61 J6

Johnson, Charles Spurgeon
Growing up in the black belt. Washing-
ton, D. C.: American Council on Edu-
cation, 1941
E185.86 J66 (Education, Social Work,
Main)

Another edition
E185.86 J66 1966 (Social Work, Main)

Into the main stream, a survey of best
practices in race relations in the
South.... Chapel Hill: The University
of North Carolina Press, 1947
E185.61 J65

The Negro in American civilization; a
study of Negro life and race relations
in the light of social research.... New
York: H. Holt & Company (c1930)
E185.6 J6

Patterns of Negro segregation.... New
York, London: Harper & Brothers
(c1943)
E185.61 J66 (Main, Education)

A preface to racial understanding. New
York: Friendship Press (c1936)
E185.61 J664 (Social Work)

To stem this tide, a survey of racial
tension areas in the United States.
Boston & Chicago: The Pilgrim Press
(1943)
E185.61 J67 (Main, Education, Social
Work)

Johnson, Edward Augustus
A school history of the Negro race in
America from 1619 to 1890, with a
short introduction as to the origin of
the race; also a short sketch of
Liberia. Revised edition. Raleigh:
Edwards & Broughton, 1881
E185 J6 1891

Another edition
E185 J6 1894

Johnson, James Weldon
Negro Americans, what now? New York:
The Viking Press, 1934
E185 J68 (Main, Social Work)

Johnson, William
William Johnson's Natchez; the ante-
bellum diary of a free Negro. (Baton
Rouge) Louisiana State University
Press (1951)
E185.97 J7 A3

Jones, LeRoi
Home; social essays. New York:
Morrow, 1966
E185.6 J64 1966

Jordan, Winthrop D comp.
The Negro versus equality, 1762-1826.
New York: Rand McNally, 1969
E185 J66

Jordan, Winthrop D
White over black; American attitudes
toward the Negro, 1550-1812.... Chapel
Hill: Publishing for the Institute of
Early History and Culture at Williams-
burg, Virginia, by the University of
North Carolina Press (1968)
E185 J67

The Journal of Negro history....
Lancaster, Pennsylvania & Washington,
D. C.: The Association for the Study
of Negro Life and History, Inc., 1916-
(annual)
E185 J7

Kahn, Tom
The economics of equality. New York:
League for Industrial Democracy (dis-
tributed by the Industrial Union De-
partment, American Federation of
Labor, Congress of Industrial Organi-
zations) 1964
E185.8 K3

Another edition
E185.8 K3 1964a

Kardiner, Abram
The mark of oppression; a psycho-
social study of the American Negro.
(1st edition) New York: Norton (1951)
E185.625 K3 (Main, Health Center,
Social Work)

Karon, Bertram P
The Negro personality: a rigorous in-
vestigation of the effects of culture.
New York: Springer Publishing Com-
pany, 1958
E185.625 K33 (Main, Social Work,
Education)

Katz, Irwin
Conflict and harmony in an adolescent
interracial group. (New York) New
York University Press, 1955
E185.61 K3

Katz, William Loren, comp.
Eyewitness; the Negro in American
history. (Chicago) Quadrangle, 1968
E185 K33 (History Graduate)

Kellogg, Charles Flint
NAACP, a history of the National
Association for the Advancement of
Colored People. Baltimore: Johns
Hopkins Press (1967-
E185.5 N276 K4

Kennedy, Robert F
Rights for Americans; the speeches of
Robert F. Kennedy. Indianapolis:
Bobbs-Merrill (1964)
E185.61 K37 (Main, Undergraduate)

Kerlin, Robert Thomas
The voice of the Negro 1919. New
York: E. P. Dutton & Company (c1920)
E185.61 K4

Another edition
E185.61 K4 1920a (Main, Undergraduate)

Killian, Lewis M
The impossible revolution? Black pow-
er and the American dream. New York:
Random House (1968)
E185.615 K48 (Browsing Room)

Racial crisis in America, leadership in
conflict. Englewood Cliffs, New Jersey: Prentice-Hall, Inc. (1964)
E185.61 K49

Killens, John Oliver
Black man's burden. New York: Tri-
dent Press, 1965
E185.61 K48

Kilpatrick, James Jackson
The Southern case for school segregation. New York: Crowell-Collier Press
(1962)
E185.61 K5 (Education, Undergraduate)

King, Martin Luther
The trumpet of conscience. (1st U. S.
edition) New York: Harper & Row
(1968)
E185.97 K5 A2

Where do we go from here: chaos or
community? (1st edition) New York:
Harper & Row (1967)
E185.615 K5 (Main, Undergraduate)

Why we can't wait. (1st edition) New
York: Harper & Row (1964)
E185.61 K54 (Browsing Room, Social
Work, Undergraduate)

Kinzer, Robert H
The Negro in American business; the
conflict between separatism and integration. (1st edition) New York: Greenberg (1950)
E185.8 K5 1950

Klineberg, Otto
Characteristics of the American Negro..
New York: Harper & Brothers (1944)
E185.6 K65

Klingberg, Frank Joseph
An appraisal of the Negro in colonial
South Carolina, a study in Americani-
zation. Washington, D. C.: The
Associated Publishers, 1941
E185.93 S7 K6

Kytle, Elizabeth Larisey
Willie Mae. New York: Knopf, 1959
(c1958)
E185.97 W62 K9

Ladd, Everett Corll
Negro political leadership in the
South. Ithaca, New York: Cornell Uni-
versity Press (1966)
E185.61 L13

LaFarge, John
The race question and the Negro, a
study of the Catholic doctrine on in-
terracial justice. New York, Toronto:
Longmans, Green & Company, 1943
E185.61 L15 (Main, Undergraduate)

Langston, John Mercer
From the Virginia plantation to the
national capital; or, The first and only
Negro representative in Congress from
the Old Dominion. Hartford, Conn.:
American Publishing Company, 1894
E185.97 L3 A3

Lectures and addresses on the Negro in
the South. (Charlottesville, Virginia:
The Michie Company printers, preface,
1915)
E185.61 L47

Lee, Frank F
Negro and white in Connecticut town.
New York: Bookman Associates (1961)
E185.93 C7 L4 (Social Work)

Lee, Hannah Farnham (Sawyer)
Memoir of Pierre Toussaint, born a
slave in St. Domingo. Boston: Crosby,
Nichols & Company, 1854
E185.97 T734

Leinwand, Gerald, comp.
The Negro in the city. New York: Wash-
ington Square Press (1968)
E185.61 L475 (Social Work)

Lester, Julius
Look out Whitey! Black power's gon'
get your mama! New York: Dial Press,
1968
E185.615 L4 (Browsing Room)

Levy, Charles J
Voluntary servitude; whites in the
Negro movement. New York: Appleton-
Century-Crofts (1968)
E185.92 L4

Lewis, Anthony
Portrait of a decade; the second Amer-
ican revolution. New York: Random
House (1964)
E185.61 L48 (Journalism, Browsing
Room)

Liberator. vol. 1, 1961- (New York: Afro-
American Research Institute, Inc.)
E185.5 L5

Liebow, Elliot
Tally's corner; a study of Negro street-
corner men. (1st edition) Boston:
Little, Brown (1967)
E185.93 D6 L5 1967 (Main, Social
Work)

Lightfoot, Claude M
Ghetto rebellion to black liberation.
(1st edition) New York: International
Publishers (1968)
E185.61 L49 (Browsing Room, Social
Work)

Lincoln, Charles Eric
The Black Muslims in America. Boston:
Beacon Press (1961)
E185.61 L5 (Main, Undergraduate, Edu-
cation, Social Work)

Another edition
E185.61 L5 1961a

Is anybody listening to black America?
New York: Seaburg Press (1968)
E185.615 L49 (Social Work)

My face is black. New York: Random
House (1964)
E185.61 L53 (Social Work)

Sounds of the struggle; persons and
perspectives in civil rights. New York:
Morrow, 1967
E185.615 L5

Little, Malcolm
Malcolm X speaks; selected speeches
and statements. (1st edition) New York:
Merit Publishing, 1965
E185.61 L58

The speeches of Malcolm X at Harvard.
New York: Morrow, 1968
E185.61 L59

Litwack, Leon F
North of slavery; the Negro in the free
states, 1790-1860. (Chicago) University of Chicago Press (1961)
E185.9 L5 (Main, Undergraduate, Education)

Lively, Earl
The invasion of Mississippi. Belmont,
Massachusetts: American Opinion,
1963
E185.93 M6 L5

Lloyd, Raymond Grann
White supremacy in the United States,
an analysis of its historical background, with special reference to the
poll tax. Washington, D. C.: Public
Affairs Press (1952)
E185.61 L6

Locke, Alain Le Roy
The new Negro; an interpretation. New
York: A. & C. Boni, 1925
E185.82 L6 (Main, Social Work)

Another edition
E185.82 L6 1925a (Undergraduate,
Social Work)

Loeb, Charles Harold
The future is yours; the history of the
Future Outlook League, 1935-1946.
Cleveland: Future Outlook League
(1947)
E185.5 L6

Logan, Frenise A
The Negro in North Carolina, 1876-
1894. Chapel Hill: University of North
Carolina Press (1964)
E185.93 N6 L6

Logan, Rayford Whittingham
The betrayal of the Negro, from Ruther-
ford B. Hayes to Woodrow Wilson....
New enl. ed. London: Collier-Mac-
millan (1969, c1965)
E185.61 L82 1965

The Negro in American life and
thought; the nadir, 1877-1901. New
York: Dial Press, 1954
E185.61 L82

What the Negro wants. Chapel Hill:
The University of North Carolina
Press (1944)
E185.61 L83

Logan, Spencer
A Negro's faith in America. New York:
The Macmillan Company, 1946
E185.61 L92

Lomax, Louis E
The Negro revolt. (1st edition) New
York: Harper (1962)
E185.61 L94 (Browsing Room)

Long, Herman Hodge
People vs. property; race restrictive
covenants in housing.... Nashville:
Fisk University Press, 1947
E185.89 H6 L6

Lord, Walter
The past that would not die. (1st edi-
tion) Harper & Row (1965)
E185.61 L96 (Main, Undergraduate,
Journalism)

Lotz, Phillip Henry
Rising above color. New York: Asso-
ciation Press, New York: Fleming H.
Revell Company, 1944
E185.96 L88

Louisiana. Legislature. Joint Committee
on Un-American Actions.
Activities of "The Nation of Islam" or
the Muslim cult of Islam in Louisiana.
(Hearings held, November 27, 1962,
Baton Rouge, La.) Baton Rouge, 1963
E185.61 L97 1963

Lubell, Samuel
White and black; a test of a nation.
(1st edition) New York: Harper & Row
(1964)
E185.61 L98

McCord, William
Mississippi: the long hot summer. (1st
edition) New York: Norton (1965)
E185.61 M15

McCulloch, Margaret Callender
Segregation a challenge to democracy.
Nashville Race Relations Department,
American Missionary Association Di-
vision, Board of Home Missions, Con-
gregational Christian, Fisk University
(1950)
E185.61 M2 (Social Work)

McDonagh, Edward C
Ethnic relations in the United States.
New York: Appleton-Century-Crofts
(c1953)
E184 A1 M13 (History Graduate, Edu-
cation, Main)

McKinley, Carlyle
An appeal to Pharoah; the Negro prob-
lem and its radical solution. New
York: Fords, Howard & Hulfert, 1890
(c1889)
E185.61 M22

McKissick, Floyd
Three-fifths of a man. (New York) Mac-
millan (1969)
E185 M3 (Browsing Room)

Manas, John Helen
The race problem, segregation or integration? Cosmic laws of evolution, the great controversy of our time. (1st edition) New York: Pythagorean Society (c1959)
E185.61 M25

Mandelbaum, David Goodman
Soldier groups and Negro soldiers. Berkeley: University of California Press, 1952
E185.63 M3 (Undergraduate)

Mangum, Charles Staples
The legal status of the Negro.... Chapel Hill, North Carolina: The University of North Carolina Press, 1940
E185.6 M27

Mark, Mary Louise
Negroes in Columbus. Columbus: The Ohio State University Press, 1928
E185.93 O2 M34 (Main, Commerce)

Marshall, Burke
Federalism and civil rights. Foreword by Robert F. Kennedy. New York: Columbia University Press, 1964
E185.61 M27

Marshall, F. Ray
The Negro and apprenticeship. Baltimore: Johns Hopkins Press (1967)
E185.8 M29 (Commerce, Social Work, Education)

The Negro and organized labor. New York: Wiley (1965)
E185.8 M3 (Main, Commerce)

The Negro worker. New York: Random House (1967)
E185.8 M32 (Social Work, Commerce)

Martin, Fletcher, ed.
Our great Americans: the Negro contribution to American progress. (Chicago: Gamma Corporation, 1953)
E185.93 M3

Martin, John Bartlow
The Deep South says "never." Foreword by Arthur Schlesinger, Jr. New York: Ballantine Books (1957)
E185.61 M3 (Education)

Marx, Gary Trade
Protest and prejudice; a study of belief in the black community. (1st edition) New York: Harper & Row (1967)
E185.61 M32 (Main, Social Work)

Mathews, Basil Joseph
Booker T. Washington. Cambridge: Harvard University Press, 1948
E185.97 W3 M3 (Main, Education)

Matthews, Donald R
Negroes and the new southern politics. New York: Harcourt, Brace & World (1966)
E185.61 M36 (Main, Undergraduate)

Matthews, Joseph Brown
Communism and the NAACP. (Atlanta: Georgia Commission on Education) Republished by Christian Education Association, Union, New Jersey (1958) 2nd version
E185.5 M3 1953a

Mayer, Edith H
Our Negro brother. New York: Shady Hill Press (1945)
E185.6 M46

Mayor's Conference on Race Relations, Chicago
...City planning in race relations. Proceedings.... Chicago: Mayor's Committee on Race Relations (1944)
E185.61 C53 (Main, Social Work)

Mecklin, John Moffat
Democracy and race friction: a study in social ethics. New York: The Macmillan Company (c1941)
E185.61 M39

Meier, August
From plantation to ghetto; an interpretative history of American Negroes. (1st edition) New York: Hill and Wang (1966)
E185 M4 (Main, Education)

Another edition
E185 M4 1966a

Negro thought in America, 1880-1915; racial idealogies in the age of Booker T. Washington. Ann Arbor, University of Michigan Press (1963)
E185.6 M5 (Main, Undergraduate, Education)

Meldon, Charles Manly
From slave to citizen. New York: Methodist Book Concern (c1921)
E185.61 M4

Meltzer, Milton
In their own words; a history of the
American Negro. New York: Crowell
(1964-1967) 3 vols.
E185 M44 (Education)

Mendelson, Wallace
Discrimination: based on the report of
the United States Commission on Civil
Rights. Englewood Cliffs, New Jersey:
Prentice Hall (1962)
E184 A1 M4

Metcalf, George R
Black profiles. (1st edition) New York:
McGraw-Hill (1968)
E185.96 M4

Miller, Abie
The Negro and the Great Society. (1st
edition) New York: Vantage Press
(c1965)
E185 M5 (Commerce)

Miller, Kelly
As to the leopard's spots: an open
letter to Thomas Dixon Jr. Washington,
D. C.: K. Müller (c1905)
E185.61 M64

The Negro in the new reconstruction.
Washington, D. C.: Howard University
(1919?)
E185.61 M66 (Social Work)

Race adjustment; essays on the Negro
in America. New York and Washington:
The Neale Publishing Company, 1908
E185.5 M54

Another edition
E185.5 M54 1908a (Main, Undergraduate)

Radicals and conservatives, and other
essays on the Negro in America. New
York: Schocken Books (1968)
E185.5 M54 1968

Miller, William Robert
Martin Luther King, Jr.; his life,
martyrdom and meaning for the world.
New York: Weybright & Talley (1968)
E185.97 K5 M5 (Social Work)

Mitchell, Glenford E., ed.
The angry black south. New York:
Corinth Books, 1962
E185.61 M7

Moon, Bucklin
The high cost of prejudice. New York:
J. Messner, Inc. (1947)
E185.61 M8

Primer for white folks.... Garden City,
N.Y.: Doubleday, Doran and Company,
Inc., 1945
E185.5 M8

Mooney, Chase Curran
Civil rights, retrospect and prospects.
Washington, D. C.: Service Center for
Teachers of History (1961)
E185.61 M825

Morris, Willie, ed.
The South today, 100 years after
Appomattox. (1st edition) New York:
Harper & Row (1965)
E185.61 M828 (Main, Undergraduate)

Moton, Robert Russa
The Negro today, remarkable growth of
fifty years.... (Tuskegee, Als.: Tuskegee Normal and Industrial Institute,
1921?)
E185.6 M5

What the Negro thinks.... Garden City,
N.Y.: Doubleday, Doran & Company,
Inc., 1930 (c1929)
E185.61 M83

Murphy, Raymond John, ed.
Problems and prospects of the Negro
movement. Belmont, California: Wadsworth Publishing Company (1966)
E185.615 M8

Murry, Pauli, ed.
States' laws on race and color, and
appendices containing international
documents, federal laws and regula-
tions, local ordinances and charts.
(Cincinnati: Woman's Division of
Christian Service, Board of Missions
and Church Extension, Methodist
Church) 1950 (i.e. 1951)
E185.6 M8 (History Graduate, Social
Work)

Supplement
E185.6 M8 Suppl. 1955 (Reference,
Social Work)

Muse, Benjamin
The American Negro revolution; from
non-violence to black power, 1963-
1967. Bloomington, Indiana: Indiana
University Press (1968)
E185.615 M83 (Browsing Room)

Ten years of prelude: the story of integration since the Supreme Court's 1954 decision. New York: The Viking Press (1964)
E185.61 M9 (Browsing Room)

Myrdal, Gunnar
An American dilemma; the Negro problem and democracy. New York: Harper & Brothers (c1944)
E185.6 M9 (Main, Social Work, History Graduate, Education)

Another edition
E185.6 M9 1962 (Education, Undergraduate, Social Work, Commerce)

Another edition
E185.6 M9 1962a

Digest of Myrdal's "An American dilemma," prepared by Samuel S. Wyer. Columbus, Ohio: The Columbus Council for Democracy, 1944
E185.6 M91 W9 (Main, Social Work)

National Association for the Advancement of Colored People.
Annual Report. no. 1- New York, 1911-
E185.5 N276 N3

National Association for the Advancement of Colored People. Labor Department.
The Negro wage-earner and apprenticeship training programs; a critical analysis with recommendations. New York (1960)
E185.8 N28 (Education)

National Committee on Segregation in the Nation's Capital.
Segregation in Washington, a report, November, 1948. (Chicago, 1948)
E185.93 D6 N3 (Social Work)

National Conference on Fundamental Problems in the Education of Negroes, Washington, D. C., 1934
Child health problems. National Conference on Fundamental Problems in the Education of Negroes. Sub-committee Report. Nashville: Julius Rosenwald Fund, Southern office, 1934
E185.88 N27

National Conference on Small Business, Washington, D. C., 1961
Problems and opportunities confronting Negroes in the field of business; report. (Washington) United States Department of Commerce, 1962 (i.e. 1963)
E185.8 N3 1961 (Commerce, Main)

National Conference on the Christian Way of Life.
And who is my neighbor? An outline for the study of race relations in America, Part I. New York: Associated Press, 1924
E185.61 N3

National Conference on the Problems of the Negro and Negro Youth. Washington, D. C., 1937.
Report of the National Conference... January 6-8, 1937. (Washington, D. C., 1937)
E185.6 N27

Another edition
E185.6 N27 1939

The national cyclopedia of the colored race. Montgomery, Alabama: National Publishing Company, Inc., 1919-
E185.96* A1 N3

National Industrial Conference Board.
Company experience with Negro employment. (New York, 1966)
E185.8 N33 (Education, Social Work)

National Negro health news.
Washington, D. C., 1945- vol. 13, no. 4; vol. 14-18 Oct.-Dec. 1945; 1946-1950 June.
E185.88 N3

National Urban League (for Social Service Among Negroes)
Economic and social status of the Negro in the United States. New York (c1961)
E185.6 N28 (Social Work)

40th anniversary yearbook, 1950. (New York, 1951)
E185.5 N33

Social aspects of reconversion; a memorandum prepared for the President of the United States by the National Urban League. New York, 1945
E185.6 N29

Neff, Lawrence Wilson
What next for the Negro? Emory University, Georgia: Banner Press (c1948)
E185.61 N4

Negro and Jew: an encounter in America; a symposium compiled by Mainstream Magazine. New York: Macmillan (1967)
E185.61 N43 (Main, Social Work)

The Negro college quarterly.
vol. 1-5 no. 2 March 1943- June 1947
Wilberforce, Ohio: Wilberforce University (1943-
E185.5 N36

Negro digest, a magazine of Negro
comment. vol. 1-10, Nov. 1942-1951
(Chicago: Negro Digest Publishing
Company, c1942-51)
E185.5 N363

The Negro handbook....
New York: W. Malliet & Company,
1942-49
E185.5 N37 (Reference, Social Work)

The Negro history bulletin.
vol. 1- Oct. 1937- Washington, D. C.:
The Association for the Study of
Negro Life and History, Inc., 1940-
E185.5 N375

The Negro problem: a series of articles
by representative American Negroes of
today. New York: J. Pott & Company,
1903.
E185.5 N38

The Negro quarterly, a review of Negro
life and culture. New York: Negro
Publication Society of America (1942-
1943)
E185.5 N388

The Negro year book, an annual encyclopedia of the Negro....1912-1952.
Tuskegee Institute, Alabama: Negro
Year Book Publishing Company,
c1912-52.
E185.5 N39 (Main, Social Work)

Nelson, Dennis Denmark
The integration of the Negro into the
United States Navy, 1776-1947, with a
brief historical introduction. (Washington, D. C.) 1948
E185.63 N4 1948

Nelson, Truman John
The right of revolution. Boston: Beacon Press (1968)
E185.61 N45

Newby, Idus A
Challenge to the court; social scientists and the defense of segregation,
1954-66. Baton Rouge: Louisiana
State University Press (1967)
E185.61 N47 (Main, Mershon)

The development of segregationist
thought. Homewood, Illinois: Dorsey
Press, 1968
E185.61 N474

Jim Crow's defense; anti-Negro thought
in America, 1900-1930. Baton Rouge:
Louisiana State University Press, 1965
E185.61 N48

Newcomb, Harvey
The "Negro pew": being an inquiry
concerning the propriety of distinctions
in the house of God, on account of
color. Boston: I. Knapp, 1837
E185 N4

Newman, Dorothy (Krall)
The Negroes in the United States,
their economic and social situation.
Washington, D. C.: United States Department of Labor, Bureau of Labor
Statistics, United States Government
Printing Office, 1966
E185.8 N48 (Social Work)

Newsome, Albert Ray
Studies in history and political
science. Chapel Hill: University of
North Carolina Press, 1947
E185.93 M6 N4 (Main, History Graduate)

New York (State) State Commission
Against Discrimination. Division of
Research.
Negroes in five New York cities; a
study of problems, achievements and
trends (by Eunice and George Grier.
New York) 1959
E185.93 N56 N46 1959 (Social Work)

Nichols, Lee
Breakthrough on the color front. New
York: Random House (c1954)
E185.63 N5

Nolan, William A
Communism versus the Negro. Chicago:
H. Regnery Company, 1951
E185.61 N6

Nolen, Claude H
The Negro's image in the South; the
anatomy of white supremacy. Lexington: University of Kentucky Press,
1967
E185.61 N64

Norgren, Paul Herbert
Employing the Negro in American
industry; a study of management
practices. New York: Industrial Relations Counselors, 1959
E185.8 N7 (Commerce)

Norris, Hoke, ed.
We dissent. New York: Saint Martin's
Press (1962)
E185.61 N68 (Browsing Room)

North Carolina. State Board of Public
Welfare.
The Negro population of North Caroli-
na; social and economic. By John R.
Larkins. Raleigh (1944?)
E185.93 N6 A5 1944

Northrup, Herbert Roof
The Negro and employment opportunity;
problems and practices. Ann Arbor:
Bureau of Industrial Relations, Graduate School of Business Administration, University of Michigan (1965)
E185.8 N85 (Social Work, Commerce)

Organized labor and the Negro. New
York, London: Harper & Brothers
(c1944)
E185.8 N87 (Main, Commerce, Social
Work)

Will Negroes get jobs now? (New York:
Public Affairs Committee, Inc., 1945)
E185.8 N872 (Main, Education,
Commerce)

Oak, Vishnu Vitthal
The Negro entrepreneur. Yellow
Springs, Ohio: Printed by the Antioch
Press 1948.
E185.8 O2

Odum, Howard Washington
Race and rumors of race: Challenge to
American crisis. Chapel Hill: Univer-
sity of North Carolina Press (c1943)
E185.61 O27

Rainbow round my shoulder; the blue
trail of black Ulysses. Indianapolis:
The Bobbs-Merril Company (c1928)
E185.86 O3

Olsen, Otto H., comp.
The thin disguise: turning point in
Negro history; Plessey v. Ferguson; a
documentary presentation, 1864-1896.
New York: Humanities Press, 1967
E185.61 O5

Oppenheimer, Martin
A manual for direct action. Chicago:
Quadrangle Press (1965)
E185.61 O6 1965

Opportunity; a journal of Negro life.
New York: National Urban League, etc.
(1923-1949)
E185.5 O6

Osofsky, Gilbert
The burden of race; a documentary
history of Negro-white relations in
America. (1st edition) New York:
Harper & Row (1967)
E185 O77 (Browsing Room, Under-
graduate, Social Work)

Other fools and their doings; or, Life
among the freedmen, by One who has
seen it. New York: J. S. Ogilvie
(c1880)
E185.2 O8

Ottley, Roi
Black odyssey, the story of the Negro
in America. New York: C. Scribner's
Sons, 1948
E185 O8

Ovington, Mary White
The walls came tumbling down. (1st
edition) New York: Harcourt, Brace
(1947)
E185.5 O9 (Main, Social Work)

Owen, Robert Dale
The wrong of slavery, the right of
emancipation, and the future of the
African race in the United States....
Philadelphia: J. B. Lippincott & Com-
pany, 1864
E185 O87

Page, Thomas Nelson
The Negro; the southerner's problem...
New York: C. Scribner's sons, 1904
E185 P13

Patterson, Dzhems Lloidvich
Khronika levoi ruki. Moscow, 1964
E185.86 P3

Paynter, John Henry
Horse and buggy days with Uncle Sam.
New York: Margent Press, 1943
E185.8 P3

Peare, Catherine Owens
Mary McLeod Bethune. New York:
Vanguard Press (1951)
E185.97 B4 P4 (Main, Education)

Peck, James
Cracking the color line; non-violent
direct action methods of eliminating
racial discrimination. (CORE, 1960?)
E185.61 P367

Freedom ride. New York: Simon &
Schuster, 1962
E185.61 P363

Sit ins; the student report. New York:
CORE (c1960)
E185.61 P36895

Perkins, Archie Ebenezer
A resume of Negro congressmen's
office-holding. New Orleans: A. E. &
J. E. Perkins, 1944
E185.8 P35

Perlo, Victor
The Negro in southern agriculture.
New York: International Publishing
(c1953)
E185.8 P4

Peterkin, Julia (Mood)
Roll, Jordan roll....
New York: R. O. Ballou (c1933)
E185.6 P46

Peters, William S
The Southern temper. (1st edition)
Garden City, N. Y.: Doubleday, 1959
E185.61 P37 (Education)

Pettigrew, Thomas Fraser
A profile of the Negro American.
Princeton, N. J.: Van Nostrand (1964)
E185.625 P4 (Reference, Under-
graduate)

Phelps-Stokes Fund.
Negro status and race relations in the
United States, 1911-1946; the thirty-
five year report of the Phelps-Stokes
Fund. New York, 1948
E185.61 P4

Pinkney, Alphonso
Black Americans. Englewood Cliffs,
New Jersey: Prentice-Hall (1969)
E185 P5

The committed: white activists in the
civil rights movement. (New Haven,
Connecticut) College and Universities
Press, 1968
E185.61 P5

Ploski, Harry A., comp.
The Negro almanac.... (1st edition)
New York: Bellwether Publishing
Company (1967)
E185 P55 (Reference, Education,
Undergraduate)

Porch, Marvin E
The Philadelphia main line Negro — a
social, economic, and educational
survey. Philadelphia, 1938
E185.93 P4 P8

Powdermaker, Hortense
After freedom; a cultural study in the
deep South.... New York: The Viking
Press, 1939
E185.6 P88 (Main, Social Work)

Powell, Adam Clayton
Marching blacks, an interpretive history of the rise of the black common
man. New York: Dial Press, 1945
E185.6 P89

Powledge, Fred
Black power, white resistance: notes
on the new civil war. Cleveland: World
Publishing Company (1967)
E185.615 P6

Preston, Edward
Martin Luther King: fighter for freedom.
Garden City, New York: Doubleday &
Company, 1969
E185.97 K5 P7 (Social Work)

Price, Hugh Douglas
The Negro and Southern politics; a
chapter of Florida history. (New York)
New York University Press, 1957
E185.93 F5 P7 1957 (History Graduate,
Undergraduate)

Procter, Samuel D
The young Negro in America, 1960-
1980.... New York: Association Press
(1966)
E185.61 P7 (Main, Social Work)

Putnam, Carleton
Race and reality; a search for solu-
tions. Washington, D. C.: Public
Affairs Press (1967)
E185.61 P79

Race and reason; a Yankee view.
Washington, D. C.: Public Affairs
Press (1961)
E185.61 P8 (Main, Undergraduate)

Quarles, Benjamin
The Negro in the making of America.
New York: Collier Books (c1967,
c1964)
E185 Q2 (Main, Education)

Radio Free Europe. Audience Research
Department.
The race issue in the United States as
seen from Poland and Hungary....
(n.p.) 1965
E185.61 R3 (History Graduate)

Rainwater, Lee
The Moynihan report and the politics of
controversy. Cambridge, Massachusetts:
Massachusetts Institute of Technology
Press (1967)
E185.86 U518 R3

Record, Wilson
The Negro and the Communist party.
Chapel Hill: University of North Caro-
lina Press (1951)
E185.61 R4

Race and radicalism; the NAACP and
the Communist Party in conflict.
Ithaca, N.Y.: Cornell University Press
(1964)
E185.5 N276 R4

Another edition
E185.5 N276 R4 1964a

Reddick, Lawrence Dunbar
Crusader without violence. New York:
Harper, (c1959)
E185.97 K5 R4

Redding, Jay Saunders
The lonesome road, the story of the
Negroes part in America. (1st edition)
Garden City, N.Y.: Doubleday, 1958
E185.61 R424 (Main, Undergraduate)

The Negro.... Washington, D. C.:
Potomac Books, 1967
E185 R38

No day of triumph. New York and
London: Harper & Brothers (1942)
E185.6 R3

On being Negro in America. (1st
edition) Indianapolis: Bobbs-Merrill
(c1951)
E185.61 R426 (Main, Social Work,
Undergraduate)

They came in chains; Americans from
Africa. (1st edition) Philadelphia:
Lippincott (1950)
E185 R4

Reid, Ira de Augustine
In minor key; Negro youth in story and
fact.... Washington, D. C.: American
Council on Education, 1940
E185.6 R35

Reimers, David M
White Protestantism and the Negro.
New York: Oxford University Press,
1965
E185.61 R428

Reuter, Edward Byron
The American race problem: a study of
the Negro. New York: Thomas Y.
Crowell Company (c1927)
E185.61 R44

Another edition
E185.61 R44 1938 (Education)

Rhode Island. Governor's Task Force on
Civil Rights
Report.... (Providence, 1964)
E185.93 R4 A56 1964

Richardson, Ben Albert
Great American Negroes. New York:
Thomas Y. Crowell Company (1949
c1945)
E185.96 R52 (Music)

Richings, G F
Evidences of progress among colored
people.... 7th edition. Philadelphia:
G. S. Ferguson Company, 1901 (c1896)
E185.6 R5 1896

Riley, Benjamin Franklin
The white man's burden; a discussion
of the interracial question with special
reference to the responsibility of the
white race to the Negro problem.
Birmingham, Ala.: B. F. Riley...
(c1910)
E185.6 R57

Rockwell, George Lincoln
White power. 2nd edition (Dallas,
Texas: Ragnarok Press, 1967)
E185.61 R6 1967a

Rohrer, John Harrison
The eighth generation: cultures and personalities of New Orleans Negroes. New York: Harper (1960)
E185.625 R6

Roman, Charles Victor
American civilization and the Negro; the Afro-American in relation to national progress.... Philadelphia: F. A. Davis Company, 1921
E185.61 R7

Romero, Patricia W., comp.
I too am America; documents from 1619 to the present. (1st edition) New York: Publishing Company (1968)
E185 R6

Rose, Arnold Marshall
Assuring freedom to be free; a century of emancipation in the U.S.A. .... With an introduction by Lyndon B. Johnson. Detroit: Wayne State University Press, 1964
E185.6 R78

The Negro in America. (1st edition) New York: Harper (1948)
E185.6 R79

The Negro in postwar America. New York: Anti-Defamation League of B'nai B'rith, c1950
E185.6 R792

The Negro's morale: group identification and protest. Minneapolis: University of Minnesota Press (1949)
E185.61 R8

Social change and the Negro problem. (New York: Anti-Defamation League of B'nai B'rith, 1964)
E185.6 R793 (Education)

Ross, Arthur Max, ed.
Employment, race, and poverty. (1st edition) New York: Harcourt, Brace and World (1967)
E185.8 R6 (Commerce, Social Work, Undergraduate)

Rousseve, Charles Barthelemy
The Negro in Louisiana; aspects of his history and his literature. New Orleans: The Xavier University Press, 1937
E185.93 L6 R8

Rowan, Carl Thomas
Go South to sorrow. New York: Random House (c1957)
E185.61 R85

South to freedom. New York: Knopf, 1952
E185.61 R86

Rudwick, Elliot M
W. E. B. DuBois; a study in minority group leadership. Philadelphia: University of Pennsylvania Press (c1960)
E185.95 D8 R8

Ruiz Suarez, Bernardo
The color question in the two Americas .... Translated by John Crosby Gordon. New York: The Hunt Publishing Company, 1922
E185.61 R93

Rutledge, Aaron L
Nineteen Negro men. San Francisco: Jossey-Bass, Inc., 1967
E185.8 R8

St. James, Warren D
The National Association for Advancement of Colored People; a case study in pressure groups....
(1st edition) New York: Exposition Press (c1958)
E185.5 N276 S3 (Social Work)

Seabrook, Isaac DuBois
Before and after; or, The relations of the races in the South. Baton Rouge: Louisiana State University Press (1967)
E185.61 S4

Secretary's Conference with College Presidents and Executives. 3rd, Fisk University, 1963
Secretary's Conference with College Presidents and Executives, April 4 and 5, 1963. (Minutes of Conference on Preparation of Minority Group Youth for Employment. Washington, 1963)
E185.8 S35 1963

Seidenberg, Jacob
Negroes in the work group; a study of selected employment practices in New York State. Ithaca: New York State School of Industrial and Labor Relations, Cornell University (1950)
E185.8 S4

Seligmann, Herbert Jacob
The Negro faces America. New York
and London: Harper & Brothers (1920)
E185.61 S43

Shannon, Alexander Harvey
The racial integrity of the American
Negro. Nashville: Parthenon Press,
1951
E185.62 S48 1951 (Main, Social Work)

Another edition
E185.62 S48 1952

Sheppard, Harold Lloyd
Civil rights, employment, and the
social status of American Negroes.
Kalamazoo: W. E. Upjohn Institute for
Employment Research, 1966
E185.61 S48

Shufeldt, Robert Wilson
A Negro menace to American civiliza-
tion. Boston: R. G. Badger, 1907
E185.61 S5

Silberman, Charles E
Crisis in black and white. New York:
Random House (1964)
E185.61 S57 (Main, Browsing Room,
Education, Undergraduate)

Simmons, William J
Men of mark; eminent, progressive and
rising. New York: Arno Press, 1968
E185.96 S5 1887a (Main, Undergraduate)

Sinclair, William Albert
The aftermath of slavery; a study of
the condition and environment of the
American Negro. Boston: Small, May-
nard & Company, 1905
E185.6 S6

Slaiman, Donald
Civil rights in the urban crisis. (Washington, D. C.) United States Department of Labor, Manpower Administration (1968)
E185.8 S5 (Education)

Sloan, Irving J
The American Negro, a chronology and
fact book.... Dobbs Ferry, N.Y.:
Oceana Publishing, 1965
E185 S5 (Main, Reference)

The Negro in modern American textbooks; a study of the Negro in selected junior and senior high school and
college level history textbooks as of
September, 1966, with additions,
December 1967.... 2nd edition (Washington) American Federation of Teachers (1967)
E185 S53 1967

Smith, Edward Staples
Selected segregation. Boston: Chris-
topher (1950)
E185.61 S6 (Health Center)

Smith, Lillian Eugenia
Now is the time. New York: The Viking
Press, 1955
E185.61 S64

Our faces, our words. (1st edition) New
York: W. W. Norton (1964)
E185.61 S66 (Browsing Room)

Smith, Samuel Denny
The Negro in Congress, 1870-1901.
Chapel Hill, N.C.: The University of
North Carolina Press, 1940
E185.6 S65

Smith, William Benjamin
The color line; a brief in behalf of the
unborn. New York: McClure, Phillips
& Company, 1905
E185.6 S66

Southern Education Reporting Service
Index to Facts on film. Nashville,
Tennessee (c1958)
E185.5 S6

Supplement.
E185.5 S6 Supplement

The Southern frontier.
vol. 1-6; January 1940- December
1945
E185.5 S63

Spencer, Samuel Reid
Booker T. Washington and the Negro's
place in American life. (1st edition)
Boston: Little, Brown (1955)
E185.97 W3 S6 (Main, Undergraduate)

Sprigle, Ray
In the land of Jim Crow. New York:
Simon & Schuster, 1949
E185.61 S76 (Main, Social Work, Under-
graduate)

Spirer, Jess
Negro crime. Baltimore: The Johns
Hopkins Press, c1940
E185.65 S75 (Social Work)

Stahl, David, ed.
The community and racial crisis. New
York: Practising Law Institute (1966)
E185.615 S7

Stanford, Peter Thomas
The tragedy of the Negro in America; a
condensed history of the enslavement,
sufferings, emancipation, present condition and progress of the Negro race
in the United States of America.... 2nd
edition 10th thousand. North Cambridge,
Mass. (1903? c1897)
E185 S8 1897a

Stang, Alan
It's very simple; the true story of civil
rights. Boston: Western Islands (1965)
E185.61 S83

Another edition
E185.61 S83 1965a

A statistical inquiry into the condition
of the people of colour, of the city and
districts of Philadelphia.
Philadelphia: Kite & Walton, 1849
E185.93 P4 S7

Sterling, Dorothy
Captain of the planter. (1st edition)
Garden City, N.Y.: Doubleday, 1958
E185.97 S6 S8 (Education)

Stewart, Maxwell Slutz
...The Negro in America. New York
(Public Affairs Commission, Inc., 1944)
E185.6 M91 S8 (Main, Education)

Stillman, Richard Joseph
Integration of the Negro in the United
States Armed Forces. New York:
Praeger (1968)
E185.63 S7

Stokes, Anson Phelps
Art and the color line; an appeal made
May 31, 1939, to the president general
and others of the Daughters of the
American Revolution to modify their
rules so as to permit distinguished
Negro artists such as Marian Anderson
to be heard at Constitution Hall. Print-
ed for the consideration of the Execu-
tive Committee of the D.A.R. at their
meeting October 23, and the Marian
Anderson Committee. Washington,
D. C., 1939
E185.61 S86

Stone, Alfred Holt
Studies in the American race problem.
New York: Doubleday, Page & Com-
pany, 1908
E185.61 S87

Stone, Chuck
Black political power in America.
Indianapolis: Bobbs-Merrill (1968)
E185 S84 (Main, Browsing Room,
Social Work)

Storey, Moorfield
The Negro question, an address delivered before the Wisconsin bar association.... June 27, 1918. (n.p., 1918)
E185.61 S875

Strana natsional'nogo hespraviia.
Moskva: Izd-vo Politicheskoi Lit-ry,
1966
E185.61 S9

Styles, Fitzhugh Lee
Negroes and the law in the race battle
for liberty, equality and justice under
the Constitution of the United States
with clauses clebres.... Boston: The
Christopher Publishing House (c1937)
E185.61 S93

Sugarman, Tracy
Stranger at the gates: a summer in
Mississippi. New York: Hill & Wang
(1966)
E185.93 M6 S8 (Main, Undergraduate)

Sutherland, Elizabeth, ed.
Letters from Mississippi. (1st edition)
New York: McGraw-Hill (1965)
E185.61 S95

Sutherland, Robert Lee
Color, class and personality. Prepared
for the American Youth Commission.
Washington, D. C.: American Council
on Education, 1942
E185.6 S96 (Main, Education, Social
Work)

Swint, Henry Lee, ed.
Dear ones at home; letters from con-
traband camps.... Nashville: Vanderbilt University Press, 1966
E185.2 S9

Tanneyhill, Ann
From school to job: guidance for minor-
ity youth. (1st edition New York:
Public Affairs Committee, 1953)
E185.8 T3 (Main, Education, Social
Work)

Tennessee. Agricultural and Industrial State University, Nashville. **Business enterprises of Negroes in Tennessee.** Prepared under the Small Business Administration Research Grant Program, Nashville, 1961 E185.8 T4 (Commerce, Main)

Terrell, Mrs. Mary (Church) **A colored woman in a white world.** Washington, D. C.: Ransdell, Inc. (c1940) E185.97 T32

Thompson, Era Bell **American daughter.** Chicago: Follett Publishing Company (1967) E185.97 T5 1967 (Main, Undergraduate)

Thomas, Charles Murdah **James F. Bundy, 1862-1914, a biography.** Washington, D. C., 1944 E185.97 B8 T4

Thomas, William Hannibal **The American Negro; what he was, what he is, and what he may become, a critical and practical discussion....** New York: Macmillan Co., London: Macmillan & Co., Ltd., 1901 E185 T4

Thornbrough, Emma Lou **The Negro in Indiana; a study of a minority.** (Indianapolis) Indiana Historical Bureau, 1957 E185.93 I6 T4

Thorpe, Earl Endris **The mind of the Negro: an intellectual history of Afro-Americans.** Baton Rouge, La.: Ortlieb Press (1961) E185.82 T5

Thurman, Sue Bailey **Pioneers of Negro origin in California.** San Francisco: Acme Publishing Company (1952) E185.93 C2 T4

Tillinghast, Joseph Alexander **...The Negro in Africa and America....** New York: For the American Economic Association by the Macmillan Co. (etc.) 1902 E185 T5 (Main, Commerce)

Another edition HB1 A52 vol. 3

Tindall, George Brown **South Carolina Negroes, 1877-1900.** Columbia: University of South Carolina Press, 1952 E185.93 S7 T5 (Main, History Graduate)

Torrence, Frederic Ridgely **The story of John Hope.** New York: Macmillan Company, 1945 E185.97 H8 T6 (Main, Education)

Tourgee, Albion Winegar **An appeal to Caesar.** New York: Fords, Howard & Hulbert, 1884 E185.61 T6

Tucker, Shirley, ed. **Mississippi from within.** New York: Arco Publishing Company (1965) E185.61 T78

Tumin, Melvin **Desegregation: resistance and readiness.** Princeton, N. J.: Princeton University Press, 1958 E185.61 T8 (Main, Undergraduate, Social Work)

Segregation and desegregation, a digest of recent research. (New York: Anti-defamation League of B'nai B'rith, 1957) E185.61 T83

U. S. Business and Defense Service Administration. **A guide to Negro marketing information.** (Prepared by Emmer Martin Lancaster under the direction of Charles H. Daly, Service Industries Division Washington: United States Government Printing Office (1966) E185.8 U53 1966

U. S. Commission on Civil Rights **Civil rights U.S.A.; housing in Washington, D. C.** (Washington, 1962) E185.89 H6 U47

Freedom to the free: century of emancipation 1863-1963. (Washington: United States Government Printing Office, 1963) E185.61 U5 1963 (Reference, Home Economics)

Hearings before the United States
Commission on Civil Rights. Hearings
held in New Orleans, La., September
27, 1960, September 28, 1960, May 5,
1961, May 6, 1961. Washington: United
States Government Printing Office,
1961
E185.93 L6 U5

Hearings held in Jackson, Mississippi,
Feb. 16-20, 1965. (Washington) United
States Government Printing Office,
1965
E185.93 M6 U5 1965

U. S. Commission on Civil Rights. Michigan State Advisory Committee
Employment problems of nonwhite
youth; report on Michigan. (Washington)
1966
E185.93 M5 U5 1966 (Main, Commerce)

U. S. Commission on Civil Rights. State
Advisory Committees Division
Reports on apprenticeship by the
Advisory Committees to the United
States Commission on Civil Rights in
California, Connecticut, Maryland, New
Jersey, New York, Tennessee, and
Wisconsin. (Washington, 1964)
E185.8 U55 1964

U. S. Department of Labor. Office of
Planning and Research
The Negro family: the case for national
action. (Washington: United States
Government Printing Office) 1965
E185.86 U5 1965 (Reference, Social
Work, Children's Hospital, Agriculture)

U. S. Library of Congress
75 years of freedom; commeration of
the 75th anniversary of the proclama-
tion of the 13th amendment to the
Constitution of the United States
(Washington: United States Government
Printing Office, 1943)
E185.6 U59

U. S. Office of Advisor on Negro Affairs
The urban Negro worker in the United
States, 1925-1936. Washington: United
States Government Printing Office
1938-39.
E185.8 U595 (Main, Commerce)

U. S. Treasury Department
Report relative to leasing abandoned
plantations and affairs of the freed
people in first special agency....
Washington, D. C.: McGill & Witherow,
printers, 1864
E185.2 U58

U. S. Women's Bureau
Negro women in the population and in
the labor force. (Washington, 1966)
E185.8 U62 1966 (Reference)

Another edition
E185.8 U62 1967 (Education)

University Commission on Southern Race
Questions
Five letters of the University Com-
mission on Southern Race Questions.
(Charlottesville, Va) 1927
E185.61 U55

Van Deusen, John George
The black man in white America.
Washington, D. C.: Associated Publish-
ing, Inc., 1938
E185.6 V24

Another edition
E185.6 V24 1944

Von Hoffman, Nicholas
Mississippi notebook. New York: D.
White (1964)
E185.61 V6 (Browsing Room)

Voegeli, V Jacque
Free but not equal; the Midwest and
the Negro during the Civil War.
Chicago: University of Chicago Press
(1967)
E185.9 V6

Wakefield, Dan
Revolt in the South. New York: Grove
Press (1960)
E185.61 W25

Walker, Anne Kendrick
Tuskegee and the black belt, a por-
trait of a race.... Richmond, Virginia:
The Dietz Press, Inc., 1944
E185.6 W17

Walker, Helen Edith
The Negro in the medical profession.
(Charlottesville) University of
Virginia, 1949
E185.82 W3

Wallace, Mike
A Mike Wallace interview with James McBride Dabbs. Produced by American Broadcasting Company in Association with the Fund for the Republic. (New York, 1958?)
E185.61 W27 (Social Work)

Warren, Robert Penn
Segregation, the inner conflict in the South. New York: Random House (c1956)
E185.61 W3 (Main, Undergraduate)

Who speaks for the Negro? New York: Random House (1965)
E185.61 W32 (Browsing Room, Undergraduate)

Washington, Booker Taliaferro
The future of the American Negro. Boston: Small, Maynard & Company, 1899
E185.6 W29

Selected speeches of Booker T. Washington.... Garden City, N.Y.: Doubleday, Doran & Company, Inc., 1932
E185.6 W3

The story of my life and work. Revised edition. Cincinnati, Ohio: W. H. Ferguson, 1901
E185.97 W3 A3 1901

Another edition
E185.97 W3 A3 1901a

The story of the Negro, the rise of the race from slavery. New York: Doubleday, Page, 1909
E185 W2

Another edition
E185 W3 1909a

Another edition
E185 W3 1909b

Up from slavery. New York: A. L. Burt Company (c1901)
Another edition
E185.97 W3 A32 1901a

Another edition
E185.97 W3 A32 1901b (Main, Browsing Room)

Another edition
E185.97 W3 A32 1901c (Rare Book Collection)

Another edition
E185.97 W3 A32 1928 (Undergraduate)

Another edition
E185.97 W3 A32 1965 (Education)

Waskow, Arthur I
From race riot to sit-in, 1919 to the 1960's; a study in the connections between conflict and violence. (1st edition) Garden City, N.Y.: Doubleday, 1966
E185.61 W34

Another edition
E185.61 W34 1966a (Social Work, Undergraduate)

Watts, Frederick Payne
...A comparative clinical study of delinquent and non-delinquent Negro boys.... Philadelphia, 1941
E185.65 W34 (Education)

Waynick, Capus M, ed.
North Carolina and the Negro. Raleigh: North Carolina Mayors' Co-operating Committee, 1964
E185.93 N6 W3

Weatherford, Willis Duke
Negro life in the South, present conditions and needs.... New York: Young Men's Christian Association Press, 1910
E185.6 W4

Race relations; adjustment of whites and Negroes in the United States. Boston; New York (etc.) D. C. Heath & Company, (c1934)
E185 W395

Weaver, Robert Clifton
Negro labor, a national problem. New York: Harcourt, Brace & Company (1946)
E185.8 W36 (Main, Commerce, Social Work)

Weltner, Charles Longstreet
Southerner. (1st edition) Philadelphia: Lippincott (1966)
E185.61 W36

Wesley, Charles Harris
In freedom's footsteps, from the African background to the Civil War. (1st edition) New York: Crown Publishing Company (1968)
E185 W397

Neglected history; essays in Negro history by a college president: Charles H. Wesley. (Washington, D. C.: Association for the Study of Negro Life and History, c1969)
E185 W398 1969

The quest for equality; from Civil War to civil rights. (1st edition) New York: Publishing Company (1968)
E185.6 W44

West Virginia. State College, Institute. Research Council
... An adventure in cooperative research .... Institute, West Virginia: West Virginia State College (1944)
E185.5 W45

Westin, Alan F, ed.
Freedom now! The civil rights struggle in America. New York: Basic Books (1964)
E185.61 W37 (Browsing Room, Undergraduate)

Weyl, Nathaniel
The Negro in American civilization. Washington, D. C.: Public Affairs Press (1960)
E185 W4 (Main, Social Work)

Wharton, Vernon Lane
The Negro in Mississippi, 1865-1890. New York: Harper & Row (1965)
E185.93 M6 W4 1947a

Another edition
F251 J28 vol. 28

White, Walter Francis
How far the promise land? New York: The Viking Press, 1955
E185.61 W4

A man called White. New York: Viking Press, 1948
E185.97 W6 A3 (Main, Undergraduate)

White, William Lindsay
Lost boundaries. (1st edition) New York: Harcourt, Brace (1948)
E185.97 J76 W5

White House Conference "to fulfill these rights," Washington, 1966.
Report, June 1-2, 1966
E185.61 W43 1966

Who's who in colored America.
vol. 1- 1927- New York: Who's Who in Colored America Corp. (c1927-
E185.96 A1 W5 (Reference)

Wilberforce University, Wilberforce, Ohio
Wilberforce University quarterly. (Wilberforce, Ohio, 1939-42)
E185.5 W66

Wiley, Bell Irvin
Southern Negroes: 1861-1865. New Haven: Yale University Press, 1938
E185.2 W67

Williams, George Washington
History of the Negro race in America from 1619 to 1880.... New York: G.P. Putnam's Sons, 1885 2 vols.
E185 W7 1883a (Undergraduate)

Williams, John Alfred
This is my country too. (New York) New American Library (1965)
E185.61 W45 (Browsing Room)

Williamson, Joel
After slavery; the Negro in South Carolina during Reconstruction, 1861-1877. Chapel Hill: University of North Carolina Press, 1965
E185.93 S7 W5 (History Graduate)

Williamson, Stanford Winfield
With grief acquainted. Chicago: Follett Publishing Company (1964)
E185.86 W5 (Browsing Room)

Willis, Garry
The second civil war: arming for Armageddon. New York: New American Library (1968)
E185.615 W5 (Browsing Room, Undergraduate)

Wilson, Joseph Thomas
The Black Phalanx. New York: Arno Press, 1968
E185.63 W5 1890a (Undergraduate)

Wilson, Theodore Brantner
The black codes of the South. University: University of Alabama Press (1965)
E185.61 W47

Winston, Henry M
Negro freedom, a goal for all Americans. New York: New Currents Publishing, 1964
E185.61 W5

Wish, Harvey, ed.
The Negro since emancipation. Engle-
wood Cliffs, New Jersey: Prentice-
Hall (1964)
E185.61 W55

Wolfgang, Marvin E
**Crime and race; conceptions and mis-
conceptions.** New York: Institute of
Human Relations Press, American
Jewish Committee (1964)
E185.65 W6 (Main, Social Work,
Reference)

Wood, Forrest G
**Black scare; the racist response to
emancipation and reconstruction.**
Berkeley: University of California
Press, 1968
E185.61 W58

Woodson, Carter Godwin
A century of Negro migration. Wash-
ington, D. C.: The Association for the
Study of Negro Life and History, 1918
E185.9 W89

**Free Negro heads of families in the
United States in 1830, together with a
brief treatment of the free Negro....**
Washington, D. C.: The Association
for the Study of Negro Life and History,
Inc. (c1925)
E185 W88

**Free Negro owners of slaves in the
United States in 1830, together with
Absentee ownership of slaves in the
United States in 1830.** New York:
Negro Universities Press (1968)
E185 W883 1924a

**The mind of the Negro as reflected in
letters written during the crisis, 1800-
1860 ....** Washington, D. C.: The
Association for Study of Negro Life
and History, Inc. (c1926)
E185 W898

The mis-education of the Negro. Washington, D. C.: The Associated Publishers, Inc., 1933
E185.82 W89

The Negro in our history .... Washing-
ton, D. C.: The Associated Publishing,
Inc. (c1922)
E185 W89

Another edition
E185 W89 1928

Another edition
E185 W89 1931

Another edition
E185 W89 1941

Another edition
E185 W89 1947

The rural Negro. Washington, D. C.:
The Association for the Study of Negro
Life and History, Inc. (c1930)
E185.86 W89 (Main, History Graduate)

The Negro wage earner. Washington,
D. C.; The Association for the Study
of Negro Life & History, 1930
E185.8 G8

**The Negro professional man and the
community.** Washington, D. C.: The
Association for the Study of Negro
Life and History, 1934
E185.82 W895

Woodward, Comer Vann
The strange career of Jim Crow. New
York: Oxford University Press (1964,
c1957)
E185.61 W6 1957a

Another edition
E185.61 W6 1966 (Main, Social Work,
Undergraduate)

Another edition
E185.61 W6 1966 (Main, Undergraduate,
Education)

Woofter, Thomas Jackson
The basis of racial adjustment.
Boston: Ginn & Company (c1965)
E185.61 W639

**Southern race progress, the wavering
color line.** Washington, D. C.: Public
Affairs Press (c1957)
E185.61 W64

Workman, William D
The case for the South. New York:
Devin-Adair Company (1960)
E185.61 W67

Wormley, Stanton Lawrence, comp
Many shades of black. New York:
Morrow, 1969
E185 W9 (Browsing Room)

Wright, Nathan
Black power and urban unrest; creative possibilities. (1st edition) New York: Hawthorne Books (1967)
E185.615 W7

Let's work together. (1st edition) New York: Hawthorne Books (1968)
E185.61 W72 (Browsing Room, Social Work)

12 million black voices; a folk history of the Negro in the United States.... New York: The Viking Press, 1941
E185.6 W9

Writers' program. Georgia
Drums and shadows; survival studies among the Georgia coastal Negroes. (by the) Savannah Unit, Georgia Writers' Project, Work Projects Administration. Athens: University of Georgia Press, 1940
E185.93 G4 W9

Writers' Program. Illinois
Cavalcade of the American Negro.... Chicago: Diamond Jubilee Exposition Authority, 1940
E185.6 W95 (Main, Education)

Writers' program. Virginia
The Negro in Virginia. New York: Hastings House, 1940
E185.93 V5 W7

Wynes, Charles E
Forgotten voices; dissenting southerners in an age of conformity. (Baton Rouge) Louisiana State University Press (1967)
E185.61 W9 (Main, Undergraduate)

The Negro in the South since 1865; selected essays in American Negro history. University: University of Alabama Press (1965)
E185.6 W97

Race relations in Virginia, 1870-1902. Charlottesville: University of Virginia Press, 1961
E185.93 V8 W92

Xavier University, New Orleans, La.
The Xavier University Occupational guidance monographs.... Monograph no. 1-25 of the Occupational Opportunities series. New Orleans, La.: Xavier University Press (c1937-38)
E185.8* X3

Yates, Elizabeth
Amos Fortune, free man. New York: Aladdin Books, 1951 (c1950)
E185.97 F73 Y3 (Education)

Another edition
E185.97 F73 Y3 1950a (Education)

Year.
Year's pictorial history of the American Negro. (Maplewood, New Jersey: C. S. Hammond, 1965)
E185 Y4

Young, Whitney Moore
To be equal. (1st edition) New York: McGraw-Hill (1964)
E185.61 Y58 (Social Work)

Young Women's Christian Associations. United States National Board. Department of Data and Trends
Toward better race relations. New York: Women's Press (1948)
E185.61 Y6 (Main, Social Work)

Zinn, Howard
SNCC: the new abolitionists. (2nd edition) Boston: Beacon Press (1965)
E185.61 S9 Z5 1965

The Southern mystique. New York: Knopf, 1968 (c1964)
E185.615 Z5

HOUSING

Advance Mortgage Corporation
Midwestern minority housing markets; a special report. Chicago, 1962
E185.89 H6 A43 (Commerce)

Babcock, Richard F
The zoning game; municipal practices and policies. Madison: University of Wisconsin Press, 1966
NA9108 B23 (Architecture)

Brandeis University, Waltham, Mass.,
Florence Heller Graduate School for
Advanced Studies in Social Welfare.
Research Center
**The middle-income Negro family faces
urban renewal.** For the Department of
Commerce & Development, Common-
wealth of Massachusetts, 1964
E185.89 H6 B7 (Social Work)

Clark, Henry
**The church and residential desegrega-
tion; a case study of an open housing
covenant campaign.** New Haven: College and University Press (1965)
E185.89 H6 C55

Commission on Race and Housing
Where shall we live? Report. Berkeley:
University of California Press, 1958
HD7293 C7 (Social Work)

Deutsch, Morton
**Interracial housing; a psychological
evaluation of a social experiment.**
Minneapolis: University of Minnesota
Press (c1951)
E185.89 H6 D4 (Education, Main)

Another edition
E185.89 H6 D4 1951a (Browsing Room,
Undergraduate)

Foley, Eugene P
The achieving ghetto. (Washington,
D. C.: National Press, 1968)
E185.8 F6 (Main, Social Work,
Commerce)

Glazer, Nathan, ed.
Studies in housing and minority groups.
Edited by N. Glazer and Davis McEn-
tire. Berkeley: University of California
Press, 1960
E185.89 H6 G5 (Main, Architecture)

Goff, Regina Mary
**Problems and emotional difficulties of
Negro children as studies in selected
communities and attributed by parents
and children to the fact that they are
Negro.** New York: Bureau of Publishing,
Teachers College, Columbia University,
1949
E185.89 C3 G6 (Health Center)

Another edition
E185.89 C3 1949a

Another edition
LB5 C72 no. 960 (Education)

Grodzius, Morton
**The metropolitan area as a racial
problem.** (Pittsburgh) University of
Pittsburgh Press (1961, c1958)
E185.89 H6 G73

Gruen, Victor
**The heart of our cities; the urban
crisis: diagnosis and cure.** New York:
Simon and Schuster, 1964
NA9108 G7 (Main, Architecture, Brows-
ing Room, Home Economics)

King, Martin Luther
**Strive toward freedom; the Montgomery
story.** (1st edition) New York: Harper
(c1958)
E185.89 T8 K5 (Browsing Room, Main,
Undergraduate)

Another edition
E185.89 T8 K5 1958a

Knight, Charles Louis
**Negro housing in certain Virginia
cities.** Richmond, Va.: The William
Byrd Press, Inc., 1927
AH439 K69

Laurenti, Luigi
**Property values and race; studies in
seven cities.** Berkeley: University of
California Press, 1960
E185.89 H6 L3 (Main, Architecture)

McEntire, Davis
Residence and race.... Berkeley: University of California Press, 1960
. HD7293 M3 (Social Work, Main, Architecture, Undergraduate)

Mayerson, Charlotte Leon, ed.
Two blocks apart.:.. New York: Holt,
Rinehart and Winston (1965)
HQ796 M36

Millea, Thomas V
Ghetto fever. Milwaukee: Bruce Pub-
lishing Company (1968)
F548.9 N3 M5 (Social Work)

Northwood, Lawrence King
**Urban desegregation: Negro pioneers
and their white neighbors.** Seattle:
University of Washington Press, 1965
E185.89 H6 N6 (Main, Social Work)

Osofsky, Gilbert
Harlem; the making of a ghetto. New
York: Harper & Row (1966)
F128.9 N3 O8 (Undergraduate, Social
Work)

Ohio. Civil Rights Commission
A survey of discrimination in housing
in Ohio. Columbus, 1963
E185.89 H6 O47 1963

Rapkin, Chester
The demand for housing in racially
mixed areas: a study of the nature of
neighborhood change. Berkeley: University of California Press, 1960
F158.9 N3 R3 (Main, Social Work,
Architecture, Health Center)

Sterner, Richard Mauritz Edvard
The Negro's share, a study of income,
consumption, housing and public
assistance. New York, London: Harper
& Brothers (1943)
E185.8 S83 (Main, Commerce, Education)

Taeuber, Karl E
Negroes in cities; residential segrega-
tion and neighborhood change. Chicago:
Aldine Publishing Company (1965)
E185.89 H6 T3 (Education, Architecture)

U. S. Commission on Civil Rights
Housing. (Washington: United States
Government Printing Office) 1961
HD7293 A4869 1961 (Architecture)

Housing; hearings. Washington: United
States Government Printing Office,
1959
HD7293 A487 1959

Housing in Washington: hearings....
(Washington: United States Govern-
ment Printing Office, 1962)
HD7304 W3 A56 1962

U. S. Commission on Civil Rights.
Massachusetts Advisory Committee.
Disorientation in housing in the Boston
metropolitan area; report.
(Washington?) 1963
E185.89 H6 U48 1963

U. S. Housing and Home Finance Agency.
Housing of the nonwhite population,
1940-1947. Washington (United States
Government Printing Office) 1946
E185.89 H2 U5 1947

Housing of the nonwhite population,
1940-1950. Washington: Housing &
Home Finance Agency, Office of the
Administrator, Division of Housing
Research, 1952
E185.89 H6 U5 1950

U. S. Housing and Home Finance Agency.
Office of Program Policy.
Our nonwhite population and its hous-
ing: the change between 1950-1960.
Washington: Housing & Home Finance
Agency, Office of the Administrator
(1963)
E185.89 H6 U52 1963

Another edition
E185.89 H6 U52 1963a (Commerce,
Architecture)

U. S. Public Housing Administration
Trends toward open occupancy in low-
rent housing programs of the Public
Housing Administration. (Washington)
Issued by the agency's Intergroup
Relations Branch.
E185.89 H6 A2 U5 (Reference)

Weaver, Robert Clifton
The Negro ghetto. (1st edition) New
York: Harcourt, Brace (1948)
E185.89 H6 W4 (Main, Social Work)

SLAVERY AND ANTI-SLAVERY

Adams, Alice Dana
The neglected period or anti-slavery in
America (1803-1831) Boston and
London: Ginn and Company, 1908
E446 A3

Adams, John Quincy, president United
States, 1767-1848
Argument of John Quincy Adams, be-
fore the Supreme Court of the United
States. New York: S. W. Benedict, 1841
E447 A3

Adams, Nehemiah
**A south-side view of slavery; or,
Three months at the South, in 1854.**
Boston: T. R. Marvin (etc.) 1854
E449 A3

Another edition
E449 A3 1860

The African repository ....
v. 1-68, 1825-1892 Washington: American Colonization Society.
E448 A25

Aikman, William
**The future of the colored race in Amer-
ica.** New York: A. D. F. Randolph,
1862
E453 A5 (Rare Book Collection)

Allen, George
**Resistance to slavery every man's
duty.** Boston: W. Crosby and H. P.
Nichols, 1847
E449 A4

American and Foreign Anti-Slavery
Society
**The annual report ... 1st-13th, 1839-
1854.** New York: American and Foreign
Anti-Slavery Society. 13 vols.
E449 A1 A5

**The American anti-slavery almanac for
1836-1847?** New York (etc.) American
Anti-Slavery Society. 12 vols.
E449 A1 A515 (Rare Book Collection)

American Anti-Slavery Society
**American slavery as it is; testimony of
a thousand witnesses.** New York:
American Anti-Slavery Society, 1839
E449 A5

Annual report .... 1834-61. New York:
American Anti-Slavery Society. 12 vols.
E449 A1 A52

American Colonization Society
**Memorial of the semi-centennial anni-
versary of the American Colonization
Society.** Washington: The Society,
1867
E448 A53

Ames, Mary
**From a New England woman's diary in
Dixie in 1865.** Springfield (Mass.: The
Plimpton Press, Norwood, Mass.) 1906
AH1665 A51

The Anti-slavery record
1835-38 New York: American Anti-
Slavery Society. 3 vols.
E449 A1 A55

Apthecker, Herbert
American Negro slave revolts. New
York: Columbia University Press,
London: P. S. King and Staples Ltd.,
1943
E447 A65

Another edition
E447 A65 1969

Another edition
Ja2 C72 no. 501

**The Negro in the abolitionist move-
ment.** New York: International (c1941)
E441 A65

**One continual cry: David Walker's
"Appeal to the Colored citizens of the
world, 1829-1830."** New York:
Humanities Press (1965)
E446 W3 A7

Armistead, Wilson
A tribute for the Negro. New York:
Manchester, Irwin, 1848
Micro-card E449

Armstrong, George Dodd
The Christian doctrine of slavery.
New York: Negro University Press
1969 (1857)
Micro-card E449

Avey, Elijah
**The capture and execution of John
Brown, a tale of martydom.** Elgin, Ill.:
Brethren Publishing House (c1906)
E451 A8

Aydelott, Benjamin Parham
Prejudice against colored people....
(Cincinnati: American Reform Tract
and Book Society, 186-?)
Micro-card E449

Bacon, Leonard
A plea for Africa. New Haven: T. G.
Woodward & Company, 1825
E448 B129

Baer, Helene (Gilbert)
**The heart is like heaven; the life of
Lydia Maria Child.** Philadelphia: Uni-
versity of Pennsylvania Press (1964)
E449 C55 B3

Bailey, Hugh C.
Hinton Rowan Helper, abolitionist-racist. University: University of Alabama Press (1965)
E449 H4 B3

Ball, Charles
Fifty years in chains; or The life of an American slave. Indianapolis, Ind.:
Asher and Company, 1860
E444 B184

Slavery in the United States Lewistown, Penn.: J. W. Shugert, 1836
E444 B182 (Rare Book Collection)

Another edition
E444 B183

Balme, Joshua Rhodes
American states, churches and slavery.
London: Hamilton, Adams, 1863
E449 B22 1863

Bancroft, Frederic
Slave trading in the Old South. Baltimore, Md.: J. H. Furst Co., 1931
E442 B3

Another edition
E442 B3 1959 (Undergraduate)

Barnes, Albert
The church and slavery. Philadelphia:
Parry and McMillan, 1857 (c1856)
E449 B23 1857

An inquiry into the Scriptual views of slavery. Philadelphia: Perkins & Purves, Boston: B. Perkins & Co., 1846
E449 B24

Barnes, Gilbert Hobbs
The anti-slavery impulse: 1830-1844.
New York, London: D. Appleton-Century (c1933)
E449 B26 (Main, Undergraduate)

Another edition
E449 B26 1933a

Another edition
E449 B26 1964a (Undergraduate)

Bartlett, Irving H
Wendell Phillips, Brahmin radical.
Boston: Beacon Press (c1961)
E449 P55 B3 (Main, Undergraduate)

Beaumont de La Bonniniere, Gustave Auguste de
Marie; or, Slavery in the United States.
Stanford, California: Stanford University Press, 1958
E443 B41 1958 (Social Work)

Benezet, Anthony
Views of American slavery, taken a century ago. Philadelphia: Published by the Association of Friends for the Diffusion of Religious and Useful Knowledge, 1858
E446 B4

Benton, Thomas Hart
Historical & legal examination of that part of the decision of the Supreme Court of the United States in the Dred Scott case .... New York: D. Appleton & Company, 1857
E450 S35 B4

Berwanger, Eugene H
The frontier against slavery; Western anti-Negro prejudice and the slavery extension controversy. Urbana: University of Illinois Press, 1967
E415.7 B45 (Main, Undergraduate)

Birckland, Lennox
A voice from the South, discussing among other subjects, slavery ....
Baltimore: J. W. Woods, printer, 1861
E449 B5

Birney, James Gillespie
The American churches the bulwarks of American slavery. 3rd American edition Concord, N. H.: P. Pillsbury, 1885
E449 B58 1885

Bittle, William Elmer
The longest way home. Detroit: Wayne State University Press, 1964
E448 B5

Blake, William O
The history of slavery and the slave trade, ancient and modern. Columbus, Ohio: J & H Miller, 1857
E441 B55 (Main, Undergraduate)

Blanchard, Jonathan
A debate on slavery, held on the 1st, 2nd, 3rd & 6th days of October, 1845...
Cincinnati: W. H. Moore & Co., New York: M. H. Newman, 1846
E449 B63

Bledsoe, Albert Taylor
An essay on liberty and slavery.
Philadelphia: J. B. Lippincott & Company, 1856
E449 B65

Boston slave riot, and trial of Anthony Burns. Boston: Fetridge and Company, 1854
E450 B8 B6

Boucher, Chauncy Samuel
In re that agressive slavocracy. (Cedar Rapids? Iowa, 1921)
E449 B68

Bradford, Sarah Elizabeth (Hopkins)
Harriet Tubman, the Moses of her people. New York: Corinth Books (1961)
E444 T88 B7 1961

Breckinridge, Robert Jefferson
Discourse of Dr. Breckinridge, delivered on the day of national humiliation, January 4, 1861, at Lexington Ky.
Baltimore: J. W. Woods, printer (c1861)
Micro-card E440.5

The great deliverance and the new career .... Philadelphia: J. S. Claxton, 1865
AH840 B82 G7

Another edition
Micro-card E649

Hints on slavery .... (Lexington, Ky.? 1843?)
Micro-card E445

The nation's success and gratitude.
Philadelphia: H. B. Ashmead, printer, 1864
Micro-card E458.3

The question of Negro slavery and the new constitution of Kentucky. (from the Biblical repertory and Princeton review. Philadelphia. 1849 V. 21, no. 4, p. 582-607)
E445 K5 B8

Breyfogle, William A
Make free. Philadelphia: Lippincott (1958)
E450 B7

Bridge, Isaac
Providential aspect and salutary tendency of the existing crisis....
New Orleans: Picayune Office printer, 1861
E449 B7

British and Foreign Anti-Slavery Society
Proceedings of the general anti-slavery convention. London, 1st, 1841
HT855 G32

Proceedings of the general anti-slavery convention. London, 2nd, 1843 British and Foreign Anti-Slavery Society (1843)
HT855 G33

Brittan, Edith H
To live in peace. (1st edition) New York: Exposition Press (c1959)
E448 B7 (Social Work)

Brooke, Samuel
Slavery and the slaveholder's religion; as opposed to christianity. Cincinnati: The author, 1846
E449 B73

Brookes, Iveson L
A defense of southern slavery. Hamburg, S. C.: Printed by Robinson & Carlisle, 1851
E449 B735

Brown, Mrs. Catharine S
Memoir of Rev. Abel Brown, by his companion .... Worcester: The author, 1849
E449 B74

Brown, David
The planter; or, Thirteen years in the South. By a northern man. Philadelphi z H. Hooker, 1853
E449 B75 (Rare Book Collection)

Brown, Isaac Van Arsdale
White diamonds better than "black diamonds"; slave states impoverished by slave labor. Trenton, N. J.: printed by Murphy & Bechtell, 1860
E449 B76

Brown, William Wells
The black man, his antecedents, his genius, and his achievements. New York: T. Hamilton, Boston: R. F. Wallcut, 1863
Micro-card E449

Clotel; or, The President's daughter; a narrative of slave life in the United States. London: Partridge & Oakley, 1853
Micro-card 449

Narrative of William W. Brown, a fugitive slave. Boston: the Anti-Slavery Office, 1848 (c1847)
E444 B7 1848

Another edition
E444 B7 1849

Brownlow, William Gannaway
Ought American slavery be perpetuated? Philadelphia: J. B. Lippincott & Co. (c1858)
E449 B78 (Main, Undergraduate)

Bruner, Clarence Vernon
An abstract of the religious instruction of the slaves in the antebellum South. Nashville, Tenn.: George Peabody's College for Teachers, 1933
E443 B717 (Main, Education)

Buckmaster, Henrietta, pseud.
Let my people go. New York and London: Harper (c1941)
E450 B77

Campbell, John
Negro-mania. Philadelphia: Campbell and Power, 1851
E449 C3

Carey, John L
Slavery in Maryland briefly considered. Baltimore: J. Murphy, 1845
E445 M3 C3

Carey, Mathew
Letters on the Colonization Society. (3rd edition) Philadelphia: Young, printer, 1832
E448 C34 1832a

Carlier, Auguste
De l'esclavage dans ses rapports avec l'union americaine. Paris: Michel Levy freres, 1862
E441 C36

Catterall, Helen Honor (Tunnicliff)
Judicial cases concerning American slavery and the Negro. Washington, D. C.: Carnegie Institute, 1926-37. 5 vols.
E441 C38

Cavanagh, Helen Marie
Anti-slavery sentiment and politics in the Northwest, 1844-60. (Chicago) 1940
E449 C37

Chambers, William
American slavery and colour. London: W. & R. Chambers, New York: Dix and Edwards, 1857
E449 C42

Channing, William Ellery
The duty of the free states. Boston: W. Crosby & Co., 1842
E447 C44

Emancipation. Boston: E. P. Peabody, 1840
E449 C43

Remarks on the slavery question, in a letter to Jonathan Phillips. Boston: J. Munroe & Company, 1839
E449 C44

Chase, Ezra B
Teachings of patriots and statesmen; or The "founders of the republic" on slavery. Philadelphia: J. W. Bradley, 1861 (c1860)
E441 C45

Cheever, George Barrell
God against slavery: and the freedom and duty of the pulpit to rebuke it, as a sin against God. Cincinnati: American Reform Tract and Book Society (1857?)
E449 C5

Another edition
E449 C5 1857a

The guilt of slavery and the crime of slaveholding. Boston: J. P. Jewett and Company, 1860
E449 C52

Chesnutt, Charles Waddell
Frederick Douglas. London: Kegan Paul, Trench, Trubner & Company (c1899)
E449 D73 C5

The house behind the cedars. Boston: Houghton, Mifflin Company (c1900)
E449 D73 C5

Child, David Lee
The American anti-slavery almanac, for 1836-1847? New York (etc.) American Anti-Slavery Society. 12v.
E449 A1 A515 (Rare Book Collection)

Rights and duties of the United States relative to slavery under the laws of war. Boston: R. F. Wallcut, 1861
E453 C45

Child, Lydia Maria (Francis)
Anti-slavery catechism. (2nd edition)
Newburyport: C. Whipple, 1839 (c1835)
E449 C527 1839

An appeal in favor of Americans called
Africans. New York: Arno Press, 1968
E449 C53 1836a (Undergraduate)

Correspondence between Lydia Maria
Child and Gov. Wise. New York: Amer-
ican Anti-Slavery Society, 1860
E451 C45

Isaac T. Hooper: a true life. Boston:
J. P. Jewett, Proctor & Worthington
(etc., etc.) 1853
E449 H59 C45 1853

The oasis. Boston: Allen and Ticknor,
1834
E449 C54

Christy, David
Cotton is king: or the culture of cotton,
and its relation to agriculture, manu-
factures and commerce.... Cincinnati:
Moore, Wilstach, Keys & Company,
1855
E449 C557

Pulpit politics; or, Ecclesiastical
legislation on slavery.... Cincinnati:
Faran & McLean 1862
E449 C5572

Clark, Calvin Montague
American slavery and Maine Congre-
gationalists. Bangor, Me.: The author,
1940
E441 C59

Clark, James Freeman
Anti-slavery days. New York: R.
Worthington, 1884 (c1883)
E441 C64

Clark, Lewis Garrard
Narratives of the sufferings of Lewis
and Milton Clarke. Boston: B. Marsh,
1846
E444 C5 1846

Clark, Rufus Wheelwright
The African slave trade. Boston: Amer-
ican Tract Society (1860)
E441 C63

Clay, Cassius Marcellus
The writings of.... New York: Harper
& Brothers, 1848
E449 C5575

Cleveland, Charles Dexter
Anti-slavery addresses of 1844 and
1845. London: S. Low, son, and
Marston, Philadelphia: J. A. Bancroft
& Company, 1867
E449 C558

Cobb, Howell
A Scriptural examination of the insti-
tution of slavery in the United States;
with its objects and purposes. (Perry?)
Ga.: printed for the author, 1856
E449 C6

Cobb, Thomas Read Rootes
An inquiry into the law of Negro slavery
in the United States of America.
Philadelphia: T. & J. W. Johnson &
Co., Savannah: W. T. Williams, 1858
E441 C7

Cochin, Augustin
The results of emancipation. Boston:
Walker, Wise & Company, 1863 (c1862)
HT1031 C61

Cockrum, William Monroe
History of the underground railroad as
it was conducted by the anti-slavery
league. Oakland City, Indiana: Press
of J. W. Cockrum Printing Company
(c1915)
E450 C6

Coffin, Levi
Reminiscences of Levi Coffin, the re-
puted president of the underground railroad. (3rd edition) R. Clarke, 1898
(c1876)
E450 C63 1898

Another edition
E450 C63 1898a

Coleman, John Winston
Slavery times in Kentucky. Chapel Hill:
The University of North Carolina Press
1940
E445 K5 C6

Coleman, Mary Haldane (Begg)
Virginia silhouettes; contemporary
letters concerning Negro slavery in the
state of Virginia. Richmond: Press of
the Dietz Printing Company, 1934
E445 V8 C6 1934a

Coleman, Mrs. Lucy Newhall
Reminiscences. Buffalo, New York:
H. L. Green, 1891
E449 C63

Collins, Winfield Hazlitt
The domestic slave trade of the southern states. New York: Broadway Publishing Company (c1904)
E442 C6

Colwell, Stephen
The South: a letter from a friend in the
North. Philadelphia: C. Sherman and
son, 1856
E449 C64

Connelley, William Elsey
John Brown. Topeka, Kansas: Crane
& Company, 1900 2 vols.
E451 C75 1900a

Conrad, Earl
Harriet Tubman ... Washington, D. C.:
The Associated Publishing, Inc.
(1943)
E444 T88 C6

Convention of Congregational Ministers
of Massachusetts
Report of the committee on slavery, to
the convention of Congregational Ministers of Massachusetts. Boston: Press
of T. R. Marvin, 1849
E449 C66

Cromwell, Otelia
Lucretia Mott. Cambridge: Harvard
University Press, 1958
E449 M92 C7

Crosby, Ernest Howard
Garrison, the non-resistant. Chicago:
The Public Publishing Company
(c1905)
E449 G24 C7

Curry, Richard Orr
The abolitionists — reformers or fanat-
ics? New York: Holt, Rinehart &
Winston (1965)
E449 C8

Curtis, George William
Wendell Phillips ... and the war for the
union. New York: J. B. Alden Publishers, 1886
E449 P55 C8

Dabney, Robert Lewis
A defence of Virginia (and through her,
of the South,) in recent and pending
contests against the sectional party.
New York: E. J. Hale & Son, 1867
E441 D3 (Main, Undergraduate)

Dew, Thomas Roderick
An essay on slavery. (2nd edition)
Richmond: J. W. Randolph, 1849
E449 D37 1849

Review of the debate (on the abolition
of slavery) in the Virginia legislature
of 1831 and 1832. Richmond: T. W.
White, 1832
E449 D4

Dewees, Jacob
The great future of America and
Africa. Philadelphia: H. Orr, 1854
E448 D5

Dillon, Merton Lynn
Benjamin Lundy and the struggle for
Negro freedom. Urbana: University of
Illinois Press, 1966
E446 L8 D5 (Main, Undergraduate)

Elijah P. Lovejoy, abolitionist editor.
Urbana: University of Illinois Press,
1961
E449 L86 D5

Donnan, Elizabeth
Documents illustrative of the history of
the slave trade to America. Washington, D. C.: Carnegie Institute, 1930-
35. 4 vols.
E441 D6

Douglas, William Orville
Mr. Lincoln and the Negroes: the long
road to equality. New York: Atheneum
(1966, c1963)
E457.2 D68 (Main, Undergraduate)

Douglass, Frederick
Life and times of Frederick Douglass,
written by himself. Hartford: Park Publishing Company, 1881
E449 D73 A1

Another edition
E449 D73 A1 1881a

Another edition
E449 D73 1881b

Another edition
E449 D73 A1 1962a (Education)

My bondage and my freedom. New
York: Miller, Orton & Mulligan, 1855
E449 D73

The life and writings of Frederick
Douglass (by) Philip S. Foner. New
York: International Publishing 1950-
55. 4 vols.
E449 D73 A2

Another edition
E449 D73 A27 1855a (Undergraduate)

Narrative of the life of Frederick
Douglass, an American slave. Boston:
Published at the Anti-Slavery Office,
1845
E449 D73 A3 (Main, Rare Book
Collection)

Another edition
E449 D73 A3 1845a (Rare Book
Collection)

Another edition
E449 D73 A3 1960 (Main, Undergraduate)

Oration by Frederick Douglass delivered on the occasion of the unveil-
ing of the Freedman's monument in
memory of Abraham Lincoln in Lincoln
Park, Washington, D. C. April 14,
1876. New York: Pathway Press 1940
E457.8 D64 1940

Drake, Charles Daniel
Union and anti-slavery speeches, delivered during the rebellion. Cincinnati: Applegate & Company, 1864
E458 D7

Drake, Daniel
Dr. Daniel Drake's letters on slavery
to Dr. John C. Warren of Boston. New
York: Schuman's, 1940
E449 D76

Drake, Thomas Edward
Quakers and slavery in America. New
Haven: Yale University Press, 1950
E441 D75

Drew, Benjamin
A north-side view of slavery. Boston:
J. P. Jewett & Company, New York:
Sheldon, Lamport & Blakeman, 1856
(c1855)
E450 D7

Drew, Thomas
The John Brown invasion; an authentic
history .... Boston: J. Campbell, 1860
(c1859)
E451 D7

Duberman, Martin B
The antislavery vanguard: new essays
on the abolitionists. Princeton, N. J.:
Princeton University Press, 1965
E449 D8 (Main, Undergraduate)

DuBois, William Edward Burghardt
The supression of the African slave
trade to the United States of America
1638-1870. New York: Russell &
Russell, 1965
E441 D8 1898a

Duignan, Peter
The United States and the African
slave trade, 1619-1862. Stanford,
California: Hoover Institute on War,
Revolution and Peace, Stanford Uni-
versity, 1963
E441 D83 (Main, Undergraduate)

Dumond, Dwight Lowell
Anti-slavery origins of the Civil War
in the United States. Ann Arbor: The
University of Michigan Press, London:
H. Milford, Oxford University Press,
1939
E449 D89

Anti-slavery; the crusade for freedom
in America. Ann Arbor: University of
Michigan Press (1961)
E441 D84 (Main, Undergraduate)

Elkin, Stanley M
Slavery: a problem in American insti-
tutional and intellectual life. Chicago:
University of Chicago Press (1959)
E443 E4 (History Graduate, Under-
graduate)

Another edition
E443 E4 1963

Another edition
E443 E4 1968 (Undergraduate)

Elliott, Charles
Sinfulness of American slavery: proved
from its evil sources .... Cincinnati:
L. Swormstedt & J. H. Power, 1850,
2 vols.
E449 E47

Elliott, E N
Cotton is king, and pro-slavery argu-
ments .... (3rd edition) Augusta, Ga.:
Pritchard, Abbott & Loomis, 1860
E449 E48 1860a

The Emancipator (complete) published
by Elihu Embree, a reprint. Nashville,
Tenn.: B. H. Murphy, 1932
E446 E53

Emerson, Ralph Waldo
An address delivered in the court-
house in Concord, Mass., on 1st Aug.,
1844. Boston: J. Munroe & Company,
1844
E449 E485 (Rare Book Collection)

The end of the irrepressible conflict.
by a merchant of Philadelphia. Philadelphia: King & Baird, 1860
E449 E49

England, John
Letters of the late Bishop England to
the Hon. John Forsythe, on the sub-
ject of domestic slavery. Baltimore:
J. Murphy, 1844.
E449 E5

Estes, Matthew
A defence of Negro slavery, as it ex-
ists in the United States. Montgomery:
Press of the "Alabama journal", 1846
E449 E8

Fay, Theodore Sedgwick
Die Sklavenmacht. Berlin: Stilke &
Van Muyden, 1865
E441 F3

Federal Writers' Project
Lay my burden down; a folk history of
slavery. Chicago: University of
Chicago Press (1945)
E444 F29

Filler, Louis
The crusade against slavery; 1830-
1860. (1st edition) New York: Harper,
1960
E173 N4 F5 (Main, Undergraduate,
History Graduate)

Fitzhugh, George
Cannibals all! or, Slaves without
masters. Richmond: A. Morris, 1857
E449 F53

Another edition
E449 F53 1960 (Main, Undergraduate)

Five slave narratives; a compendium.
New York: Arno Press, 1968
E444 F5 (Main, Undergraduate)

Flanders, Ralph Betts
Plantation slavery in Georgia. Chapel
Hill: University of North Carolina
Press, 1933
E445 G3 F55 (Main, Commerce)

Fletcher, John
Studies on slavery, in easy lessons.
Natchez: J. Warner, 1852 (c1851)
E449 F6

Foner, Philip Sheldon
Frederick Douglass, a biography. New
York: Citadel Press (1964)
E449 D73 F6 1964 (Main, Under-
graduate)

The life and writings of Frederick
Douglass. New York: International
Publishers 1950-55.
E449 D73 A2

Franklin, John Hope
The emancipation proclamation. New
York: Doubleday, 1963
E453 F7 (Undergraduate, Main)

Fredrickson, George M
William Lloyd Garrison. Englewood
Cliffs, N. J.: Prentice-Hall (1968)
E449 G24 F7

Free negroism; or Results of emancipa-
tion in the North, and the West India
Islands. 2nd edition revised and en-
larged. New York: Van Evrie, Horton
& Company, 1966
E449 F68 1866

Freeman, Frederick
Yaradee. Philadelphia: J. Whetham,
1836
E448 F7

French, Mrs. A M
Slavery in South Carolina and the ex-
slaves; or, The Port Royal Mission.
New York: W. M. French, 1862
E185.93 S7 F7

Friends, Society of London Yearly
meeting.
Proceedings in relation to the presentation of the address of the yearly
meeting.... Cincinnati: Printed by E.
Morgan & Sons, 1855
E449 F7 1855

Furnas, Joseph Chamberlain
Goodbye to Uncle Tom. New York:
W. Sloane Associates, 1956
E441 F8 (Main, Undergraduate)

The road to Harper's Ferry. New York:
W. Sloane Associates, 1959
E448 F8 (Browsing Room)

Gara, Larry
The liberty line; the legend of the
Underground Railroad. Lexington:
University of Kentucky Press (1961)
E450 G3

Garrison, William Lloyd
Selections from the writings and
speeches of William Lloyd Garrison.
Boston: R. F. Wallcut, 1852
E449 G24

Thoughts on African colonization...
Boston: Garrison and Knapp, 1832
E448 G3

Another edition
E448 G3 1832a (Undergraduate)

Genovese, Eugene D
The political economy of slavery:
studies in the economy and society of
the slave South. New York: Pantheon
Books (1965)
E442 G4 (Main, Undergraduate)

George, James Zachariah
The political history of slavery in the
United States. New York: The Neale
Publishing Company, 1915
AH778 G34

Giddings, Joshua Reed
The exiles of Florida. Columbus, Ohio:
Follett, Foster, 1858
E83.817 G45

Another edition
E83.817 G45 1964

Speeches in Congress (1841-1852)
Boston: J. P. Jewett & Co., Cleveland: Jewett, Proctor and Worthington,
1853
E415.6 G5

Gilbert, Olive
Narrative of Sojourner Truth. Boston,
1850
E185.97 T8 G5

Another edition
E185.97 T8 G5 1878a (Main, Undergraduate)

Gill, John
Tide without turning: Elijah P. Love-
joy and freedom of the press. Boston:
Starr King Press (c1958)
E449 L86 G5

Goodell, William
The American slave code in theory
and practice. (2nd edition) New York:
American and Foreign Anti-Slavery
Society, 1853
E441 G6 1853a

Goodloe, Daniel Reaves
The southern platform: or, a Manual of
southern sentiment on the subject of
slavery. Boston: J. P. Jewett & Company, 1858
E449 G6

Goodwin, Daniel Raynes
Southern slavery in its present aspects.
Philadelphia: J. B. Lippincott & Com-
pany, 1864
E449 H5518 G6

Graham, Shirley
There was once a slave. New York: J.
Messner, Inc. (1947)
E449 D73 G7 (Main, Undergraduate)

Your most humble servant. New York:
Messner (1949)
QB36 B3 G7

Another edition
QB36 B3 G7145

Grayson, W J
James Louis Petigru. A biographical
sketch. New York: Harper & Brothers,
1866
AH1674 P48 G7

Greeley, Horace
A history of the struggle for slavery
extension or restriction in the United
States, from the Declaration of Inde-
pendence to the present day. New
York: Dix, Edwards & Company, 1856
E441 G7

Gregory, James Monroe
Frederick Douglass, the orator. Spring-
field, Mass.: Wiley & Co. (c1893)
E449 D73 G73

Griffiths, Julia
Autographs for freedom. Boston: J. P.
Jewett & Company, Cleveland: Jewett,
Proctor, & Worthington, 1853
E449 G7 Ser. 1 (Rare Book Collection)

Autographs for freedom. (2nd series)
Auburn, Alden, Beardsley & Company,
Rochester: Wanzer, Breadsley & Company, 1854
E449 G7 Ser 2 (Rare Book Collection)

Grimke, Archibald Henry
William Lloyd Garrison, the abolitionist. New York: Funk & Wagnalls,
1891
E449 G24 G8

Gurley, Ralph Randolph
Mission to England. Washington, D.C.:
W. W. Morrison, 1841
E448 G8

Halasz, Nicholas
**The rattling chains: slave unrest and
revolt in the antebellum South.** New
York: McKay (1966)
E447 H3

Hall, Marshall
**The two-fold slavery of the United
States.** London: A. Scott, 1854
E449 H3

Hallowell, Anna (Davis)
**James and Lucretia Mott. Life and
letters.** Boston, New York: Houghton,
Mifflin & Company, 1884
E449 M9 H3

Another edition
E449 M9 1890

Hare, Lloyd Custer Mayhew
**The greatest American woman,
Lucretia Mott.** New York: The American Historical society, inc., 1937
E449 M92 H2

Harris, Alexander
**The causes of the war shown; or The
inquiries.** Philadelphia, 1863
E448 H3

Harris, Norman Dwight
**The history of Negro servitude in
Illinois, and of the slavery agitation in
that state, 1719-1864.** Chicago: A. C.
McClurg & Company, 1904
E445 I2 H3

Haviland, Laura (Smith)
A woman's life-work; labors and experiences. Chicago: C. V. Waite,
1887 (c1881)
E450 H3 1887

Headley, Joel Tyler
**The great rebellion; a history of the
civil war in the United States.** Hartford: Hurlbut, Williams & Company,
Chicago: E. B. & R. C. Treat, 1863
(c1862) 2 vols.
E468 H4

Another edition
E468 H4 1866

Hedrick, Charles Embury
**Social and economic aspects of slavery
in the transmontane prior to 1850.**
Nashville, Tenn.: George Peabody
College for Teachers, 1927
E449 H38 1927a

Helper, Hinton Rowan
**The impending crisis of the South: how
to meet it.** New York: Burdick Brothers,
1857
E449 H4

Another edition
E449 H4 1860 (Commerce, Main, Undergraduate)

Henson, Josiah
Father Henson's story of his own life.
New York: Corinth Books (1962)
E444 H52 A3 1962

**Truth stranger than fiction. Father
Henson's story of his own life.**
Boston: J. P. Jewett & Company,
Cleveland: H. P. B. Jewett, 1858
E444 H52 A3 (Main, Rare Book
Collection)

Another edition
E444 H52 A3 1879

Hinton, Richard Josiah
John Brown and his men. New York:
Funk & Wagnalls, 1894
AH825 B87 H6

Another edition
E451 H5 1894a (Undergraduate)

Hodgman, Stephen Alexander
**The nation's sin and punishment; or
The land of God visible in the overthrow of slavery.** New York: American
News Company, 1864
E449 H53

Holland, Frederic May
Frederick Douglass, the colored orator. New York: Funk & Wagnalls Company, 1895
E449 D73 H7 1895

Another edition
E449 D73 H7 1895a

Hopkins, John Henry
A Scriptural, ecclesiastical, and historical view of slavery.... New York: W. I. Pooley & Company (1864)
E449 H55

Hopkins, Vincent Charles
Dred Scott's case. New York: Fordham University Press, D. X. McMullen Company, distributors (1951)
E450 S35 H6 1951

Hoppe, Anna
Negro slavery: a review of conditions preceding the Civil War. St. Louis: Rudolph Volkening (1935)
AH439 H79

Hosmer, William
The higher law, in its relations to civil government: with particular reference to slavery, and the fugitive slave law. Auburn, New York, Derby & Miller, 1852
E449 H595

Hoss, Elijah Embree
Elihu Embree, abolitionist. Nashville: University Press Company, 1897
E446 E55 H6

Hough, Sabin
The Union: how shall it be reconstructed and saved? (Cincinnati, 1861)
E449 H598 (Rare Book Collection)

Howard, Warren S
American slaves and the Federal law, 1837-1862. Berkeley: University of California Press, 1963
E449 H6

Howe, Samuel Gridley
The refugees from slavery in Canada West. Report to the Freedmen's inquiry commission. Boston: Wright & Potter, printers, 1864.
AH755 H85

Humphries, Eck
The underground railroad. McConnelsville, Ohio: Herald Printing Company, 1931
E450 H92

Hurd, John Codman
The laws of freedom and bondage in the United States. Boston: Little, Brown & Company, New York: D. Van Nostrand, 1858-62. 2 vols.
E441 H8

An inquiry into the condition and prospects of the African race in the United States: and the means of bettering its fortunes. By an American. Philadelphia: Haswell, Barrington & Haswell, 1839
E449 I5

James, H F
Abolitionism unveiled! hypocrisy unmasked! and knavery scouraged.... New York: T. V. Paterson, 1850
E449 J3

Jameson, Melvin
Elijah Parish Lovejoy as a Christian. Rochester, N.Y.: Scranton, Wetmore & Company (1910?)
E449 L86 J3

Jay, William
Miscellaneous writings on slavery. Boston: John P. Jewett & Company, Cleveland, Ohio: Jewett, Proctor & Worthington, 1853
AH755 J42

Jefferson, Isaac
Memoirs of a Monticello slave. Charlottesville: University of Virginia Press, 1951
E444 J4

A view of the action of the federal government in behalf of slavery. New York: J. S. Taylor, 1838
E441 J3

Jenkins, William Sumner
Pro-slavery thought in the old South. Chapel Hill: University of North Carolina Press, 1935
E441 J4

Johnson, Charles Spurgeon
Shadow of the plantation.... Chicago, Illinois: The University of Chicago Press (1934)
AH439 J68

Johnson, Frank Roy
The Nat Turner slave insurrection. Murfreesboro, North Carolina: Johnson Publishing (1966)
F232 S7 J6

Johnson, Oliver
  William Lloyd Garrison and his times.
  Boston: B. B. Russel & Company, New
  York: C. Drew, 1880 (c1879)
  E449 G24 J6

Junkin, George
  The integrity of our national union, vs.
  abolitionism, an argument from the
  Bible. Cincinnati: R. P. Donogh, 1843
  E449 J8 (Rare Book Collection)

Kansas. University.
  A check list of an exhibition of John
  Brown, 1800-1859. (Lawrence) 1959
  E451 K27

Karsner, David
  John Brown, terrible "saint." New
  York: Dodd, Mead & Company, 1934
  E451 K3

Keckley, Mrs. Elizabeth (Hobbs)
  Behind the scenes. New York: Carleton,
  1868
  E457.15 K4

  Another edition
  E457.15 K4 1868a (Undergraduate)

Keifer, Joseph Warren
  Slavery and four years of war; a politi-
  cal history of slavery in the United
  States. New York and London: G. P.
  Putnam's Sons, 1900
  E470 K4

Korngold, Ralph
  Thaddeus Stevens; a being darkly
  wise and rudely great. (1st edition)
  New York: Harcourt, Brace (c1955)
  E415.9 S84 K6

  Two friends of man; the story of
  William Lloyd Garrison and Wendell
  Phillips. (1st edition) Boston: Little
  Brown, 1950
  E449 G24 K6 (Main, Undergraduate)

Kraditor, Aileen S
  Means and ends in American aboli-
  tionism: Garrison and his critics on
  strategy and tactics, 1834-1850. (New
  York) Pantheon Books (1969)
  E449 K7

Kuhns, Frederick Irving
  The American Home Missionary Society
  in relation to the anti-slavery con-
  troversy in the Old Northwest.
  Billings, Mont., 1959
  E449 K8

Lader, Lawrence
  The bold Brahmins; New England's
  war against slavery, 1831-1863. (1st
  edition) New York: Dutton, 1961
  E449 L3

Larned, Edwin Channing
  The new fugitive slave law. Chicago:
  Printed at the Democrat Office, 1850
  E450 L3 (Rare Book Collection)

Laurens, Henry
  A letter from Henry Laurens to his son,
  John Laurens, Aug. 14, 1776. New
  York: privately printed for the Columbia
  University Libraries,1964
  E446 L3

The legion of liberty! and force of truth,
  containing the thoughts, words, and
  deeds of some prominent apostles ....
  New York: American Anti-Slavery
  Society, 1857
  E449 L4 1857

Lerner, Gerda
  The Grimke sisters from South Caroli-
  na; rebels against slavery. Boston:
  Houghton Mifflin, 1967
  E449 G8 L4

The Liberator.
  Documents of upheaval; selections
  from William Lloyd Garrison's the
  Liberator, 1831-1865. (1st edition)
  New York: Hill & Wang (1966)
  E449 L47 (History Graduate)

The liberty bell, by friends of freedom.
  Boston: Anti-slavery Fair, 1839-46,
  National Anti-slavery Bazaar, 1847-58.
  E449 L5

Liberty or slavery; the great national
  question. Boston: Congressional
  Board of Publication, 1857
  E449 L53

Livermore, George
  An historical research respecting the
  opinions of the founders of the republic on Negroes as slaves, as citizens,
  and as soldiers. Boston: J. Wilson &
  son, 1862
  AH540 L78

Lloyd, Arthur Young
  The slavery controversy, 1831-1860.
  Chapel Hill: University of North
  Carolina Press, 1939
  E449 L79

Loguen, Jermain Wesley
The Rev. J. W. Loguen, as a slave and as a freedman. Syracuse: Truair, 1859
AH755 L84

Long, John Dixon
Pictures of slavery in church and state. Philadelphia: the author, 1857
E449 L8

Lovejoy, Owen
The barbarism of slavery. (Washington, D. C.: Buell & Blanchard, printers, 1860)
E449 L84

Lowell, James Russel
The anti-slavery papers of James Russel Lowell. Boston: Houghton, Mifflin, 1902, 2 vols.
E449 L87 (Rare Book Collection)

Lutz, Alma
Crusade for freedom; women of the anti-slavery movement. Boston: Beacon Press, (1968)
E449 L89

Lyman, Darius
Leaven for doughfaces; or Threescore and ten parables touching slavery. Cincinnati: Bargs & Company, Cleveland: L. E. Barnard & Company, 1856
E449 L9

McColley, Robert
Slavery and Jeffersonian Virginia. Urbana: University of Illinois Press, 1964
E445 V8 M3 1964 (Main, Undergraduate)

McConnell, John Preston
Negroes and their treatment in Virginia from 1865 to 1867. Pulaski, Va.: B. D. Smith & Brothers (c1910)
AH1210 V8 M12

McDougall, Mrs. Frances Harriet (Whipple) Greene
Shahmah in pursuit of freedom; or The branded hand. New York: Thatcher & Hutchinson, 1858
E449 M13 1858 (Rare Book Collection)

McDougall, Mrs. Marion Gleason
... Fugitive slaves (1619-1865). Boston: Ginn & Company, 1891
AH755 M13

McKitrick, Eric L
Slavery defended: the views of the old South. Englewood Cliffs, N. J.: Prentice Hall (1963)
E449 M16

McManus, Edgar J
A history of Negro slavery in New York. (1st edition Syracuse, N. Y.) Syracuse University Press (1966)
E445 N56 M3

MacNaul, Willard Carey
The Jefferson-Lemen compact. (Chicago) The University of Chicago Press, 1915
E445 I2 M16

McPherson, James M
The struggle for equality: abolitionists and the Negro in the Civil War and Reconstruction. Princeton: Princeton University Press, 1964
E449 M19 (Main, Undergraduate)

Magdol, Edward
Owen Lovejoy, abolitionist in Congress. New Brunswick, N. J.: Rutgers University Press (1967)
E415.9 L89 M3

Mandel, Bernard
Labor; free and slave, working men and the anti-slavery movement in the U. S. New York: Association Authors (c1955) :
E449 M3 (History Graduate, Undergraduate)

Martyn, Carlos
Wendell Phillips: the agitator. New York: Funk & Wagnalls Company (c1890)
E449 P55 M3

Massie, James William
America; the origin of her present conflict; her prospect for the slave, and her claim for anti-slavery sympathy. London: J. Snow, 1864
AH778 M41

Mathews, Donald G
Slavery and Methodism; a chapter in American morality 1780-1845. Princeton, N.J.: Princeton University Press, 1965
E449 M32

Matlack, Lucius C
  The antislavery struggle and triumph
  in the Methodist Episcopal church.
  New York: Phililips & Hunt, Cincin-
  nati: Walden & Stove, 1881
  E449 M34

May, Samuel Joseph
  Some recollections of our anti-slavery
  conflict. New York: Arno Press, 1968
  E449 M37 1869a (Undergraduate)

Mellen, George W F
  An argument on the unconstitutionality
  of slavery, embracing an abstract of
  the proceedings of the national and
  state conventions on this subject.
  Boston: Saxton & Peirce, 1841
  E449 M4

Mellon, Matthew Taylor
  Early American views on Negro
  slavery; from the letters and papers of
  the founders of the republic. New
  York: Bergman Publishers (1934)
  AH755 M52

Meltzer, Milton
  Tongue of flame; the life of Lydia
  Maria Child. New York: Crowell (1965)
  E449 C55 M4

Merkel, Benjamin
  The antislavery controversy in Mis-
  souri 1819-1865. St. Louis: Washington
  University, 1942
  E445 M67 M5

  Another edition
  AH755 M52 1969

Merrill, Walter McIntosh
  Against wind and tide, a biography of
  Wm. Lloyd Garrison. Cambridge: Har-
  vard University Press, 1963
  E449 G24 M4 (Main, Undergraduate)

Merriman, George Spring
  The Negro and the nation; a history of
  American slavery and enfranchisement.
  New York: Henry Holt & Company
  (c1906)
  AH439 M56

Moore, George Henry
  Notes on the history of slavery in
  Massachusetts. New York: Negro
  Universities Press, 1886
  E445 M4 M6 1866a

Morse, Jedidiah
  A discourse, delivered at the African
  meeting - house, in Boston, July 14,
  1808. Boston: Printed by Lincoln and
  Edmands, 1808.
  E446 M6 (Rare Book Collection)

Muelder, Hermann Richard
  Fighters for freedom. New York:
  Columbia University Press, 1959
  E445 I2 M8

The national era.
  Washington, 4 vols.
  E449* A1 N3

New-England Educational Commission
  for Freedmen.
  Extracts from letters of teachers and
  superintendents of the New-England
  Educational Commission for Freedmen.
  Boston: D. Clapp, 1864
  AH1205 N54

Nichols, Charles Harold
  Many thousand gone. Leiden: Brill,
  1963
  E444 N5

Nichols, Roy Franklin
  Disruption of American democracy.
  New York: Macmillan, 1948
  E436 N62 (Main, History Graduate)

Northrup, Solomon
  Twelve years a slave. Auburn: Derby
  & Miller, Buffalo: Derby, Orton &
  Mulligan, 1853
  E444 N6

  Another edition
  E444 N6 1968

Nye, Russel Blaine
  William Lloyd Garrison and the
  humanitarian reformers. (1st edition)
  Boston: Little, Brown (c1955)
  E449 G24 N8 (Main, Undergraduate)

Olson, Edwin
  Negro slavery in New York. New York,
  1947
  E445 N56 O5

Owen, Robert Dale
  The policy of emancipation: in three
  letters.... Philadelphia: J. B. Lippincott & Company, 1863
  E453 O9

Owens, William A
Black mutiny; the revolt on the
schooner Amistad. Philadelphia:
Pilgrim Press (1968)
E447 O9 1968

Paine, Lewis W
Six years in a Georgia prison. Narra-
tive of Lewis W. Paine. Boston: B.
Marsh, 1852 (c1851)
E450 P3

Palfrey, John Gorham
Papers on the slave power. Boston:
Merrill, Cobb & Company (1846)
E449 P3 1846a

Parker, Theodore
The trial of Theodore Parker, for the
misdemeanor of a speech in Faneuil
hall.... Boston: Published for the
author, 1855
E450 P35

Parsons, Theophilus
Slavery. Its origins, influence, and
destiny. Boston: W. Carter & Brothers,
1863
E453 P3

Patton, William Weston
Slavery and infidelity. Cincinnati:
American Reform Book & Tract Society
(c1856)
E449 P38

Pease, William Henry
The antislavery argument. Indianap-
olis: Bobbs - Merrill (c1965)
E446 P4

Phelps, Amos Augustus
Lectures on slavery, and its remedy.
Boston: New England Anti-Slavery
Society, 1834
E449 P53

Phillips, Ulrich Bonnell
American Negro slavery: a survey of
the supply, employment and control of
Negro labor as determined by the
Plantation Regime. New York: D.
Appleton & Co., 1940 (c1918)
E441 P45

Another edition
E441 P45 1918a (Main, Undergraduate)

Phillips, Wendell
Review of Lysander Spooner's essay
on the unconstitutionality of slavery.
Boston: Andrews & Prentiss, 1847
E441 S618 P4 1847

Wendell Phillips on civil rights and
freedom. Edited by Louis Filler. (1st
edition) New York: Hill & Wang (1965)
E449 P55 (History Graduate)

Pillsbury, Parker
Acts of the anti-slavery apostles. Con-
cern,N. H. (Clague, Wegman, Schlicht
& Co., printers) 1883
E449 P58 1883

Pollard, Edward Alfred
Black diamonds gathered in the darkey
homes of the South. New York: Pudney
& Russell, 1859
E449 P75 1859

Another edition
E449 P75 1860

Poole, William Frederick
Anti-slavery opinions before the year
1800; read before the Cincinnati
literary club, Nov. 16, 1872.
Cincinnati: R. Clarke & Company, 1873
E446 P6

The pro-slavery argument; as main-
tained by the most distinguished
writers.... Charleston: Walker, Richards
& Company, 1852
E449 P96

Quarles, Benjamin
Frederick Douglass. Washington, D.C.:
Associated Publishers (c1948)
E449 D73 Q3

Another edition
E449 D73 Q32

Lincoln and the Negro. New York:
Oxford University Press, 1962
E457.2 Q3 (Main, Undergraduate)

The Negro in the Civil War. Boston:
Little, Brown, 1953
E450 N3 Q3

Quarterly anti-slavery magazine
Edited by Elizur Wright, June, v. 1-2,
Oct., 1835-July 1837. New York:
American Anti-Slavery Society.
Micro card E449

Quincy, Josiah
Address illustrative of the nature and
power of the slave states, and the
duties of the free states. Boston:
Ticknor and Fields, 1856
E453 Q7

Ratner, Lorman
Powder keg; Northern opposition to
the anti-slavery movement. New York:
Basic Books (1968)
E449 R3

Read, Hollis
The Negro problem solved; or, Africa
as she was, as she is, and as she
shall be. New York: A. A. Constantine,
1864
E448 R4

Redpath, James
The public life of captain John Brown.
Boston: Thayer and Eldrige, 1860
E451 R4

Reese, David Meredith
Letters to the Honorable William Jay.
New York: Leavitt, Lord and Company,
Boston: Crocker and Brewster, 1835
E449 J42 R3

Robinson, John Bell
Picture of slavery and anti-slavery.
Advantageous of Negro freedom.
Philadelphia, 1863
AH755 R66

Ross, Alexander Milton
Memoirs of a reformer. Toronto: Hunter
Rose & Co., 1893
E450 R8

Recollections and experiences of an
abolitionist; from 1855-1865. Toronto:
Rowsell & Hutchison, 1875
E450 R82 (Rare Book Collection)

Ross, Frederick Augustus
Slavery ordained of God. Philadelphia:
J. B. Lippincott & Company, 1857
E449 R82

Ruchames, Louis
The abolitionists. New York: Putnam
(1963)
E449 R88 (History Graduate)

A John Brown reader. New York:
Abelard-Schuman, 1959
E451 R8 (Main, Undergraduate)

Russell, Charles Edward
The story of Wendell Phillips: a soldie
of the common good. Chicago: C. H.
Kerr and Company (c1914)
E449 P55 R8

Sanborn, Franklin Benjamin
D. S. G. Howe, the philanthropist.
New York: Funk & Wagnalls, 1891
E449 H64 S3

The life and letters of John Brown,
liberator of Kansas. Boston: Roberts
Brothers, 1885
E451 S19

Recollections of seventy years.
Boston: R. G. Badger, 1909 2 vols.
E449 S19

Another edition
E449 S19 1909a

Savage, William Sherman
The controversy over the distribution
of abolition literature 1830 - 1860.
(Washington, D. C.) The Association
for the study of Negro life and history,
inc., 1938
E449 S264

Sawyer, George S
Southern institutes; or, An inquiry into
the origin and early prevalence of
slavery and the slave-trade. Philadelphia: J. B. Lippincott & Company,
1858
E449 S3

Scarborough, Ruth
The opposition to slavery in Georgia
prior to 1860. Nashville, Tenn.: George
Peabody College for Teachers, 1933
E445 G3 S3 (Main, Education)

Schuckers, Jacob William
The life and public services of Salmon
Portland Chase. New York: D. Apple-
ton & Company, 1874
E415.9 C4 S3

Seabury, Samuel
American slavery distinguished from
the slavery of English theorists and
justified by the laws of nature. New
York: Mason Brothers, 1861
E449 S4

Sears, Lorenzo
Wendell Phillips, orator and agitator.
New York: Doubleday Page & Compan'
1909
E449 P55 S4

Sellers, James Benson
Slavery in Alabama. University, Al'
University of Alabama Press, 195('
E445 A3 S4

Sherwin, Oscar
Prophet of liberty; a biography of Wendell Phillips. New York: New York University, 1943
E449 P55 S5

Shipherd, Jacob R
History of the Oberlin - Wellinton rescue. New York: Sheldon & Company, 1859
E450 S55

Siebert, Wilbur Henry
Light on the underground railroad. Re-printed from the American historical review, vol. 1, no. 3, April 1896
AH755 S56

Slavery and white servitude in East Florida. Gainsville, Florida: Florida Historical Society, c1931
AH1715 S563

The Underground Railroad from slavery to freedom. New York: Macmillan, 1898
E450 S567

The Underground Railroad in Ohio. Columbus, Ohio, 1895
AH755 S573

Another edition
E450 S567 1899

Another edition
E450 S567 1898a (Undergraduate)

Another edition
E450 S567 1898b (Undergraduate)

The Underground Railroad in Massa-chusetts. Worcester, Massachusetts: American Antiquarian Society (Pro-ceedings) 1935
E172 A47 n.s. V.45, pt. 1

Another edition
AH755 S574

Vermont's anti-slavery and under-ground railroad record. Columbus: Spahr & Glenn, 1937
E450 S57

Sillen, Samuel
Women against slavery. New York: Masses & Mainstream (1955)
E449 S5

Simms, Henry Harrison
Emotion at high tide: abolition as a controversial factor, 1830-45. (Baltimore?) 1960
E449 S525 (Main, Undergraduate)

Simpson, Albert Franklin
The political significance of slave representation 1787-1821. (Baton Rouge, La.) 1941
E446 S6

Smedley, Robert C
History of the underground railroad in Chester, and neighboring counties of Pennsylvania. Lancaster: Office of The Journal, 1883
E450 S63

Smith, Elbert B
The death of slavery; the United States, 1837-65. Chicago: University of Chicago Press (1967)
E415.7 S6 (History Graduate)

Smith, Goldwin
Does the Bible sanction American slavery? Cambridge: Sever & Francis, 1863
E449 S53

Smith, James L
Autobiography of James L. Smith. Norwich (Conn.) Press of the Bulletin Company, 1881
E444 S65 A2

Smith, Jeremiah
Is slavery sinful? being partial dis-cussions of the proposition, Slavery is sinful, between Ovid Butler, esq.,.....
Indianapolis: Dodd, 1863
E449 S55

Smith, William Andrew
Lectures on the philosophy and prac-tice of slavery. Nashville, Tenn.: Stevenson & Evans, 1856
E449 S56

Smith, William Henry
A political history of slavery. New York, London: G.P. Putnam's sons, 1903. 2 vols.
E441 S55

The South vindicated from the treason and fanaticism of the northern aboli-tionists. Philadelphia: H. Manly, 1836
E449 S6

Spooner, Lysander
The unconstitutionality of slavery.
Boston: B. Marsh, 1845
E441 S6

Another edition
E441 S6 1860

Stampp, Kenneth Milton
And the war came: the north and the secession crisis, 1860-1861. Baton Rouge: Louisania State University Press (c1950)
E440.5 S8 (Main, Undergraduate)

The peculiar institution . New York: Knopf, 1956
E441 S8 (Main, Undergraduate)

Staudenraus, Philip John
The African colonization movement, 1816-1865. New York: Columbia University, 1961
E448 S8 (Main, History Graduate)

Stevens, Charles Emery
Anthony Burns, a history. Boston: J.P. Jewett & Co., 1856
E450 B8 S7

Steward, Austin
Twenty-two years a slave, and forty years a freeman. Rochester, N.Y.: W. Alling, 1857 (c1856)
E444 S7

Stiles, Joseph Clay
Speech on the slavery resolutions, delivered in the general assembly.... New York: M.H. Newman & Co., 1850
E449 S7

Still, William
The underground railroad. Philadelphia: Porter and Coates, 1872
AH755 S85

Another edition
E450 S8 1872a (Undergraduate)

Stuart, Moses
Conscience and the constitution. Boston: Crocker & Brewster, 1850
E449 S898

Sumner, Charles
The barbarism of slavery.... Washington, D.C.: T. Hyatt, 1860
E449 S9 (Rare Book Collection)

Another edition
E449 S9 1860a

Another edition
E449 S9 1863

The suppressed book about slavery. New York: Carleton, 1864
E449 S95

Another edition
E449 S95 1864a (Main, Undergraduate)

Swaney, Charles Baumer
Episcopal Methodism and slavery. Boston: R. G. Badger (c1926)
E449 S96

Sydnor, Charles Sackett
Slavery in Mississippi. Gloucester, Mass.: P. Smith, 1965 (c1933)
E445 M6 S9 1933a (Undergraduate)

Tannenbaum, Frank
Slave and citizen: The Negro in the Americas. New York: Knopf, 1947
E29 N3 T16 (Main, Social Work, Undergraduate)

Another edition
E29 N3 T16 1946a (Journalism)

Tappan, Lewis
A side-light of Anglo-American relations, 1839-1858. (Lancaster, Pa.) The Association for the study of Negro life and history, inc., 1927
E449 T3

Taylor, Joe Gray
Negro slavery in Louisiana. (Baton Rouge) Louisiana Historical Association (1963)
E445 L8 T3

Taylor, Orville Walters
Negro slavery in Arkansas. Durham, N.C.: Duke University Press, 1958
E445 A8 T3 (Social Work)

Taylor, Susie King
Reminiscences of my life in camp.
New York: Arno Press, 1968
E492.94 33d T3 1902a (Main, Undergraduate)

Ten Broek, Jacobus
The antislavery origins of the fourteenth amendment. Berkeley: University of California Press, 1951
E449 T4

Thomas, Benjamin Platt
Theodore Weld, crusader for freedom.
New Brunswick: Rutgers University Press, 1950
E449 W4 T45 (Main, Undergraduate)

Thomas, John L
The liberator, William Lloyd Garrison, a biography. (1st edition) Boston: Little, Brown (1963)
E449 G24 T5

Slavery attacked: the abolitionist crusade. Englewood Cliffs: Prentice-Hall (1965)
E449 T5

Thompson, George
Prison life and reflections; or, A narrative of the arrest.... Oberlin: J.M. Fitch, 1847
E450 T4

Another edition
E450 T4 1847a

Another edition
E450 T4 1848

Another edition
E450 T4 1850

Another edition
E450 T4 1860

Thompson, John
The life of John Thompson, a fugitive slave. Worcester: J. Thompson, 1856
E444 T4

Torrey, Jesse
A portraiture of domestic slavery in the United States. Philadelphia: published by the author, John Bioren, printer, 1817
E446 T68 (Rare Book Collection)

Treadwell, Seymour Boughton
American liberties and American slavery. New York: J.S. Taylor, Boston: Weeks, Jordan & Company, 1838
E449 T7

Trefousse, Hans Louis
The radical Republicans; Lincoln's vanguard for racial justice. (1st edition) New York: Knopf, 1969 (c1968)
E449 T75

Tyson, John Shoemaker
Life of Elisha Tyson, the philanthropist. Baltimore: printed by B. Lundy, 1825
E446 T9 T9

United States Civil War Centennial Commission
Emancipation centennial, 1962; a brief anthology of the preliminary proclamation. Washington, 1962
E453 U5 1962

United States Supreme Court
A report of the decision of the Supreme Court of the United States, and the opinions of the judges thereof, in the case of Dred Scott versus John F.A. Sandford. New York: D. Appleton & Company, 1857
E450 S35 U5

Van Dyke, Henry Jackson
The character and influence of abolitionism. New York: D. Appleton, 1860
E449 V3

Van Eurie, John H
White supremacy and negro subordination; or Negroes a subordinate race, and (socalled) slavery its normal condition. 2nd edition. New York: Van Eurie, Horton & Company, 1868
AH755 V25

Van Rensselaer, Cortlandt
Slaveholding and colonization. Philadelphia: J.M. Wilson, 1858
E448 V27

Villard, Oswald Garrison
John Brown, 1800-1859, a biography.
Boston and New York: Houghton Mifflin Company, 1911 (c1910)
E451 V7 (Main, Undergraduate)

Another edition
E451 V7 1943

Voorhees, Daniel W
Argument of Hon. Daniel W. Voorhees of Terra Haute, Indiana....
1859
E451 V8

Wade, Richard C
  Slavery in the cities. New York: Ox
  ford University Press, 1964
  E443 W3 (Main, Undergraduate)

Walker, David
  David Walker's appeal, in four articles, together with a preamble, to the
  colored citizens of the world, but in
  particular, and very expressly, to
  those of the United States of America.
  Boston: D. Walker 1829
  E446 W3 (Rare Book Collection)

  Another edition
  E446 W3 1965

Ward, Samuel Ringgold
  Autobiography of a fugitive Negro. New
  York: Arno Press, 1968
  E449 W3 1855a (Main, Undergraduate)

Washington, Booker Taliaferro
  Frederick Douglass. Philadelphia:
  G.W. Jacobs & Company, (1907)
  E449 D73 W3

Webb, Richard Davis
  The life and letters of Captain John
  Brown who was executed at Charles-
  town, Virginia, December 2, 1859....
  London: Smith, Elder & Company, 1861
  E451 W4 1861

Webster, Noah
  Effects of slavery, on morals and industry. Hartford (Connecticut) Printed
  by Hudson and Goodwin, 1793
  E446 W38 (Rare Book Collection)

Weinstein, Allen, comp.
  American Negro slavery. New York:
  Oxford University Press, 1968
  E441 W4

Weld, Theodore Dwight
  Letters of Theodore Dwight Weld,
  Angelina Grimke Weld and Sarah
  Grimke, 1822-1844. New York, London:
  D. Appleton-Century Company, inc.
  (c1934) 2 volumes
  E449 W4 A3

Wells, Tom Henderson
  The slave ship Wanderer. Athens:
  University of Georgia Press (c1967)
  E449 W42

Weston, George M
  The progress of slavery in the United
  States. Washington, D.C.: Published
  by the author, 1857.
  AH755 W53

Wheat, Marvin T
  The progress and intelligence of Americans; collateral proof of slavery. 2nd
  edition (Louisville, Ky., 1863, c1862)
  E449 W45 1863

Wheatley, Phillis, afterwards Phillis
  Peters
  Works... in Readex microprint edition
  of Early American Imprints...
  Microprint AC1 E2

Willey, Austin
  The history of the antislavery cause
  in state and nation. Portland, Maine:
  B. Thurston, 1886
  E441 W5

Williams, James
  Narrative of James Williams. New York:
  The American Anti-Slavery Society, 1838
  E444 W5 (Rare Book Collection)

Wilson, Henry
  History of the antislavery measures of
  the 37th and 38th United States Con-
  gresses, 1861-1864. Boston: Walker,
  Wise, & Company, 1864
  E453 W5 1864

  Another edition
  E453 W5 1865

Wilson, Hill Peebles
  John Brown, soldier of fortune; a cri-
  tique. Lawrence, Kansas: H.P. Wilson,
  1913
  E451 W5

Wish, Harvey
  George Fitzhugh, propagandist of the
  old South. Baton Rouge, Louisiana:
  Louisiana State University Press, 1943
  E449 F55 W8

Wolf, Hazel Catherine
  On freedom's altar; the martyr complex
  in the abolition movement. Madison:
  University of Wisconsin Press, 1952
  E449 W6

Woodberry, George Edward
  Wendell Phillips; the faith of an American. (Boston) Printed for the Woodberry society (by D. B. Updike) 1912
  E449 P55 W6 (Rare Book Collection)

Woodman, Harold D, ed.
  Slavery and the Southern economy.
  New York: Harcourt, Brace & World
  (1966)
  E441 W6

Yarbrough, William Henry
Economic aspects of slavery in relation to southern and southwestern
migration. Nashville, Tennessee:
George Peabody College for Teachers,
1932
E441 Y3 (Main, Education)

Zakharova, Maria Nikolaevna
Narodnoe dvlzhenie v SShA protio
rabstva. Moskva Nauka, 1965
E449 Z3

Zilversmit, Arthur
The first emancipation; the abolition
of slavery in the North. Chicago: University of Chicago Press (1967)
E446 Z5

CIVIL WAR

Ayers, James T
The diary of James T. Ayers, Civil
War recruiter .... Springfield, Printed
by the authority of the State of Illinois,
1947
F536 I35 no. 50

Burchard, Peter
One gallant rush; Robert Gould Shaw
and his brave Black Regiment. New
York: St. Martin's Press (1965)
E513.5 54th B8

Cornish, Dudley Taylor
The sable arm; Negro troops in the
Union Army. (1st edition) New York:
Longmans, Green, 1956
E540 N3 C6

Higginson, Thomas Wentworth
Army life in a black regiment. East
Lansing: Michigan State University
Press, 1960
E492.94 33rd H5 1960

Long, Francis Taylor
The Negroes of Clarke County, Georgia, during the great war. (Athens,
Georgia, 1919)
AH439 L84

McPherson, James M
Marching toward freedom; the Negro in
the Civil War, 1861-1865. New York:
Knopf (c1967)
E540 N3 M23 (Main, Education)

The Negro's civil war: how American
Negroes felt and acted during the war
for the Union. New York: Pantheon
(1965)
E540 N3 M25 (Main, Undergraduate)

Nell, William Cooper
The colored patriots of the American
revolution with sketches of several
distinguished colored persons; to
which is added a brief survey of the
condition and prospects of colored
Americans .... With an introduction by
Harriet Beecher Stowe. Boston: R. F.
Wallcut, 1855
E269 N3 N4 (Rare Book Collection)

Another edition
E269 N3 N4 1855a (Undergraduate)

The Negro in the American revolution.
Chapel Hill: University of North Carolina Press, 1961
E269 N3 Q3

Trowbridge, John Townsend
The South: a tour of its battlefields
and ruined cities. Hartford, Conn.:
L. Stebbins, 1866
AH1606 T86

Wagandt, Charles Lewis
The mighty revolution: Negro emancipation in Maryland, 1862-1864. Baltimore: Johns Hopkins Press (1964)
E512 W3

Wesley, Charles Harris
  Negro Americans in the Civil War. (1st edition) New York: Publishers Company (1967)
  E540 N3 W4

Ohio Negroes in the Civil War. (Columbus) Ohio State University Press (1962)
E525 O33 no. 6 (Main, OSU Collection)

RECONSTRUCTION

Allen, James Stewart
  Reconstruction: the battle for democracy (1865-1876). New York: International (c1937)
  E668 A42 1937a

Ashmore, Harry S
  The man in the middle. Columbia: University of Missouri Press (1966)
  E846 A8 (Main, Journalism)

Brown, William Wells
  The Negro in the American rebellion: his heroism and his fidelity. New edition Boston: A. G. Brown & Company, 1885
  AH1130 B87

Buck, Paul Herman
  The road to reunion, 1865-1900. Boston: Little, Brown (c1937)
  E661 B8 1937a (Main, Undergraduate)

Cable, George Washington
  The Negro question. (New York: American Missionary Association, 1888)
  AH1205 C11

Campbell, Sir George
  White and black; the outcome of a visit to the United States. London: Chatta & Windus, 1879
  AH370 C18

Carter, Hodding
  The angry scar: the story of reconstruction. (1st edition) Garden City, New York: Doubleday, 1959
  E668 C3 (Browsing Room, Undergraduate)

Coulter, Ellis Merton
  The South during reconstruction 1865-1877. (Baton Rouge)Louisiana State University Press, 1947
  F216 C85 (Main, History Graduate, Undergraduate)

Cox, LaWanda C (Fenlason)
  Politics, principle and prejudice, 1865-66; the dilemma of Reconstruction America. (New York) Free Press of Glencoe, (1963)
  E666 C6 (Main, Undergraduate)

Current, Richard Nelson,ed.
  Reconstruction, 1865-1877. Englewood Cliffs, N. J.: Prentice-Hall (1965)
  E668 C8 (History Graduate)

De Forest, John William
  A Union officer in the Reconstruction. New Haven: Yale University Press, 1948
  E185.93 S7 D4

DeMond, Albert Lawrence
  Certain aspects of the economic development of the American Negro, 1865-1900. Washington, D. C.: The Catholic University of American Press, 1945
  E185.8 D4

Donald, David Herbert
  The politics of reconstruction, 1863-1867. Baton Rouge:Louisiana State University Press (1965)
  E668 D58

Du Bois,William Edward Burghardt
  Black reconstruction; an essay toward a history of the part black folk played in the attempt to reconstruct democracy in America, 1860-1880. New York: Harcourt, Brace and Company (c1935)
  E668 D8 (Main, History Graduate)

  Another edition
  E668 D8 1962

Franklin, John Hope
Reconstruction: after the Civil War.
(Chicago) University of Chicago Press
(1961)
E668 F7 (Main, History Graduate,
Undergraduate)

Hero, Alfred O
The Southerner and world affairs.
Baton Rouge: Louisiana State
University Press, 1965
E744 H47 (Main, Mershon)

Hickey, Neil
**Adam Clayton Powell and the politics
of race.** New York: Fleet (1965)
E784 P79 H5 (Browsing Room)

Hirshson, Stanley P
**Farewell to the bloody shirt: northern
Republicans and the southern Negro,
1877-1893.** Bloomington: Indiana Uni-
versity Press (1962)
E661 H65 (Main, Undergraduate)

Huff, Warren, ed.
Famous Americans.2nd series. Los
Angeles, California: C. Webb & Com-
pany (c1941)
E663 H882

Hyman, Harold Melvin, ed.
**New frontiers of the American Recon-
struction.** Urbana: University of Illinois Press, 1966
E668 H9 (Main, History Graduate)

Kennedy, Robert F
To seek a newer world. (1st edition)
Garden City, New York: Doubleday,
1967
E840 K4 (Browsing Room, Social Work)

Kugelmass, J Alvin
Ralph J. Bunche, fighter for peace.
New York: Messner (1952)
E748 B885 K8 (Browsing Room)

Lubell, Samuel
The future of American politics. New
York: Harper (1952)
E743 L8 1952 (Main, Undergraduate,
History Graduate)

Another edition
E743 L8 1965

Lynch, John Roy
The facts of reconstruction. New York:
Neale, 1913
AH1210 M6 L9

Another edition
E668 L88 1913a (Undergraduate)

Morrow, Everett Frederic
**Black man in the White House: diary of
the Eisenhower years....** New York:
Coward-McCann (1963)
E835 M58

Morton, Richard Lee
**The Negro in Virginia politics, 1865-
1902.** Charlottesville: The University
of Virginia, 1919
AH439 M89

Powell, Aaron Macy
**Personal reminisces of the anti-slavery
and other reforms and reformers.** Plain-
field, N. J.: A. R. Powell, New York:
Caulon Press, 1899
AH755 P88

Another edition
E449 P8

Randel, William Peirce
The Ku Klux Klan: a century of infamy.
(1st edition) Philadelphia: Chilton
(1965)
E668 R18 (Main, Browsing Room, Undergraduate)

Richardson, Joe Martin
**The Negro in the reconstruction of
Florida.** Tallahassee: Florida State
University, 1965
AS36 F57 no. 46

Sefton, James E
**The United States army and recon-
struction, 1865-1877.** Baton Rouge:
Louisiana State University Press
(1967)
E668 S37

Sherwin, Mark
The extremists. New York: St. Martin's
(1963)
E743 S54 (Browsing Room)

Singletary, Otis A
Negro militia and reconstruction.
Austin: University of Texas Press
(c1957)
E668 S5

Smith, Frank Ellis
Congressman from Mississippi. New
York: Pantheon (1964)
E748 S656 A3 (Main, Undergraduate)

Stampp, Kenneth Milton
The era of Reconstruction, 1865-1877.
New York: Knopf, 1965
E668 S7

Another edition
E668 S7 1965a (Undergraduate)

U. S. Dept. of Labor. Division of Negro
Economics.
1st-2nd study on Negro labor. (1919,
1921)
AH439 U58

**The Negro at work during the world
war and during Reconstruction.** Washington: Government Printing Office,
1921
AH439 U58 no. 2

Negro migration in 1916-17. Washington: Government Printing Office, 1919
AH439 U58 no. 1

U. S. Supreme Court
**Extracts from the Dred Scott decision,
1957.** New York: A. Lovell & Company,
1895
AH429 A51 H no. 23

Van Deusen, John George
**Did Republicans "colonize" Indiana
in 1879?** (Bloomington, Indiana: Indiana
magazine of history) 1934
AH1930 V24

Wesley, Charles Harris
...The collapse of the confederacy....
Washington, D. C., 1922
AH865 W51

Williams, William H
**The Negro in the District of Columbia
during Reconstruction.** (Washington,
D. C., 1924)
AH439 W72

Wilson, Joseph Thomas
**The black phalanx; a history of the
Negro soldiers in the wars of 1775-
1812, 1861-1865.** Hartford, Conn.:
American Publishing Company, 1888
AH1130 W75

HISTORY – LOCAL

Andrews, Sidney
The South since the war. Boston:
Ticknor & Fields, 1866
F216 A5

Apthecker, Herbert
Nat Turner's slave rebellion. New
York: Humanities Press (1966)
F232 S7 A8

Ashmore, Harry S
An epitaph for Dixie. (1st edition) New
York: Norton (c1958)
F209 A8 (Main, Undergraduate,
Journalism)

The other side of Jordan. (1st edition)
New York: Norton (1960)
F185.61 A73

Barksdale, James Worsham
**A comparative study of contemporary
white and Negro standards in health,
education and welfare, Charlottesville,
Virginia.** (Charlottesville) University
of Virginia, 1949
F234 C47 B3

Barnwell, William H
**In Richard's world; the battle of
Charleston, 1966.** Boston: Houghton
Mifflin, 1968
F279 C49 N4 B3

Barton, Rebecca Chalmers
**Our human rights; a study in the art of
persuasion.** Washington, D. C.: Public
Affairs Press (c1955)
F586 B3

Bates, Daisy (Gatson)
The long shadow of Little Rock, a memoir. New York: David McKay Company (1962)
F419 L7 B3 (Main, Education)

Beckwourth, James P
The life and adventures of James P. Beckwourth. Westwood Village, Los Angeles: The United States Library Association, Inc. (c1932)
F592 B39 A3 1932

Another edition
F592 B39 A3

Blood, Robert O
Northern breakthrough. Belmont, Calif.: Wadsworth Publishing Company (1968)
F614 M6 B55 (Commerce)

Blossom, Virgil T
It has happened here. (1st edition) New York: Harper (c1959)
F419 L7 B5 (Main, Education)

Braden, Anne
The wall between. New York: Monthly Review Press, 1958
F459 L8 B7

Brotz, Howard
The Black Jews of Harlem: Negro nationalism and the dilemmas of Negro leadership. (New York) Free Press of Glencoe (1964)
F128.68 H3 B7

Brown, Earl Louis
...Why race riots? Lessons from Detroit .... (New York: Public Affairs Committee, Inc.) 1944
F574 D4 B8 (Main, Education)

Bullock, Henry Allen
Pathways to the Houston Negro market. (Ann Arbor, Michigan: J. W. Edwards, c1957)
F394 H8 B8 1957

California. Governor's Commission on the Los Angeles Riots.
Violence in the city — an end or a beginning; a report. (Los Angeles) 1965
F869 L8 C3 1965

Carmer, Carl Lamson
Stars fell on Alabama. New York: Farrar & Rinehart, Inc., 1934
F325 C3 (Main, Undergraduate)

Another edition
F326 C3 1934a

Carter, Hodding III
So the Heffners left McComb. Garden City, N. Y.: Doubleday, 1965
F349 M16 C3 (Main, Browsing Room)

Another edition
F215 C3 1950a (Undergraduate)

Southern legacy. Baton Rouge: Louisiana State University Press (1950)
F215 C3 (Main, Journalism)

Carter, Wilmoth Annette
The urban Negro in the South. (1st edition) New York: Vantage Press (c1961)
F264 R1 C3

Another edition
F209 C33 1941a (Undergraduate, Journalism)

Cash, Wilbur Joseph
The mind of the South. New York: Knopf, 1941
F209 C33 (History Graduate, Undergraduate)

Cason, Clarence
90° in the shade. Chapel Hill: University of North Carolina Press (c1935)
F215 C33

Chicago. Mayor's Committee on Race Relations
Race relations in Chicago, December 1944. (Chicago, 1944)
F548.9 N3 A5 1944

Chicago Conference on Home Front Unity, 1945
Human relations in Chicago, reports of commissions and charter of human relations, adopted by Chicago Conference on Home Front Unity, October 30, November 6, 1945. Chicago: Mayor's Committee on Race Relations (1946)
F548.5 C53 1945b

Chicago urban league
Annual report. 4th- 1919/20- Chicago, 1920 -
F548.9 N3 A1 C5

Childs, Benjamin Guy
The Negroes of Lynchburg, Virginia. Charlottesville, Virginia: Surber-Arundale Company, Inc., 1923
AH439 C53

Clark, Kenneth Bancroft
Dark ghetto; dilemmas of social power..
New York: Harper & Row (1965)
F128.9 N3 C6

Another edition
F128.9 N3 C6 1965a (Education, Undergraduate)

Clark, Thomas Dionysius
The emerging South. New York: Oxford
University Press, 1961
F209 C5 (Main, Undergraduate)

Another edition
F209 C5 1968

Clarke, John Henrik
**Harlem U.S.A.; the story of a city
within a city.** Told by James Baldwin
(and others) Berlin: Seven Seas Publishers (c1964)
F128.68 H3 C5 (Browsing Room)

Cohen, Jerry
Burn, baby, burn! New York: Dutton,
1966
F869 L8 C6 (Main, Undergraduate,
Journalism)

Conot, Robert E
Rivers of blood, years of darkness.
Toranton, New York: Bantam Books
(1967)
F869 L8 C65 1967a (Main, Social Work)

Another edition
F869 L8 C65

Cox, Samuel Sullivan
**Emancipation and its results - is Ohio
to be Americanized?** (Washington: L.
Towers, 1862)
AH840 C87 E

Crump, Spencer
**Black riot in Los Angeles; the story of
the Watts tragedy.** (1st edition) Los
Angeles: Trans-Anglo Books (1966)
F869 L8 C7

Current, Richard Nelson
Three carpetbag governors. Baton
Rouge: Louisiana State University
Press, (1967)
F316 R27 C8

Dabbs, James McBride
Who speaks for the South? New York:
Funk & Wagnalls (1964)
F209 D3

Daniels, John
**In freedom's birthplace: a study of
Boston Negroes.** Boston and New York:
Houghton Mifflin Company, 1914
AH439 D18

DeCarava, Roy
The sweet flypaper of life. New York:
Hill & Wang (1967, c1955)
F128.9 N3 D4 (Browsing Room)

DeCorse, Helen Camp
**Charlottesville - a study of Negro life
and personality.** (Charlottesville,
1933?)
AH439 D29

Dollard, John
Caste and class in a southern town.
New Haven: Yale University Press,
London: H. Milford, Oxford University
Press, 1937
AH1606 D66 (Main, Social Work,
Commerce)

Douglass, Frederick
**Addresses of the Hon. W. D. Kelley,
Miss Anna E. Dickinson and Mr.
Frederick Douglass, at a mass meet-
ing, Philadelphia, July 6, 1863 for the
promotion of colored enlistments.**
Philadelphia, 1863
AH1130 K29

Drake, St. Clair
Black metropolis. (revised and enlarged
edition) New York: Harper & Row
(1962)
F548.9 N3 D6 1962 (Main, Undergraduate)

Another edition
F548.9 N3 D6 (Main, Social Work,
Undergraduate)

**Churches and voluntary associations
in the Chicago Negro community.** Report of Official project 465-54-3-386
conducted under the auspices of the
Work Projects Administration.
(Chicago) 1940
F548.9 N3 D7

DuBois, William Edward Burghardt
**Dark water; voices from within the
veil.** New York: Harcourt, Brace and
Howe, 1920
AH439 D79

Duncan, Otis Dudley
The Negro population of Chicago.
(Chicago) University of Chicago Press
(1957)
F548.9 N3 D8 (Main, Social Work)

Durham, Philip
The Negro cowboys. New York: Dodd,
Mead (c1965)
F596 D8

Dutcher, Dean
**The negro in modern industrial
society; an analysis of changes in the
occupations of negro workers, 1910-
1920.** Lancaster, Pa., 1930
AH439 D97

Ehle, John
The free men. (1st edition) New York:
Harper & Row (1965)
F264 C38 E4

Elman, Richard M
Ill-at-ease in Compton. New York:
Pantheon Books (1967)
F869 C7 E4 (Social Work)

Elwang, William Wilson
The Negroes of Columbia, Missouri.
(Columbia, Missouri) University of
Missouri, 1904
F474 C72 E5

Epstein, Abraham
The Negro migrant in Pittsburgh.
Pittsburgh, Pa., 1918
AH1558 P6 E6

Estupinan Tello, Julio
El negro en Esmeraldas. Quito,
Ecuador, 1967
F3741 E6 E8

Everett, Faye Philip, ed.
The colored situation. Boston:
Meador, 1936
AH439 E93

Ezell, John Samuel
The South since 1865. New York:
Macmillan (1963)
F215 E8

Federal Writers' Project
These are our lives. Chapel Hill: The
University of North Carolina Press,
1939
F210 F29 (Main, Social Work)

Fiske, John
....**Unpublished orations: "The discovery of the Columbia River, and the
Whitman controversy"; "The Crispus
Attucks memorial," and "Columbus
memorial."** Boston: Printed for members only, The Bibliophile Society,
1909
F880 F54 (Rare Book Collection)

Fleming, Walter Lynwood
....**I. Freedmen's bureau documents.
II. The Freedmen's savings bank.**
Morgantown, West Virginia, 1904
AH1205 F59 D

**Studies in southern history and poli-
tics.** New York: Columbia University
Press, 1914
AH1606 S93 (History Graduate)

Franklin, John Hope
The militant South, 1800-1861. Cambridge: Belknap Press of Harvard University Press, 1956
F213 F7 (Main, Undergraduate)

Frazier, Edward Franklin
The Negro family in Chicago. Chicago, Illinois: The University of Chicago Press (c1932)
AH439 F85

Frontiers of America. Columbus Chapter.
**Advancement: Negroes contribution in
Franklin County, 1803-1953.** (Colum-
bus, 1954)
F497 F8 F76 (Reference)

Gaines, Francis Pendelton
The Southern plantation. New York:
The Columbia University Press, 1925
AH1606 G14

Garner, James Wilford
Reconstruction in Mississippi. New
York, London: The Macmillan Com-
pany, 1901
F341 G3 (History Graduate)

Georgia. Governor, 1917-1921 (Hugh M
Dorsey)
**A statement from Governor Hugh M.
Dorsey as to the Negro in Georgia.**
(Atlanta? 1921)
AH439 D71

Gladden, Washington
**The Negro's southern neighbors and
his northern friends.** New York: n.d.
AH439 G54

Glazer, Nathan
Beyond the melting pot. Cambridge:
Massachusetts Institute of Technology
Press and Harvard University Press
(1964, c1963)
F128.9 A1 G55 (Main, Social Work)

Grayson, William John
**Memoir of James Louis Petigru, a
biographical sketch ....** New York:
Harper & Brothers, 1866
AH1674 P48 G7

Green, Constance (McLaughlin)
Washington: capital city, 1879-1950.
Princeton, New Jersey: Princeton
University Press, 1963
F194 G7 (Main, Architecture, Under-
graduate)

Grunsfeld, Mary-Jane (Loeb)
Negroes in Chicago. (Chicago: Mayor's
Committee on Race Relations, 1944)
F548.9 N3 G7 (Social Work)

Hammond, Mrs. Lily (Hardy)
In the vanguard of a race. New York:
Council of women for home missions
and Missionary education movement of
the United States and Canada (c1922)
AH439 H215

Southern women and racial adjustment.
(Lynchburg, Virginia: J. P. Bell) 1917
AH439 H22

Handlin, Oscar
**The newcomers: Negroes and Puerto
Ricans in a changing metropolis.** Cam-
bridge: Harvard University Press, 1959
F128.9 A1 H3 (Social Work, Archi-
tecture, Browsing Room, Undergraduate)

Hardin, Clara Alberta
The Negroes of Philadelphia. Bryn
Mawr, Pa., 1945 (c1943)
F158.9 N3 H3

Harlan, Howard Harper
Zion Town—a study in human ecology.
(Charlottesville) West Virginia, 1935
AH439 H28

Harris, William Charles
**Presidential reconstruction in Missis-
sippi.** Baton Rouge: Louisiana State
University Press (c1967)
F341 H3 1967

Haskin, Sara Estelle
The handicapped winners. Nashville,
Tennessee, Dallas, Texas: M. E.
Church South, 1922
AH439 H35

Hawkins, William George
**Lunsford Lane, or Another Helper from
North Carolina.** Boston: Crosby &
Nichols, 1863
AH439 H39

Hayden, Thomas
Rebellion in Newark. New York:
Random (1967)
F144 N6 H3 (Social Work)

Hearn, Lafcadio
Children of the levee .... (Lexington)
University of Kentucky Press (c1957)
F499 C5 H4 (Main, Journalism)

Helper, Hinton Rowan
**Compendium of the impending crisis
of the South.** New York: A. B. Burdick,
1860
AH775 H48

Herskovits, Melville Jean
**Rebel destiny: among the bush Negroes
of Dutch Guiana.** New York and
London: Whittlesey House, McGraw-
Hill Book Company, Inc., 1934
F2431 N3 H4

Hesslink, George K
**Black neighbors; Negroes in a northern
rural community.** Indianapolis: Bobbs-
Merrill (1968)
F572 C3 H4

Holt, Len
An act of conscience. Boston: Beacon
Press (1965)
F234 D3 H6

Horsmanden, Daniel
**The New-York conspiracy, or A his-
tory of the negro plot.** New York:
Southwick and Pelsue, 1810
AH1527 H8

Huie, William Bradford
Three lives for Mississippi. New York:
WWC Books, 1965
F347 N4 H8 (Main, Browsing Room)

Illinois. Chicago Commission on Race Relations.
The Negro in Chicago; a study of race relations and a race riot in 1919. New York: Arno Press, 1968
F548.9 N3 I4 1922a (Undergraduate)

Another edition
AH439 I3 (Main, Social Work)

Irwin, Marjorie Felice
The Negro in Charlottesville and Albemarle county. (Charlottesville? Virginia, 1929)
AH439 I72

Jackson, Giles B
The industrial history of the Negro race in the United States .... Richmond, Virginia: Negro Educational Association, 1911
AH439 J13

Jarrell, Hampton M
Wade Hampton and the Negro; the road not taken. Columbia: University of South Carolina Press, 1949
F274 H3 J3

Johnson, Guion Griffis
A social history of the Sea Islands. Chapel Hill: University of North Carolina Press, 1930
F277 B3 J6

Johnson, Guy Benton
Folk culture on St. Helena Island, South Carolina. Chapel Hill: University of North Carolina Press, 1930
AH439 J665

Johnson, James Weldon
Black Manhattan. New York: A. A. Knopf, 1930
F128.9 N3 J6 (Main, Social Work)

Another edition
F128.9 N3 J6 1930a (Undergraduate)

Johnson, Philip A
Call me neighbor, call me friend: the case history of the integration of a neighborhood on Chicago's south side. (1st edition) Garden City, N. J.: Doubleday, 1965
F548.9 N3 J6

Johnston, Sir Harry Hamilton
The Negro in the New world. London: Methuen & Company, ltd. (1910)
AH439 J72

Jones, Katherine M
The plantation south. Indianapolis: Bobbs-Merrill (c1957)
F213 J6 (Main, Undergraduate)

Jones, William Henry
Recreation and amusement among negroes in Washington, D. C.; a sociological analysis of the negro in an urban environment. Washington, D. C., Howard University Press, 1927
AH439 J795

Kelsey, Carl
The Negro farmer. Chicago: Jennings & Pyle, 1903
AH439 K29

Key, Valdimar Orlando
Southern politics in state and nation. (1st edition) New York: Knopf, 1949
F215 K4 (History Graduate)

Kirwan, Albert Dennis
Revolt of the Rednecks; Mississippi politics, 1876-1925. Lexington: University of Kentucky Press, 1951
F341 K5 (History Graduate)

Korngold, Ralph
Citizen Toussaint. Boston: Little, Brown, 1944
F1923 T73 K8 (Main, Undergraduate)

Langhorne, Orra Henderson Moore (Gray)
Southern sketches from Virginia, 1881-1901. Charlottesville: University Press of Virginia (1964)
F231 L3

Lee, Alfred McClung
Race riot. New York: The Dryden Press, Inc., 1943
F574 D4 L4 (Main, Social Work)

Lee, George Washington
Beale street, where the blues began. New York: R. O. Ballou (c1934)
F444 M5 L4

Leigh, Frances Butler
Ten years on a Georgia plantation since the war. London: R. Bentley & Son, 1883
AH1210 G4 L5

Lerche, Charles Olsen
The uncertain South: its changing patterns of politics in foreign policy. Chicago: Quadrangle Books (1964)
F215 L53

Locke, Alain LeRoy
The Negro in America. Chicago: American Library Association, 1933
AH439 L79 (Education)

Lofton, John
Insurrection in South Carolina: the turbulent world of Denmark Vesey. Yellow Springs, Ohio: Antioch Press (1964)
F279 C4 L6

Love, Nat
The life and adventures of Nat Love. New York: Arno Press, 1968
F594 L65 1907a (Main, (Undergraduate)

Lowery, Irving E
Life on the old plantation in antebellum days; or, a story based on facts. Columbia, South Carolina: The State Company, printers, 1911
AH755 L91

Mabry, William Alexander
The Negro in North Carolina politics since reconstruction. Durham, North Carolina: Duke University Press, 1940
F251 D9 ser. 23

Martin, Asa Earl
Our Negro population. Kansas City, Mo.: Franklin Hudson Publishing Company (c1913)
F474 K2 M3

McGill, Ralph Emerson
The South and the southerner. (1st edition) Boston: Little, Brown (1963)
F215 M3 (Browsing Room, Journalism, Mershon)

McKay, Claude
Harlem: Negro metropolis. New York: E. P. Dutton & Company, Inc. (c1940)
F128,68 H3 M15

Miller, Kelly
The primary needs of the Negro race, an address delivered before the Alumni association of the Hampton Normal and Agricultural Institute. Washington, D. C.: Howard University Press, 1899
AH1206 M65

Race adjustment. 3rd edition. New York, Washington: the Neale Publishing Company, 1910
AH439 M64 1909

Minor, Richard Clyde
James Preston Poindexter, elder statesman of Columbus. (Columbus) 1947
F496 P6 M5

Nelson, Truman John
The torture of mothers. Boston: Beacon Press (1968, c1965)
F128.9 N3 N4 (Browsing Room)

Nicholls, William Hord
Southern tradition and regional progress. Chapel Hill: University of North Carolina Press. (c1960)
F209 N5 (Main, Commerce)

Odum, Howard Washington
An American epoch; southern portraiture in the national picture. New York: H. Holt & Company (c1930)
F215 O3

Folk, region, and society: selected papers. Chapel Hill: University of North Carolina Press (1964)
F209 O3

Ohio. Civil Rights Commission
Discrimination in public accomodations in Ohio. Columbus, Ohio, 1960
F496.2 A1 A5 1960 (Reference)

Olmsted, Frederick Law
The cotton kingdom. New York: Knopf, 1953
F213 O53 1953 (Commerce)

A journey in the back country. New York: Mason Brothers, 1860
F213 O532 1860

A journey in the back country in the winter of 1853-4. New York: G. P. Putnam's Sons, 1907
F213 O532 1907

A journey in the seaboard slave states, with remarks on their economy. New York: Dix & Edwards (etc.) 1856
F213 O533

Another edition
Micro-card E449

Another edition
F213 O533 1859

Another edition
F213 O533 1904

Another edition
(Apply Rare Book Collection)

A journey through Texas. New York:
Dix, Edwards & Company, London:
S. Low (etc.) 1857
F391 O5

**Journeys and explorations in the
cotton kingdom.** London: S. Low, Son
& Company, 1862
F213 O535 1862 (History Graduate)

The slave states. New York: Mason
Brothers, 1859 (half-title of "A journey in the seaboard states with remarks on their economies")
F213 O533 1859

O'Reilly, Charles Terrance
The people of the inner core-north.
New York: LePlay Research (1965)
F589 M6 O7

Ottley, Roi
The Negro in New York. New York:
New York Public Library, 1967
F128.9 N3 O88

'New world a-coming?' Boston:
Houghton Mifflin, 1943
F128.9 N3 O9 (Main, Social Work)

Another edition
F128.9 N3 O9 1943a (Undergraduate)

Patterson, Caleb Perry
The Negro in Tennessee, 1790-1865.
Austin, Texas: The University (1922)
AH755 P31

Pierce, Edward Lillie
**The freedmen of Port Royal, South
Carolina.** New York: Rebellion record,
1863
AH1140 P61

**The Planter; or, Thirteen years in the
South, by a northern man.** Philadelphia:
H. Hooker, 1853
AH755 P71

Polk, William Tannahill
**Southern accent: from Uncle Remus to
Oak Ridge.** New York: Morrow (1953)
F215 P6

Porter, Anthony Toomer
**Led on! Step by step; scenes from
clerical, military, educational and
plantation life in the South, 1828-
1898.** New York & London: G. P.
Putnam's Sons, 1899
AH895 P84 A1

Proudfoot, Merrill
Diary of a sit-in. Chapel Hill: Univer-
sity of North Carolina Press (1962)
F444 K7 P7

Reddick, Lawrence Dunbar
**The Negro in the New Orleans press,
1850-1860.** (Chicago) 1941
F349 N4 R3

Reilley, Edward C
**Politico-economic considerations in
the Western Reserve's early slavery
controversy.** Columbus, Ohio: Ohio
State Archaelogical and Historical
Quarterly, 1943
F486 O372 vol. 52.

Riker, James
**Revised history of Harlem (city of
New York.)** New York: New Harlem
Publishing Company, 1904
F128.68 H3 R6 1904

Rose, Willie Lee Nichols
**Rehearsal for Reconstruction: the Port
Royal experiment.** Indianapolis: Bobbs-
Merrill (1964)
F277 B3 R6 (Main, Undergraduate)

Rubin, Louis Decimus, ed.
The lasting South. Chicago: H.
Regnery Company, 1957
F209 R8 (Main, Undergraduate)

Rubin, Morton
Plantation county. (Chapel Hill) Uni-
versity of North Carolina Press, 1951
F215 R8

Rudwick, Elliott M
**Race riot at East St. Louis, July 2,
1917.** Carbondale: Southern Illinois
University Press, (1964)
F549 E2 R8 (Main, Undergraduate)

Saunders, Doris E., ed.
The day they marched. Chicago:
Johnson (c1963)
F200 S3

Scheiner, Seth M
Negro mecca. (New York) N. Y. Uni-
versity Press, 1965
F128.9 N3 S3

Scott, Emmett Jay
Booker T. Washington, builder of a civilization. Garden City, New York: Doubleday, Page & Company, 1916
AH395 W3 S4

Sellers, Charles Grier, ed.
The southerner as American. Chapel Hill: University of North Carolina Press (c1960)
F209 S4 (Main, Undergraduate)

Sherwood, Henry Noble
Paul Cuffe. Washington, D. C.: The Association for the study of Negro life and history, 1923
AH439 S55

Shogan, Robert
The Detroit race riot; a study in violence. (1st edition) Philadelphia: Chilton Books (1964)
F574 D4 S5

Silver, James Wesley
Mississippi: the closed society. New York: Harcourt, Brace & World (1964)
F345 S5 1964 (Main, Journalism, Undergraduate, Social Work, Browsing Room)

Another edition
F345 S5 1966 (Undergraduate)

Simkins, Francis Butler
The everlasting South. (Baton Rouge) Louisiana State University Press (1963)
F209 S579 (Main, Undergraduate)

Sindler, Allan P, ed.
Change in the contemporary South. Durham, N. C.: Duke University Press, 1963
F216.2 S5

Smith, Frank Ellis
Look away from Dixie. (Baton Rouge) Louisiana State University Press (1965)
F216.2 S6

Society for the Preservation of Spirituals
The Carolina low-country. New York: The Macmillan Company, 1931
F269 S67 (Rare Book Collection)

Another edition
F269 S67 1931a

Spear, Allan H
Black Chicago: the making of a Negro ghetto, 1890-1920.... Chicago: University of Chicago Press (1967)
F548.9 N3 S65 (Social Work, Main, Undergraduate)

Spellman, Cecil Lloyd
Elm City, a Negro community in action. Tallahassee: Florida A & M College, c1947
F264 E22 S7 (Social Work)

Steiner, Bernard Christian
History of slavery in Connecticut. Baltimore: Johns Hopkins Press, 1893
JA2 J65 vol. 11

Strickland, Arvarh E
History of the Chicago Urban League. Urbana: University of Illinois Press, 1966
F548.9 N3 S7

Stringfellow, William
My people is the enemy: an autobiographical polemic. New York: Holt, Rinehart & Winston (1964)
F128.9 N3 S8 (Browsing Room)

Sumner, Charles
Memoirs and letters of Charles Sumner. 2nd edition.London: Sampson, Low Marston, Searle & Rivington, 1878-1894. Volumes 3-4 published in Boston: Roberts Brothers, 1894
AH395 S95 P

Tate, Thaddeus W
The Negro in eighteenth-century Williamsburg. Charlottesville: University Press of Virginia (c1965)
F234 W7 T3

Taylor, Alrutheus A.
The Negro in South Carolina during Reconstruction. Washington: Association for the Study of Negro Life and History (c1924)
AH1210 S6 T3

The Negro in Tennessee, 1865-1880. Washington, D. C.: The Associated Publishers, Inc., 1941
E185.93 T3 T2 (Journalism, History Graduate)

The Negro in the Reconstruction of Virginia. Washington: Association for the Study of Negro Life and History (1926)
AH439 T23

Terkel, Louis
Division Street: America. New York:
Pantheon Books (1967)
F548.52 T4 (Main, Undergraduate,
Browsing Room)

Thompson, Daniel Calbert
The Negro leadership class. Engle-
wood Cliffs, New Jersey: Prentice-
Hall (1963)
F379 N5 T5

Turner, Edward Raymond
**The Negro in Pennsylvania; slavery,
servitude, freedom, 1639-1861.** Washington: American Historical Association, 1911
AH1555 T95

Tuskegee Normal and Industrial Institute.
**Program (with addresses); memorial
exercises held under the direction of
the Board of Trustees in memory of Dr.
Booker T. Washington, late Principal
of Tuskegee Normal and Industrial
Institute.** Institute Chapel, Sunday
evening, Dec. 12, 1915. (Tuskegee,
Students of the Tuskegee Normal and
Industrial Institute, 1915)
AH395 W3 T9

U. S. Commission on Civil Rights
**Hearings before the U. S. Commission
on Civil Rights.** Hearings held in
Memphis, Tennessee, June 25-26,
1962. (Washington: United States
Government Printing Office, 1963)
F444 M5 U5 1962

**Hearings before the U. S. Commission
on Civil Rights, Newark, New Jersey,
Sept. 11-12, 1962.** (Washington: United
States Government Printing Office,
1963)
F144 N6 U5 1963

**Hearings before the U. S. Commission
on Civil Rights, Phoenix, Arizona,
February 3, 1962.** (Washington: United
States Government Printing Office,
1962)
F819 P57 1962

**Hearing held in Cleveland, Ohio, April
1-7, 1966.** Washington: United States
Government Printing Office, 1966
F499 C6 U43 1966

U. S. Commission on Civil Rights.
South Dakota Advisory Committee.
**Negro airmen in a northern community:
discrimination in Rapid City, South
Dakota; a report.** (Washington: United
States Government Printing Office)
1963
F659 R2 U5 1963

U. S. Work Progress Administration.
Illinois.
**Occupational changes among Negroes
in Chicago.** (Chicago) 1939
F548.9 N3 A55 1939a

The Chicago Negro community.
(Chicago) 1939
F548.9 N3 A55 1939

Vandiver, Frank Everson, ed.
**The idea of the South: pursuit of a
central theme.** (Chicago) University of
Chicago Press (1964)
F209.5 V3 (Main, Undergraduate)

Warner, Robert Austin
New Haven Negroes, a social history.
New Haven: Yale University Press,
London: H. Milford, Oxford University
Press, 1940
F104 N6 W28

Warner, William Lloyd
Color and human nature. Washington,
D. C.: American Council on Education,
1941
F548.9 N3 W28 (Main, Education,
Social Work)

Washington, Booker Taliaferro
**An autobiography, the story of my life
and work.** Atlanta, Georgia: J. L.
Nichols & Company, 1901
AH395 W3 A15

Working with the hands. New York:
Doubleday, Page & Company, 1904.
AH395 W3 A1

Weinberg, Kenneth G
**Black victory; Carl Stokes and the
winning of Cleveland....** Chicago:
Quadrangle Books, 1968
F499 C6 S8 W4 (Browsing Room)

Whalen, Richard J
**A city destroying itself; an angry view
of New York.** New York: Morrow, 1965
F128.52 W4

Williams, Eric Eustace
  The Negro in the Caribbean. Washington, D. C.: The Associates in Negro Folk Education, 1942
  F1623 W72

Wood, Junius, B
  The Negro in Chicago. (Chicago: Chicago Daily News, 1916)
  AH1946 C58 W8

Woodward, Comer Vann
  The burden of Southern history. Baton Rouge: Louisiana State University Press (c1960)
  F209 W6 (Main, History Graduate, Undergraduate, Browsing Room)

Origins of the new South 1877-1913. (Baton Rouge) Louisiana State University Press, 1951
  F215 W6 (Main, History Graduate, Undergraduate)

Woofter, Thomas Jackson
  Black yeomanry. New York: H. Holt & Company (c1930)
  F277 B3 W9

FOLKLORE

Abrahams, Roger D
  Deep down in the jungle...; Negro folklore from the streets of Philadelphia. Hatboro, Pa.: Folklore Associates, 1964
  GR103 A2 (Rare Book Collection)

Bennett, John
  The doctor to the dead; grotesque legends and folk tales of old Charleston. New York, Toronto: Rinehart & Company ,Inc. (1946)
  GR103 B4

Boatright, Mody Coggin
  From hell to breakfast. Dallas: University Press, Southern Methodist University, 1944
  GR1 T35 vol. 19

Bradford, Roark
  How come Christmas, a modern morality. 3rd edition. New York, London: Harper and Brothers, 1934 (c1930)
  PS3503 R128 H6 1934

  Another edition
  PS3503 R128 O42 1944

  John Henry. New York and London: Harper & Brothers, 1939
  EL140 B7995 Jo2

Kingdom coming.... New York and London; Harper & Brothers, 1933
  PS3503 R128 K5

Let the band play Dixie and other stories. New York: Harper & Brothers, 1934
  PS3503 R128 L4

Ol' King David an' the Philistine boys. New York and London: Harper & Brothers, 1930
  PS3503 R128 O4

Ol' man Adam an' his chillun; being the tales they tell about the time when the Lord walked the earth like a natural man. New York, London: Harper & Brothers (c1928)
  PS3503 R128 O42 1928

The three-headed angel. 2nd edition. New York and London: Harper & Brothers, 1937
  PS3503 R128 T4 1937a

Brewer, John Mason, comp.
  American Negro folklore. Chicago: Quadrangle Books, 1968
  GR103 B66 (Browsing Room)

Aunt Dicy tales; snuff-dipping tales of the Texas Negro. (Austin? Texas) 1956
GR103 B67 (Rare Book Collection)

Dog ghosts, and other Texas Negro folk tales. Austin: University of Texas Press (c1958)
GR103 B68

The word on the Brazos. Austin: University of Texas Press, 1953 (i.e. 1954, c1953)
GR103 B7

Connelly, Marcus Cook
The green pastures; a fable suggested by Roark Bradford's southern sketches "Ol' Man Adam an' his chillun". New York: Farrar & Rinehart, Inc. (c1929)
PS3505 P48 G7 1929

Another edition
EL140 C753 Gr

Another edition
PR1271 D96

Dobie, James Frank
Follow de drinkin' gou'd. Austin, Texas: Publishing by the Texas Folklore Society, c1928
GR1 T35 v. 7

Texan stomping grounds. Austin: Texas Folk-lore Society, 1941
GR1 T35 v. 17

Tone the bell easy. Austin, Texas: Texas Folk-lore Society, 1932
GR1 T35 vol. 10

Dorson, Richard Mercer, ed.
Negro folktales in Michigan. Cambridge: Harvard University Press, 1956
GR103 D6

Negro tales from Pine Buff, Arkansas, and Calvin, Michigan. Blomington: Indiana University Press, 1958
GR15 I4 no. 12

Edwards, Charles Lincoln
Bahama songs and stories. Boston and New York: Houghton, Mifflin & Company, 1895
GR1 A5 vol. 3

Hughes, Langston, ed
The book of Negro folklore. New York: Dodd Mead Inc., 1958
GR103 H8 (Reference, Main, Undergraduate)

Hurston, Zora Neale
Mules and men. Philadelphia, London: J. B. Lippincott Company, 1935
GR103 H96

Jackson, Bruce
The Negro and his folklore in nineteenth century periodicals. Austin: University of Texas Press (1967)
GR103 J3 (Main, Music)

Jones, Charles Colcock
Negro myths from the Georgia coast told in the vernacular. Boston and New York: Houghton, Mifflin & Company, 1888
GR103 J7

Owen, Mary Alicia
Voodoo tales, as told among the Negroes of the Southwest. New York, London: G. P. Putnam's Sons, 1893
GR103 O8

Puckett, Newbell Niles
Folk beliefs of the southern Negro. Chapel Hill: University of North Carolina Press, London: H. Milford, 1926
GR103 P8 1926

Stoney, Samuel Gaillard
Black Genesis. New York: Macmillan, 1930
GR103 S88

Wittke, Carl Frederick
Tambo and bones; a history of the American minstrel stage. Durham, North Carolina: Duke University Press, 1930
GT3650 W53 (Main, Music)

RACE

Alpenfels, Ethel Josephine
Sense and nonsense about race. New and Revised edition. New York: Friendship Press, 1957 (i.e. 1958, c1957)
GN29 A4 1957 (Physical Education-Women)

Barzun, Jacques
Race: a study in modern superstition. New York: Harcourt, Brace and Company (c1937)
GN315 B29

Benedict, (Mrs.) Ruth (Fulton)
Race: science and politics. New York: Modern Age Books, 1940
GN315 B46 (Main, Social Work)

Another edition
GN315 B46 1945 (Education)

Another edition
GN315 B46 1959 (Undergraduate)

Congrès international des écrivains et artistes noirs. 2nd, Rome, 1959
Deuxieme Congrès des écrivains et artistes noirs. (Rome: 26 mars-1er avril 1959) (Paris, 1959-
GN654 C6 1959

Coon, Carleton Stevens
The living races of man. (1st edition) New York: Knopf, 1965
GN315 C64 (Main, Undergraduate)

The origin of races. (1st edition) New York: Alfred A. Knopf, 1966 (c1962)
GN350 C6 (Main, Undergraduate, Botany & Zoology)

Dowd, Jerome
The Negro races, a sociological study. New York: The Macmillan Company, London: Macmillan & Company, Ltd., 1907-
GN545 D74

Fanon, Frantz
Black skin, white masks. Translated by Charles Lam Markmann. New York: Grove Press (1967)
GN645 F31 (Main, Social Work)

Fausett, Arthur Huff
...Black gods of the metropolis.... Philadelphia: University of Pennsylvania Press, 1944
GN4 P5 vol. 3

Finot, Jean
Race prejudice.... New York: E. P. Dutton & Company (1907?)
GN320 F5

Garn, Stanley M
Human races. Springfield, Illinois: Thomas (c1961)
GN315 G3

Another edition
GN315 G3 1965 (Main, Undergraduate, Health Center)

Hoffman, Frederick Ludwig
Race traits and tendencies of the American Negro. New York: Macmillan, 1896
HB1 A5 vol. 11 (Main, Commerce)

Logan, Rayford Whittingham
The Negro and the post-war world, a primer. Washington, D. C.: The Minorities Publishing, 1945
GN645 L83 (Commerce)

Ly, Abdoulaye
Mercenaires noirs, notes sur une forme de l'exploitation des Africaines. Paris: Présence africaine (1957)
GN645 L9

Morand, Paul
Magie noire. Paris: B. Grasset, 1928
GN645 M82

Mphahlele, Ezekiel
The African image. London: Faber & Faber (1962)
GN645 M85

Another edition
GN645 M85 1962a

The National Association for the
Advancement of Colored People
Purpose. New York: Trades Council
(n.d.)
AH439 N26 A2

Robinson, Bradley
Dark companion. New York: R. M.
McBride (1947)
G635 H4 R6

Rose, Arnold Marshall, ed.
Minority problems: a book of readings.
New York: Harper (1965)
GN315 R6 (Social Work)

Stanton, William Ragan
**The leopard's spots: scientific atti-
tudes toward race in America, 1815-
1859.** (Chicago) University of Chicago
Press (1960)
GN17 S75

United Nations Educational, Scientific
and Cultural Organization.
**The race. question in modern science;
race and science.** New York: Columbia
University Press, 1961
GN320 U52 1961 (Main, Social Work)

SPORTS

Boyle, Robert H
Sport—mirror of American life. (1st
edition) Boston: Little, Brown and
Company (1963)
GV583 B6 (Browsing Room)

Cozens, Frederick Warren
Sports in American life. (Chicago) The
University of Chicago Press (1953)
GV583 C6

Fraley, Lester Martin
**A comparison of the general athletic
ability of white and Negro men of
college age.** Nashville, Tennessee:
George Peabody College for Teachers,
1939
GV436 F8 (Main, Education)

Gibson, Althea
I always wanted to be somebody. New
York: Harper (c1958)
GV994 G5 A3 (Browsing Room)

Henderson, Edwin Bancroft
The Negro in sports. (Revised edition)
Washington, D. C., The Associated
Publishers Inc. (c1939)
E185.88 H49

Howard, Elston
Catching. New York: Viking (1966)
GV872 H6

Johnson, John Arthur
Jack Johnson in the ring and out.
Chicago: National Sports Publishing
Company, 1927
GV1132 J7 A3

Louis, Joe
My life story. New York: Duell, Sloan,
& Pearce (1947)
GV1132 L8 A3 1947

Mays, Willie
**Willie Mays: my life in and out of base-
ball, as told to Charles Einstein.** New
York: Dutton, 1966
GV865 M4 A3

Nilsson, Tore, ed.
**Den stora matchen om VM-titeln i
tungviktsboxning Floyd Patterson-
Ingemar Johansson.** New York, 1959...
Stockholm: Ahlen & Akerlund, 1959
GV1132 J6 N5

Robinson, John Roosevelt
**Breakthrough to the big league; the
story of Jackie Robinson and Alfred
Duckett.** New York: Harper & Row
(1965)
GV865 R6 A27 (Education)

**Jackie Robinson, my own story, as
told to Wendell Smith.** New York:
Greenberg (1948)
GV865 R6 A3

Roeder, Bill
Jackie Robinson. New York: Barnes
(c1950)
GV865 R6 R6

Waterman, Julian Seesel
The aftermath of Moore vs. Dempsey.
(Fayetteville, Ark., 1933)
AS36 A72 no. 299

Young, Andrew Sturgeon Nash
Negro firsts in sports. Chicago: John-
son Publishing Company (1963)
GV697 A1 Y6

ECONOMIC CONDITIONS

American Management Association
The Negro worker. New York: Ameri-
can Management Association, c1942
HD21 A5 no. 1 (Commerce, Main)

Avins, Alfred
**Open occupancy vs. forced housing
under the Fourteenth amendment....**
New York: Bookmailer (c1963)
HD7293 A9 (Main, Social Work)

Bancroft, Gertrude
**The American labor force: its growth
and changing composition.** New York:
Wiley (c1958)
HD5724 B3 (Reference, Commerce)

Banfield, Edward C
**Government and housing in metropoli-
tan areas.** New York: McGraw-Hill,
1958
HD7293 B3 (Main, Social Work, Architecture, Commerce, Home Economics)

Becker, Gary Stanley
The economics of discrimination.
(Chicago) University of Chicago Press
(1957)
HD4903.5 U58 B4 (Main, Commerce)

Bitting, Samuel Tilden
**....Rural land ownership among the
Negroes of Virginia, with special
reference to Abbemarle County.** (Charlottesville, Virginia: The Michie Company Printers, 1915)
HD1156 V8 B6

Blood, Kathryn
Negro women war workers. (Washing-
ton) Women's bureau, United States
Department of Labor (1945)
HD6093 A3 no. 205 (Main, Commerce,
Education)

Brazeal, Brailsford Reese
**The Brotherhood of sleeping car
porters; its origin and development.**
New York and London: Harper &
Brothers (1946)
HD6515 R36 B8 (Main, Commerce)

Bright, James Rieser
Automation and movement. Boston:
Division of Research, Graduate School
of Business Administration, Harvard
University, 1958
HD45 B7 (Commerce)

Brown, Mrs. Jean (Collier)
The Negro woman worker. Washington:
United States Government Printing
Office, 1938
HD6093 A3 no. 165 (Main, Commerce)

Brown, Thomas Isaacs
**Economic co-operation among the
negroes of Georgia.** Atlanta, Georgia:
The Atlanta University Press, 1917
HT1521 A1 A8 no. 19

Bryson, Winfred Octavus
Negro life insurance companies. Phil-
adelphia, 1948
HG8951 B7

Bullock, Paul
Merit employment: non-discrimination in industry. Los Angeles: University of California. (1960)
HD4903.5 U58 B8 (Commerce)

Caplovitz, David
The poor pay more .... (New York) Free Press of Glencoe (1963)
HC110 C6 C3 (Main, Social Work, Commerce, Home Economics)

Another edition
HC110 C6 C3 1967 (Commerce)

Carpenter, Niles
Nationality, color and economic opportunity in the city of Buffalo. New York (c1927)
AS36 B94 vol. 5 no. 4 (Commerce)

Casstevens, Thomas W
Politics, housing, and race relations: California's Rumford act and Proposition 14. Berkeley: Institute of Governmental Studies, University of California, 1967
HD7303 C2 C3

Chapin, Francis Stuart, ed.
Urban growth dynamics. New York: Wiley (1962)
HT123 C4 (Main, Architecture)

Cleland, Herdman Fitzgerald
The black belt of Alabama. New York: American Geographical Society, 1920
HC107 A13 C6 (Orton)

Chilman, Catherine S
Growing up poor; an overview and analysis of child rearing and family life patterns associated with poverty... Washington: United States Department of Health Education, & Welfare, Welfare Administration, Division of Research (United States Government Printing Office, 1966)
HC110 P6 C5 (Children's Hospital)

Columbia University. Conservation of Human Resources Project.
Democratic values and the rights of management. New York: Columbia University Press, 1963
HD8072 C727 (Commerce)

Commerce Clearing House
Fair employment practices under Federal law: laws, regulations, executive orders, rules, forms. New York (1966)
HD4903.5 U58 C57 (Commerce)

Conference of Community Leaders on Equal Employment Opportunity Washington, D. C., 1962
The American dream — equal opportunity .... (Washington: United States Government Printing Office, 1962)
HD4903.5 U58 C6 1962

Conference on Equal Employment Opportunity. West Virginia State College, Institute, 1963
Equal employment opportunity; report. Charleston: West Virginia State College, Institute, 1963
HD4903.5 U6 W43 C6 1963

Conference on Poverty-in-Plenty: The Poor in Our Affluent Society, Georgetown, University, Washington, D. C., 1964
Poverty in plenty. New York: P. J. Kennedy (1964)
HC106.5 C774 1964 (Main, Social Work)

Cox, Oliver Cromwell
Capitalism and American leadership. New York: Philosophical Library (1962)
HB501 C78 (Commerce)

Caste, class and race; a study in social dynamics. (1st edition) Garden City, N. Y.: Doubleday, 1948
HT609 C6 (History Graduate)

Another edition
HT609 C6 1959

Crossland, William August
...Industrial conditions among Negroes in St. Louis.... St. Louis, Mo. (Press of Mendle Printing Company) 1914
HD6305 N3 C9

Duncan, Beverly
Housing a metropolis — Chicago. Glencoe, Illinois: Free Press (1960)
HD7304 C4 D8 (Main, Social Work, Architecture)

Fanning, John William
Negro migration .... (Athens, Georgia, 1930)
HD211 G4 F2

Federal council of the churches of Christ in America. Commission on the church and race relations.
Better houses for Negro homes.... New York, 1925
HD7293 A3 F29

Ferman, Louis A
The Negro and equal employment opportunities.... (Washington?) 1966
HD4903.5 U58 F4 (Commerce)

Ferman, Louis A, ed.
Poverty in America. Ann Arbor: University of Michigan Press (1965)
HC110 P6 F4 (Social Work, Education)

Another edition
HC110 P6 F4 1968 (Social Work)

Fleming, Walter L
The freedman's saving bank. Chapel Hill: University of North Carolina Press, 1927
HG2613 W34 F6 1927

Foote, Nelson N
Housing choices and housing constraints. New York: McGraw-Hill, 1960
HD7293 F65 (Architecture, Home Economics)

Ginzberg, Eli
The American worker in the twentieth century, a history through biographies. (New York) Free Press of Glencoe (1964, c1963)
HD8072 G4 (History Graduate, Undergraduate, Commerce)

The development of human resources. New York: McGraw-Hill (1966)
HD5724 G49 (Commerce, Education)

Manpower agenda for America. New York: McGraw-Hill (c1968)
HD5724 G52 (Commerce, Undergraduate, Social Work)

The pluralistic economy. New York: McGraw-Hill (1965)
HD3885 G5 (Commerce)

Goldner, William
New housing for Negroes: recent experience. (Berkeley) University of California (c1958)
HD268 S4 C3 no. 12

Greenhut, Melvin Leonard, ed.
Essays in Southern economic development. Chapel Hill: University of North Carolina Press (1964)
HC107 A13 G7 (Commerce)

Greer, Scott Allen
Last man in; racial access to union power. Glencoe, Illinois: Free Press (c1959)
HD6490 R2 G7

Grier, George W
Equality and beyond.... Chicago: Quadrangle Books, 1966
HD7293 G79 (Social Work)

Herbst, Alma
The Negro in the slaughtering and meat-packing industry in Chicago. Boston and New York: Houghton Mifflin, Company, 1932
HD6305 C7 H5 (Main, Commerce)

Hiestand, Dale L
Economic growth and employment opportunities for minorities. New York: Columbia University, 1964
HD4903.5 U58 1964 (Main, Commerce, Social Work)

Hines, George Washington
Negro banking institutions in the United States. Washington, D. C., 1924
HG2001 H66

Hope, John
Equality of opportunity; a union approach to fair employment. Washington: Public Affairs Press (c1956)
HD4903.5 U58 H6

Irelan, Lola M, comp.
Low-income life styles. Washington: United States Department of Health, Education and Welfare, United States Government Printing Office (1966)
HC110 P6 I7 1966 (Reference, Social Work, Home Economics)

Jacobs, Paul
The state of the unions. New York: Atheneum, 1966 (c1963)
HD6508 J3 (Main, Undergraduate)

Johnson, Charles Spurgeon
The economic status of Negroes.... (Nashville) Fisk University Press, 1933
HD6305 C7 J6 (Main, Commerce)

Johnson, Joseph T
The potential Negro market. (1st edition) New York: Pageant Press (1952)
HF3031 J6 (Commerce)

Kennedy, Robert F
The enemy from within. New York:
Harper & Row (c1960)
HD8072 K4 (Browsing Room, Under-
graduate)

Kesselman, Louis Coleridge
The social politics of FEPC. Chapel
Hill: University of North Carolina
Press, 1948
HD4903 K4 (Main, History Graduate)

Klein, Woody
Let in the sun. New York: Macmillan
(1964)
HD7304 N5 K55

Lampman, Robert J
**The low income population and
economic growth.** Washington: United
States Government Printing Office,
1959
HC110 I5 L3 (Main, Commerce)

Leggett, John C
Class, race and labor .... New York:
Oxford University Press, 1968
HD8085 D6 L4 (Commerce)

Leventhal, Sharon
Job discrimination is illegal.... (1st
edition, New York: Public Affairs
Committee, 1967)
HD4903.5 U58 L48 (Main, Education,
Social Work)

Litwack, Leon F
The American labor movement. Engle-
wood Cliffs, New Jersey: Prentice-
Hall (1962)
HD6508 L68 (Commerce)

Lowry, Herbert J
**Vocational opportunities for Negroes
in Cleveland.** (Cleveland) 1938
HF5381 U5 O33 no. 1 (Main, Commerce,
Social Work, Education)

Mayhew, Leon H
Law and equal opportunity.... Cam-
bridge: Harvard University Press, 1968
HD4903.5 U6 M33 M39

Meyerson, Martin
Housing, people, and cities. New York:
McGraw-Hill, 1962
HD7293 M4 (Architecture, Home
Economics)

Meyerson, Martin
**Politics, planning, and the public
interest.** Glencoe, Ill.: Free Press
(c1955)
HD7304 C4 M4 (Main, Architecture)

Another edition
HD7304 C4 M4 1955a (Undergraduate)

Michael, Donald N
Cybernation: the silent conquest.
(Santa Barbara, California: Center for
the Study of Democratic Institutions,
1962)
HD45 M5 (Education)

The next generation. New York:
Random House (1965)
HQ796 M44 (Education)

Michigan. Employment Security Commis-
sion.
**Detroit metropolitan area survey of
training needs, 1962-1963.** Mayor's
Committee for Economic Growth of the
City of Detroit (and) Michigan Em-
ployment Security Commission.) Lan-
sing? 1964?)
HF5382.5 U6 D4 M5 1962-63
(Commerce)

Miller, Herman Phillip
Income of the American people. New
York: Wiley (c1955)
HC110 I5 M5 (Main, Reference, Home
Economics, Commerce, Agriculture)

Rich man, poor man. New York:
Crowell (1964)
HC110 I5 M54 (Social Work, Commerce)

Millspaugh, Martin
Human side of urban renewal .... New
York: Washburn, 1960 (c1958)
HD7293 M55 (Main, Social Work,
Architecture)

Missouri. Negro Industrial Commission.
Semi-annual report, 2nd-3rd 1920-1921.
(Jefferson City: The Hugh Stephens
Company, 1920-1921)
HD6305 C7 M8

Mitchell, James B
**The collapse of the National benefit
life insurance company; a study in
high finance among Negroes.** Washington, D. C.: Howard University, 1939
HG8963 N352 M5

Moore, Truman E
The slaves we rent. New York: Random House (1965)
HD1525 M6 (Browsing Room, Undergraduate)

Myrdal, Gunnar
Challenge to affluence. New York: Pantheon Books (1963)
HC106.5 M8 (Main, Social Work, Commerce, Browsing Room, Undergraduate)

Values in social theory.... London: Routledge & K. Paul (1958)
H61 M9

National Association of Manufacturers of the United States of America.
A tale of 22 cities.... (New York, 1965)
HD4903.5 U58 N38 (Commerce)

National Community Relations Advisory Council.
FEPC reference manual prepared by the Committee on Employment Discrimination of the National Community Relations Advisory Council. New York (1948)
HD4903 N3 1948 (Social Work)

National Manpower Council
A policy for skilled manpower.... New York: Columbia University Press, 1954
HD5724 N2725 (Engineering-Industrial)

National Opinion Research Center
Do Negroes have equal economic opportunities? Why? Denver, Colorado, 1944
HM261 A1 N2 no. 22 (Education)

National responsibility for education of the colored people: A. The status of Negro education.... (Washington, D.C.: National Education Association, 1918)
LZ13 N52 1918

National Urban League
Negro membership in American labor unions.... New York (The Alexander Press, 1930)
HD6305 C7 N26 (Commerce)

National Urban League. Department of Industrial Relations
How unemployment affects Negroes. New York, 1931
HD5724 N28 (Main, Commerce)

Unemployment status of Negroes.... New York: National Urban League, 1931
HD6305 C7 N27 (Commerce)

New York (City) City Commission on Human Rights
The ethnic survey by CCHR. (New York, 1964)
HD4903.5 U6 N7 N35 1964

New York (City) New School for Social Research
Discrimination and low incomes. (New York) State of New York Interdepartmental Committee on Low Incomes, 1959
HD4903.5 U6 N7 N4 (Social Work)

Nicol, Helen (Osterrieth)
Negro women workers in 1960. Washington: United States Government Printing Office, 1964
HD6093 A3 no. 287

Norgren, Paul Herbert
Toward fair employment. New York: Columbia University Press, 1964
HD4903.5 U58 N6 (Main, Social Work)

Ohio Civil Rights Commission
Report. 1st- 1959/60- Columbus, Ohio
HD4903 A2 O3 (Main, Education)

Ohio. State Employment Service
....The Negro in defense. (Columbus, Ohio, 1941)
HD6305 C7 O3 (Social Work)

Oneal, James
The next emancipation.... New York: The Emancipation Publishing Company (1922?)
HD6305 C7 O5

Philadelphia Afro-American
The new Philadelphia story, a report on the characteristics of the Philadelphia Negro market. (Baltimore) Philadelphia Afro-American, c1946
HF3163 P5 P4

Pidgeon, Mary Elizabeth
Negro women in industry in 15 states. Washington; United States Government Printing Office, 1929
HD6093 A3 no. 70 (Main, Commerce, Education, Social Work)

Pinchback, Raymond Bennett
The Virginia Negro artisan and trades-
man. Richmond, Virginia: The William
Byrd Press, Inc., 1926
AH439 P64

Prentice Hall, Inc.
How the new civil rights law affects
your employment practices.... (Englewood Cliffs, New Jersey, c1964)
HD4903.5 U58 P7 (Commerce)

President's Conference on Home Build-
ing and Home Ownership, Washington,
D. C., 1931
Negro housing. Washington, D. C.
(c1932)
HD7286 P93 1932 vol. 6 (Commerce,
Architecture, Social Work)

Rackow, Felix
Combating discrimination in employ-
ment in New York State. Ithaca (1949)
HD4903 R22 (Commerce, Main)

Richberg, Donald Randall
Nor can government: analysis and
criticism of S.984- "A bill to prohibit
discrimination in employment because
of race, religion, color, national origin,
or ancestry." (New York: National
Industrial Conference Board, 1948)
HD4903 R5

Rosen, Harry M
But not next door. New York: I.
Obolensky (1962)
HD7304 D38 R6 (Main, Social Work,
Browsing Room)

Ross, Malcolm Harrison
All manner of men. New York: Reynal
& Hitchcock (1948)
HD4903 R6 (Main, Commerce, Under-
graduate)

Rossi, Peter Henry
Why families move.... Glencoe, Illinois:
Free Press (c1955)
HD7287.5 R6

Ruchames, Louis
Race, jobs and politics; the story of
the FEPC. New York: Columbia Uni-
versity Press, 1953
HD4903.5 U58 R8 (History Graduate,
Commerce)

Scarborough, Donald Dewey
An economic study of Negro farmers
as owners, tenents, and croppers.
(Athens, Georgia, 1923)
HD211 G4 S28

Smith, Clarence G
Containment of minority groups through
housing. (Toledo? Ohio, 1968)
HD7303 O3 S6 (Commerce)

Smith, Stanley Hugh
Freedom to work. New York: Vantage
Press (1955)
HD4903.5 U6 W3

Snavely, Tipton Ray
The taxation of Negroes in Virginia.
(Charlottesville, Virginia: the Michie
Company, 1916)
AH439 S66

Southall, Sara Elizabeth
Industry's unfinished business....
(1st edition) New York: Harper (1950)
HD8072 S69 (Commerce, Main)

Southern Regional Council
The price we pay (for discrimination)
Prepared by Barbara Patterson and
other members of the SRC and the
Anti-Defamation League. (Atlanta,
Georgia: SRC) 1964
HC107 A13 S76 (Education)

Sovern, Michael I
Legal restraints on racial discrimina-
tion in employment. New York:
Twentieth Century Fund, 1966
HD4903.5 U58 S68

Spero, Sterling Denhard
The Black worker; the Negro and the
labor movement. New York: Columbia
University Press, 1931
HD6305 C7 S7 (Main, Commerce)

Another edition
HD6305 C7 S7 1959

Street, James Harry
The new revolution in the cotton
economy.... Chapel Hill: University of
North Carolina Press (c1957)
HD9075 S8 (Commerce)

Stuart, Merah Steven
An economic detour. New York: W.
Malliet & Company, 1940
HG8799 S93

Taft, Philip
Organized labor in American history.
(1st edition) New York: Harper & Row
(1964)
HD6508 T25 (History Graduate, Undergraduate, Commerce)

Testing and fair employment.
New York: New York University Press,
1968
HF5549.5 E5 T4 1968 (Commerce,
Main, Education)

U. S. Commission on Civil Rights. Mary-
land Advisory Committee.
Report on Maryland: employment.
(Washington) 1964
HD4903.5 U58 A45 1964

U. S. Committee on Fair Employment
Practice (1943)
Report. 1st- (2nd) 1943/44- 1945/46
Washington: United States Government
Printing Office, 1945-47.
HD4903 U47

U. S. Congress. Senate. Committee on
Education and Labor
Fair employment practices act. Wash-
ington: United States Government
Printing Office, 1944
HD4903 U5 1944b

U. S. Equal Employment Opportunity
Commission
Newsletter. vol. 1- Nov. (1965)
Washington
HD4903.5 U58 A26

U. S. Government Contract Committee
Five years of progress, 1953-1958.
(Washington: United States Govern-
ment Printing Office, 1958)
HD4903.5 U58 A5

U. S. Housing and Home Finance
Agency. Intergroup Relations Service
**State statutes and local ordinances
and resolutions prohibiting discrimina-
tion in housing and urban renewal
operations.** Revised December, 1961.
Washington, 1961 (i.e. 1962)
HD7293 A535 1961 (Reference)

U. S. Housing and Home Finance
Agency. Office of Program Policy
Equal opportunity in housing.... (Wash-
ington: United States Government
Printing Office) 1964
HD7293 A5 1964 (Social Work)

United States. National Youth Admini-
stration. Ohio
**Job opportunities for Negro youth in
Columbus.** Columbus, Ohio, 1938
HF5381 U5 O33 no. 2 (Education,
Social Work, Commerce)

U. S. President's Committee on Equal
Employment Opportunity
**Guide for investigations and com-
pliance reviews in equal employment
opportunity.** Washington, 1962
HD4903.5 U58 A63 1962 (Main, Davis
Welding)

Report. 1961/62- (Washington)
HD4903.5 U58 A35 (Main, Social Work,
Commerce)

U. S. Women's Bureau
**Current data on nonwhite women work-
ers.** (Washington) 1965
HD6093 A6 A35 1965 (Reference)

Negro women in industry. Washington:
United States Government Printing
Office, 1922
HD6093 A3 no. 20 (Main, Commerce,
Social Work)

Women in Mississippi industries.
Washington: United States Government
Printing Office, 1926
HD6093 A3 no. 55

Women in Florida industries. Washing-
ton: United States Government Printing
Office, 1930
HD6093 A3 no. 80 (Main, Commerce,
Education, Social Work)

U. S. Works Progress Administration.
Georgia
**....Father-son occupations among
Negroes in Atlanta, Georgia.** (Atlanta,
1937)
HD6305 C7 U5 1937 (Education)

Washington Afro American
**....Report on characteristics of the
Washington Negro market; its product
buying and brand preference in 1945....**
Washington, D. C.: The Afro American
(1946)
HF3163 W4 W3

Washington (State) University Institute
of Labor Economics
**Job opportunities for racial minorities
in the Seattle area.** Seattle: University
of Washington Press (1948)
HD4903 W3

Wesley, Charles Harris
Negro labor in the United States, 1850-1925.... New York: Vanguard Press (1927)
HD6305 C7 W5 (Main, Commerce)

West Virginia. Bureau of Negro Welfare and Statistics
Negro housing survey of Charleston. (Charleston: Jarrett Printing Company, 1934?)
AH439 W4

Woodson, J H Harmon, jr.
The Negro as a business man. Washington, D. C.: The Association for the study...., 1929
HT1523 H28

Woofter, Thomas Jackson
....The Negroes of Athens, Georgia. (Athens, Georgia: The University, 1913)
HD6305 N38 W9

Wright, Dale
They harvest despair: the migrant farm worker. Boston: Beacon Press (1965)
HD1525 W7 (Commerce)

COMMUNITY RACE RELATIONS

Abrahamson, Julia
A neighborhood finds itself. New York: Harper (c1959)
HN80 C5 A6 (Main, Architecture, Social Work)

Abrams, Charles
The city is the frontier. New York: Harper (1965)
HT123 A65 (Main, Home Economics, Undergraduate, Architecture)

Forbidden neighbors.... (1st edition) New York: Harper (c1955)
HD7293 A588 (Architecture)

Alexander, Charles C
The Ku Klux Klan in the Southwest. (Lexington) University of Kentucky Press (1965)
HS2330 K63 A43

Allport, Gordon Willard
The resolution of intergroup tensions; a critical appraisal of methods. (New York: National Conference of Christians and Jews, 1952)
HT1525 A5 (Education)

Amter, Israel
Mirovoe osvoboditel noe dvizhenie negrov. 1925
HT1581 A516 R9

Anderson, Martin
The federal bulldozer: a critical analysis of urban renewal: 1949-1962. Cambridge, Mass.: Institute of Technology Press (1965, c1964)
HT175 U6 A84 1964a (Architecture, Commerce)

Atlanta University
Atlanta University publications, no. 1-1897- . Atlanta, Georgia: Atlanta University Press, 1897-
HT1521 A1 A8

Bagramov, Eduard Aleksandrovich
Ideology of hatred. (Moscow: Novosti Press Agency Publishing House, 1966)
HT1521 B31

Baker, Paul Ernest
Negro-white adjustment. New York: Association Press, 1934
AH439 B154

Banton, Michael P
Race relations. New York: Basic Books (c1967)
HT1521 B34 (Main, Education)

Baughman, Laurence E Alan
Southern rape complex; hundred year psychosis. Atlanta: Pendulum Books (1966)
HN79 A13 B3 (Education)

Beasley, Deliah Leontium
The Negro trail blazers of California.
Los Angeles, California (Times Mirror
Printing & Binding House) 1919
AH439 B36

Bell, Daniel
The end of ideology. Glencoe, Illinois:
Free Press (c1960)
HN57 B4 (Main, Mershon, Social Work,
History Graduate)

Another edition
HN57 B4 1961 (Commerce)

Another edition
HN57 B4 1962 (Commerce, Undergraduate)

Berry, Brewton
Race and ethnic relations. Boston:
Riverside Press, 1951
Precat A25072

Another edition
HT1521 B4 1958 (Main, Social Work)

Another edition
HT1521 B4 1965 (Main, Undergraduate)

Beshers, James M
Urban social structure. (New York)
Free Press (1962)
HT151 B4 (Main, Home Economics)

Bettelheim, Bruno
**Dynamics of prejudice; a psychologi-
cal and sociological study of veterans..**
(1st edition) New York: Harper (1950)
HM291 B4 (Education, Social Work)

Social change and prejudice. (New
York) Free Press (1964)
HM291 B4 1964

Bigham, John Alvin
Select discussions of race problems.
Atlanta, Georgia: The Atlanta Univer-
sity Press, 1916
HT1521 A1 A8 no. 20

Black, Algernon David
Who's my neighbor? (1st edition. New
York: Public Affairs Committee, 1958)
HD7293 B6 (Main, Education, Social
Work)

Another edition
HD7293 B6 1966

Blalock, Hubert M
**Toward a theory of minority group re-
lations.** New York: Wiley (1967)
HT1521 B5 (Main, Social Work)

Brawley, Benjamin Griffith
Your Negro neighbor. New York: The
Macmillan Company, 1918
AH439 B84

Burgess, Ernest Watson
Contributions to urban sociology.
Chicago: University of Chicago Press
(1964)
HT108 B8 (Main, Architecture, Under-
graduate, Commerce)

Campbell, Byram
**Race and social revolution: twenty-one
essays on racial and social problems.**
New York: Truth Seeker, 1958
HT1521 C3

Chalmers, David Mark
**Hooded Americanism: the first century
of the Ku Klux Klan.** (1st edition)
Garden City, N.Y.: Doubleday, 1965
HS2330 K63 C5

Christie, Richard
**Studies in the scope and method of
"The Authoritarian Personality."**
Glencoe, Illinois: Free Press (c1954)
HM271 A818 C4 (History Graduate,
Education)

Columbus Urban League. Youth Department
**Community service available to the
youth of Columbus.** (Columbus, Ohio,
1943?)
HQ796 C75

Conference of Negro Land-Grant Col-
leges for Co-ordinating a Program of
Cooperative Social Studies, Atlanta
University
Report. 1st-2nd; 1943-44. Atlanta, Ga.
HT1521 A1 A8 no. 22

Conneau, Théophile
Capitan Canot, an African slaver. New
York: Arno Press, 1968
HT1322 C6 1854a (Undergraduate)

Davis, Allison
Deep South. Chicago: The University
of Chicago Press (1941)
HN79 A2 D2 (Main, Social Work, Undergraduate, Education)

The relation between color caste and economic stratification in two "black" plantation counties. (Chicago, 1942)
HN79 A2 D3

Dean, John Peebles
A manual of intergroup relations. (Chicago) University of Chicago Press (1955)
HT1525 D4 (Education, Social Work)

Another edition
HT1525 D4 1955a (Health Center)

Detroit. City Plan Commission
Renewal and revenue; an evaluation of the urban renewal program in Detroit... Detroit, 1962
HT177 D4 A5 1962 (Architecture)

Diaz Soler, Luis M
Historia de la esclavitud Negro en Puerto Rico. (2nd edition, corr.) Rio Piedras: Editorial Universitaria, Universidad de Puerto Rico, 1965
HT1086 D5 1965

Dubois, William Edward Burghardt
Black folk then and now; an essay in the history and sociology of the Negro race.... New York: H. Holt & Company (c1939)
HT1581 D81 (Main, Social Work)

The college-bred Negro, a report of a social study made under the direction of Atlanta University, together with the proceedings of the 5th Conference for the study of the Negro problems held at Atlanta University, May 29-30, 1900. Atlanta, Georgia: Atlanta University Press, 1900
HT1521 A1 A8 no. 5

Another edition
HT1521 A1 A8 no. 5 1902

The college-bred Negro American. Atlanta, Georgia: the Atlanta University Press, 1910
HT1521 A1 A8 no. 15

The common school and the Negro American; report of a social study made by Atlanta University under the patronage of the trustees of the John F. Slater fund, with the proceedings of the 16th annual conference for the study of the Negro problems, held at Atlanta University, on Tuesday, May 30th, 1911.... Atlanta, Georgia: The Atlanta University Press 1911
HT1521 A1 A8 no. 16

Economic cooperation among Negro Americans. Atlanta, Georgia: The Atlanta University Press, 1907
HT1521 A1 A8 no. 12

Efforts of social betterment among Negro Americans; report of a social study made by Atlanta University under the patronage of the trustees of the John F. Slater fund; together with the proceedings of the 14th annual conference for the study of the Negro problems, held at Atlanta University, on Tuesday, May 24th, 1909.... Atlanta, Georgia: The Atlanta University Press, 1909
HT1521 A1 A8 no. 14

Morals and manners among Negro Americans...report of the 18th conference for the study of the Negro problems held at the Atlanta University on Monday, May 26th, 1913. Atlanta, Georgia: The Atlanta University Press, 1913
HT1521 A1 A8 no. 18

The Negro American artisan; report of a social study made by Atlanta University ... 17th annual Conference ... May 27th, 1912. Atlanta, Georgia: The Atlanta University Press, 1912
HT1521 A1 A8 no. 17

Another edition
HT1521 A1 A8 no. 7

The Negro American family; a report of the 13th Conference ... Tuesday, May 26, 1908. Atlanta, Georgia: Atlanta University Press, 1908
HT1521 A1 A8 no. 13

The Negro artisan. Atlanta, Georgia: The Atlanta University Press, 1902
HT1521 A1 A8 no. 7

Race prejudice. New York: The Republican Club of the city of New York (c1910?)
HT1521 D8

Some notes on Negro crime. Atlanta, Georgia: The Atlanta University Press, 1904
HT1521 A1 A8 no. 9

Duncan, Otis Dudley
Metropolis and region. Baltimore: Johns Hopkins Press (c1960)
HT123 D78 (Main, Architecture, Reference, Commerce)

The edge of the ghetto; a study of
church involvement in the community
organization. (by) John Fish (and
others. 1st edition) New York: Seabury Press (1968, c1966)
HN80 C5 E3 (Main, Undergraduate)

Eldredge, Hanford Wentworth
Taming megalopolis. New York: F. A.
Praeger (1967)
HT151 E4 (Architecture, Under-
graduate, Social Work)

Another edition
HT151 E4 1967a (Education)

Embree, Edwin Rogers
Balance sheet in race relations.
(n.p., n.d.)
HT1521 E53

Investment in people: the story of the
Julius Rosenwald fund. (1st edition)
New York: Harper (1949)
HV97 J8 E5

Encyclopedia of the Negro .... New
York: The Phelps-Stokes fund, Inc.,
1945
HT1581 E56 (Main, Social Work)

English, David
Divided they stand. (American elec-
tion, 1968) Englewood Cliffs: Prentice-
Hall, 1969
E851 E5 (Browsing Room)

Evans, Arthur M
Working out the race problem. Tuskee-
gee, Alabama: Tuskegee Institute
(1912?)
LC2851 T9 E9

Fortune.
The exploding metropolis. Garden City,
N. Y.: Doubleday, 1958
HT123 F69 1958a (Browsing Room,
Commerce, Undergraduate, Journalism)

Frazier, Edward Franklin
Race and culture contacts in the
modern world. (1st edition) New York:
Knopf, 1957
HT1521 F7

Gilmore, Harlan Welch
Racial disorganization in a southern
city. Nashville, Tennessee: McQuiddy
(1931?)
HN80 N2 G4

Ginzburg, Ralph, ed.
100 years of lynchings. New York:
Lancer Books, 1962
HV6464 G5

Gist, Noel Pitts
Urban society. New York: Thomas Y.
Crowell (c1933)
HT151 G53

Another edition
HT151 G53 1940

Another edition
HT151 G53 1956 (Architecture)

Another edition
HT151 G53 1964 (Undergraduate)

Gordon, Milton Myron
Assimilation in American life. New
York: Oxford University Press, 1964
HN57 G6 (Main, Undergraduate,
Social Work)

Gordon, Mitchell
Sick cities. New York: Macmillan
(1963)
HT123 G6 (Browsing Room,
Architecture)

Green, Constance (McLaughlin)
The rise of urban America. (1st edi-
tion) New York: Harper (1965)
HT123 G72 (Main, Browsing Room,
Undergraduate, Architecture)

Gregoire, Henri
An inquiry concerning the intellectual
and moral faculties and literature of
Negroes. College Park, Maryland:
McGrath Publishing Company, 1967
HT1581 G71 1810a

Gregory, John Walter
The menace of colour. 2nd edition
London: Seeley, Service & Company,
Ltd., 1925
HT1621 G82 1925

Handlin, Oscar, ed.
The historian and the city. (Cambridge,
Mass.) Massachusetts Institute of
Technology Press, 1963
HT155 H3 (History Graduate, Fine Arts,
Education, Commerce, Architecture)

Harlem Youth Opportunities Unlimited,
New York.
Youth in the ghetto. (3rd edition) New
York, 1964
HN80 N5 H32 1964 (Social Work)

Harmon, J H Jr.
The Negro as a businessman. Washington, D. C.: The Association for the Study of Negro Life and History (c1929)
HT1523 H28

Harris, Abram Lincoln
Economic foundations of American race division. (Chapel Hill: The University of North Carolina Press, 1927)
HT1521 H28

Harte, Thomas Joseph
Catholic organizations promoting Negro-white race relations in the United States. Washington, D. C.: The Catholic University of America Press, 1947
HM15 C36 vol. 24

Harvard University. Dept. of Psychology
ABC's of scapegoating. Revised edition (New York: Anti-Defamation League of B'nai B'rith, 1948)
HM291 H338 1948

Haselden, Kyle
The racial problem in Christian perspective. New York: Harper & Row (c1959)
HT1521 H3

Hayford, Casely
Ethiopia unbound. London: C. N. Phillips, 1911
HT1581 H4

Herskovits, Melville Jean
The myth of the Negro past. New York: Harper (c1941)
HT1581 H57 (Main, Education)

Another edition
HT1581 H57 1958a (Undergraduate)

Hill, Walter Barnard
Rural survey of Clarke County, Ga., with special reference to the negroes. (Athens, Ga., 1915)
HN79 G4 H6

Hoover, Edgar Malone
Anatomy of a metropolis.... Cambridge: Harvard University Press, 1959
HC108 N5 H6 (Main, Commerce, Architecture)

Horowitz, Eugene Leonard
The development of attitude toward the Negro. New York, 1936
HT1583 H81 1936 (Main, Social Work)

Another edition
BF21 A6 no. 194 (Education)

Hunter, Floyd
Community power structure: a study of decision makers. Chapel Hill: University of North Carolina Press, (1953)
HM141 H8 (Main, Education, Agriculture, Social Work, Undergraduate)

Interracial Conference, 3rd, Columbus, 1929
Third interracial conference, Columbus, Ohio. (Columbus, Ohio) 1929
HT1581 A1 I6 1929

Jackson, Kenneth T
The Ku Klux Klan in the city, 1915-1930. New York: Oxford University Press, 1967
HS2330 K63 J3 (Main, Undergraduate)

Jennings, M Kent
Community influentials: the elites of Atlanta. (New York) Free Press of Glencoe (c1964)
HM141 J44 (Education)

Johnson, Manning
Color, communism, and common sense. (Belmont, Mass.: American Opinion, 1963)
HX61 J6 1958a

Josephine (pseud.)
Tell me Josephine. New York: Simon and Schuster, 1964
HQ734 J85 (Browsing Room)

Josephson, Halsey D
Discrimination; a study of recent developments in American life insurance. New York: Wesley Press, (1960)
HG8961 N5 J6 (Commerce)

Kahl, Joseph Alan
The American class structure. New York: Rinehart (c1957)
HN57 K3 1957 (Education, Commerce, Social Work, Undergraduate, Main)

Kheel, Theodore Woodrow .
How race relations affect your business. Englewood Cliffs, N.J.: Prentice-Hall, c1963
HT1523 K5 (Commerce)

La Farge, John
The Catholic viewpoint on race relations. Garden City, N.Y.: Hanover House, 1960
HT1521 L22 1960

Landry, Stuart Omer
The cult of equality. New Orleans:
Pelican (1945)
HT1581 L3 1945a

Leap, William Lester
Red Hill - neighborhood life and race
relations in a rural section. (Charlottesville, Va.: The Michie Company,
printers) 1933
AH439 L43

Leconfield, Hugh Archibald Wyndham
The Atlantic and emancipation. London, New York (etc.) Oxford University Press, 1937
HT867 L4

The Atlantic and slavery. London:
Oxford University Press, H. Milford,
1935
HT867 L42

Lewin, Julius
The struggle for racial equality. (Lon-
don) Longsman (1967)
HT1521 L52

Lewin, Kurt
Resolving social conflicts, selected
papers on group dynamics (1935-46)
(1st edition) New York: Harper & Row
(1948)
HM251 L67 (Main, Education, Commerce, Social Work, Undergraduate)

Lewis, Helen Matthews
The woman movement and the Negro
movement, parallel struggles for
rights. (Charlottesville) University of
Virginia, 1949
HQ1310 L4

Lieberson, Stanley
Ethnic patterns in American cities.
(New York) Free Press of Glencoe
(1963)
HN57 L72 1963 (Main, Social Work)

Lipset, Seymour Martin
Social mobility in industrial society.
Berkeley: University of California
Press, 1959
HT609 L7 (Main, Agriculture, Educa-
tion, Commerce, Undergraduate)

Another edition
HT609 L7 1959a (Social Work)

Lowe, David
Ku Klux Klan: the invisible empire.
(1st edition) New York: W. W. Norton
(1967)
HS2330 K63 L63 (Browsing Room,
Undergraduate)

Lowe, Jeanne R
Cities in a race with time; progress
and poverty in America's cities. New
York: Random House (1967)
HT175 U6 L6 (Browsing Room, Social
Work, Architecture, Undergraduate)

Lyford, Joseph P
The airtight cage. (1st edition) New
York: Harper & Row (1966)
HN80 N5 L9 (Social Work, Main,
Undergraduate)

McKinney, John C., ed.
The South in continuity and change.
Durham, N. C.: Duke University Press,
1965
HN79 A13 M2

Mailer, Norman
The white Negro. (San Francisco)
City Lights Books (c1957)
HN57 M22

Mannix, Daniel Pratt
Black cargoes: a history of the Atlantic
slave trade, 1518-1865. New York:
Viking (1963, c1962)
HT1049 M3 (Main, Undergraduate,
Commerce)

Marrow, Alfred Jay
Changing patterns of prejudice: a new
look at today's racial, religious, and
cultural tensions. Philadelphia: Chilton Company, Book Division (1962)
HN57 M26 (Social Work)

Marx, Gary Trade
The social basis of the support of a
depression era extremist: Father
Coughlin. Berkeley: Survey Research
Center, University of California, 1962
HN57 M28

Mason, Philip
An essay on racial tension. London,
New York: Royal Institute of Inter-
national Affairs (1954)
HT1521 M3

Massachusetts. Commission Against
Discrimination
Report. 1948/49- 1950/51- 1955/56
Boston, 1950-
HD4903.5 U6 M33

Masuoka, Jitsuichi
Race relations: problems and theory.
Chapel Hill: University of North
Carolina Press (1961)
HT1521 P3 M3

Miller, William Robert
**Non-violence: a Christian interpreta-
tion.** New York: Association Press
(1964)
HM278 M5 (Social Work)

Moffat, Adelene
Views of a southern woman. (New
York: National Association for the
Advancement of Colored People) n.d.
AH439 M69

National Advisory Commission on Civil
Disorders
Report. (Washington: United States
Government Printing Office, 1968)
HV6477 N3 1968 (Reference, Educa-
tion, Social Work)

Another edition
HV6477 N3 1968a (Main, Journalism,
Reference, Commerce)

Another edition
HV6477 N3 1968b (Education, Social
Work)

National Association for the Advance-
ment of Colored People
**An appeal to the world; a statement on
the denial of human rights to minori-
ties in the case of citizens of the
Negro descent in the United States of
America and an appeal to the United
Nations for redress.** (New York, 1947)
HT1523 N3 (Social Work, Main)

**Thirty years of lynching in the United
States, 1889-1918.** New York: National
Association for the Advancement of
Colored People, 1919
HV6457 N27

Another edition
HV6457 N27 1919

Nearing, Scott
Black America. New York: The Van-
guard Press, 1929
HT1581 N35

Negroes in the United States. Washing-
ton: United States Government Printing
Office, 1904
HA201 1900 A12 no. 8

New Jersey Conference of Social Work.
Interracial Committee
The Negro in New Jersey. (Newark)
1932
AH439 N5 A3 1932

New York Herald Tribune
**New York City in crisis (a study in
depth of urban sickness)....** New York:
McKay (1965)
HN80 N5 N53 (Main, Architecture)

Newark, New Jersey. Mayor's Commis-
sion on Group Relations
Newark, a city in transition. Newark,
N. J.: Market Planning Corp., 1959
HN80 N525 N4

Ottley, Roi
No green pastures. New York: Scribner,
1951
HT1581 O8

Ovington, Mary White
**Half a man: The status of the Negro in
New York.** London: Longmans, Green
and Company, 1911
AH439 O96

Packard, Vance Oakley
**The status seekers: an explanation of
class behavoir in America and the
hidden barriers that affect you, your
community, your future.** New York: D.
McKay Company, 1959
HT609 P3 (Main, Browsing Room,
Agriculture, Undergraduate, Social
Work, Commerce)

Park, Robert Ezra
Race and Culture. Glencoe, Illinois:
Free Press (1950)
HT1521 P3

Petersen, William
American social patterns. Garden City,
N.Y.: Doubleday (1956)
HN57 P45 (Main, Undergraduate)

Phylon, v.1-
1940- Atlanta, Atlanta University
HM1 P57

Pitts, Nathan Alvin
The cooperative movement in Negro communities of North Carolina. Washington, D. C.: Catholic University of America Press, 1950
HM15 C36 v.33

Raper, Arthur Franklin
The tragedy of lynching. Chapel Hill: The University of North Carolina Press, 1933
HV6464 R2

Reed, Ruth
The Negro women of Gainsville, Georgia. (Athens, Ga., 1921)
AH439 R32

Reuter, Edward Byron
The mulatto in the United States. Boston: R. G. Badger (c1918)
AH439 R44

Rice, Arnold S
The Ku Klux Klan in American politics. Washington, D. C.: Public Affairs Press (1962)
HS2330 K63 R5 (History Graduate)

Riley, Benjamin Franklin
The life and times of Booker T. Washington. New York, Chicago: Fleming H. Revell Company, 1916
AH439 W3 R5

Robinson, James Herman
Tomorrow is today. Philadelphia: Christian Education Press (1954)
HN18 R6

Rose, Arnold M., ed.
Human behavior and social processes. Boston: Houghton, Mifflin (c1962)
HM131 R79 (Main, Education, Social Work, Commerce)

Schlivek, Louis B
Man in metropolis. (1st edition) Garder City, N.Y.: Doubleday, 1965
HN80 N5 S3 (Architecture)

Schmid, Calvin Fisher
Growth and distribution of minority races in Seattle, Washington. (Seattle) Seattle Public Schools, 1964
HN80 S6 S3 (Education)

Schnore, Leo Francis
The Urban scene: human ecology and demography. New York: Free Press (1965)
HT123 S3 (Main, Architecture, Commerce)

Sherif, Muzafer
Groups in harmony and tension. New York: Harper (1953)
HM131 S4 (Education, Agriculture, Main, Social Work)

Intergroup conflict and cooperation: the Robbers Cave experiment. Norman, Oklahoma: Institute of Group Relations, University of Oklahoma, 1961
HM253 S4 (Education, Social Work)

Intergroup relations and leadership. New York: Wiley (1962)
HM131 S42 (Main, Commerce, Education, Social Work)

Reference groups: explorations in conformity and deviance of adolescents. New York: Harper & Row (1964)
HQ797 S45 (Main, Education, Social Work)

Sherrard, Owen Aubrey
Freedom from fear. New York: St. Martin's (1961, c1959)
HT1162 S35 1959a

Another edition
HT1162 S35 (Commerce)

Sibley, Eldridge
Differential morality in Tennessee, 1917-1928. Nashville: The Fisk University Press, 1930
HB1355 T2 S5

Sibley, Mulford Q., ed.
The quiet battle: writings on the theory and practice of non-violent resistence. (1st edition) Garden City, N. Y.: Doubleday, 1963
HM278 S5

Another edition
HM278 S5 1963a (History Graduate)

Simpson, Bertram Lenox
The conflict of colour. London: Macmillan, 1910
HT1521 S6

Simpson, George Eaton
Racial and cultural minorities; an analysis of prejudice and discrimination. New York: Harper & Row (1965)
HT1521 S62 1965 (Main, Social Work, Education)

Another edition
HT1521 S62 1958 (Social Work, Main)

Another edition
HT1521 S62 1953 (Social Work, Main)

Another edition
HM251 S72 1958 (Main, Commerce,
Social Work, Education)

Another edition
HM251 S72 1950 (Main, Social Work)

Another edition
HM251 S72 1952 (Education, Social
Work, Main)

Spring, Lindley
The Negro at home. New York: the
Author, 1868
AH1205 S76

Stoddard, Theodore Lothrop
**The rising tide of color against white
world-supremacy.** New York: C.
Scribner's sons, 1920
HT1521 S86

Stuart, Charles
A memoir of Granville Sharp. New York:
American Anti-Slavery Society, 1836
HT867 S92

Sumner, Charles
White slavery in the barbary states.
Boston: W. D. Ticknor, 1847
HT1345 S85 1847

Tannenbaum, Frank
Darker phases of the South. New York
and London: G. P. Putnam's Sons, 1924
HN79 A2 T2

Thompson, Edgar Tristram
**Race: individual and collective be-
havior....** Glencoe, Illinois: Free
Press (c1958)
HT1521 T46 (Education)

U. S. Commission on Civil Rights
**Children in need; a study of federally
assisted programs of aid to needy
families with children in Cleveland and
Cuyahoga County, Ohio.** (Washington)
1966
HV742 O3 U45 1966 (Social Work)

U. S. Congress. Joint Committee on the
Economic Report
**Characteristics of the low-income pop-
ulation and related federal programs.**
Washington: United States Government
Printing Office, 1955
HN57 A5 (Main, Social Work)

U. S. Securities and Exchange Commission
**Report on the feasibility and advisabil-
ity of the complete segregation of the
functions of dealer and broker.** Washington: United States Government
Printing Office, 1936
HG4621 U6 1936

Vance, Rupert Bayless
The urban South. Chapel Hill: Univer-
sity of North Carolina Press, 1954
HT123 V3 (History Graduate)

Warner, Sam Bass, ed
Planning for a nation of cities. Cam-
bridge: Massachusetts Institute of
Technology Press (1966)
HT123 W28 (Engineering-Civil, Archi-
tecture, Education)

Warner, William Lloyd
American life: dream and reality.
(Chicago) University of Chicago Press
(1953)
HN57 W29 1953 (Main, Social Work,
Undergraduate)

Another edition
HN57 W29 1962

Yankee city. New Haven: Yale University
versity Press, 1963
HN57 W3317 (Main, Education)

Wattenberg, Ben J
**This U. S. A.; An unexpected family
portrait of 194,067,296 Americans
drawn from the census.** Garden City,
N.Y.: Doubleday (1965)
HA215 W3 (Reference, Journalism,
Commerce, Undergraduate, Social
Work)

Wattenberg, William W, ed
"All men are created equal." Detroit:
Wayne State University Press, 1966
HM146 W3 (Main, Social Work)

Weatherford, Willie Duke
Negro life in the South. Revised edition. New York: Association Press,
1924
AH439 W35

Present forces in Negro progress. New
York: Association Press, 1915
AH439 W36

Weaver, Robert Clifton
Dilemmas of urban America. Cambridge, Mass.: Harvard University Press, 1965
HT175 U6 W4 (Main, Commerce)

The urban complex; human values in urban life. (1st edition) New York: Doubleday, 1964
HT123 W38 (Browsing Room, Architecture, Undergraduate, Social Work)

Why colored people in Philadelphia are excluded from the streetcars. Philadelphia: B. C. Bacon, 1866
AH755 W62

Williams, Eric Eustace
Capitalism and slavery. Chapel Hill: University of North Carolina Press (1944)
HC254.5 W72

Another edition
HC254.5 W72 1944a

Williams, Robin Murphy
The reduction of intergroup tensions. New York (1947)
HT1523 W72 (Main, Education, Social Work)

Wood, Robert Coldwell
Suburbia. Boston: Houghton Mifflin (c1958)
HT351 W6 (Main, Architecture, Undergraduate)

Wright, Nathan
Ready to riot. (1st edition) New York: Holt, Rinehart & Winston (c1968)
HN80 N525 W7 (Social Work)

Wright, Richard
White man, listen! (1st edition) Garden City, N.Y.: Anchor Books (1957)
HT1581 W7 1964

Another edition
Precat A16906

Another edition
Precat A23796

Wu, Charles Ling
Attitudes toward Negroes, Jews, and Orientals in the United States. (Columbus, Ohio: H. L. Hedrick) 1930
HT1521 W95

Yates, William
Rights of colored men to suffrage, citizenship and trial by jury. Philadelphia: Merrihew and Gunn, 1838
AH439 Y39

Young, Marechal Neil Ellison
Some sociological aspects of vocational guidance of Negro children. Philadelphia, 1944
HF5381 Y72

SOCIAL PROBLEMS

American Academy of Political and Social Science, Philadelphia
The Negro's progress in fifty years. Philadelphia: American Academy of Political and Social Science (c1913)
AH439 A52

Amos, William E
Counseling the disadvantaged youth. Englewood Cliffs, New Jersey: Prentice-Hall (1968)
HF5382.5 U5 A65 (Education, Social Work)

Asbell, Bernard
The new improved American. (1st edition) New York: McGraw-Hill (c1965)
HC110 A9 A8 (Browsing Room, Social Work)

Association for the care of colored orphans of Philadelphia.
Annual report. 6th- 1841-
Philadelphia, 1842-
HV995 P5 A5

Bagdikian, Ben H
In the midst of plenty: the poor in America. Boston: Beacon (1964)
HV91 B3 (Social Work, Home Economics, Journalism)

Bandura, Albert
Adolescent aggression. New York: Ronald Press Company (c1959)
HV9069 B29 (Education, Social Work, Agriculture)

Barron, Milton Leon
People who intermarry. (Syracuse, N.Y.) Syracuse University Press, 1946 (i.e. 1947, c1946)
HQ557 D4 B3

Bensing, Robert C
Homicide in an urban community. Springfield, Illinois: Thomas (c1960)
HV6534 C55 B4 (Main, Social Work)

Berelson, Bernard
Human behavior: an inventory of scientific findings. New York: Harcourt, Brace, 1964
HM51 B48 (Main, Undergraduate, Education, Botany and Zoology, Social Work, Journalism, Commerce, Agriculture, Health Center, Reference)

Another edition
HM51 B48 1967 (Education)

Bernstein, Saul
Alternatives to violence; alienated youth and riots, race and poverty. New York: Association Press (1967)
HV9104 B425 (Main, Social Work)

Youth on the streets: work with alienated youth groups. New York: Association Press (1964)
HV9104 B43 (Social Work)

Bohannan, Paul
African homicide and suicide. Princeton, N.J.: Princeton University Press, 1960
HV6513 B6 (Main, Social Work, Undergraduate, Education)

Bremner, Robert Hamlett
From the depths: the discovery of poverty in the United States. New York: New York University Press (1956)
HV91 B83 (Social Work, Commerce, Main, Undergraduate)

Buell, Charles Edwin
The education of the Negro blind in the United States. Ann Arbor, Michigan, 1945
HV1791 D8

Cantril, Hadley
The psychology of social movements. New York: Wiley, 1941
HM291 C23 (Main, Education, Undergraduate, Social Work)

Another edition
HM291 C23 1941a (Main, Undergraduate)

Chambliss, Rollin
What Negro newspapers in Georgia say about some social problems, 1933.... Athens, Georgia, 1934
AH439 C44

Child Welfare League of America
Child care facilities for dependent and neglected Negro children in three cities, New York City, Philadelphia, Cleveland. New York: Child Welfare League of America, Inc., 1945
HV3181 C53 (Social Work)

Cloward, Richard A
Delinquency and opportunity: a theory of delinquent gangs. Glencoe, Illinois: Free Press (c1960)
HV9069 C62 (Main, Social Work)

Another edition
HV9069 C62 1960a (Education)

Cohen, Albert Kircidel
Delinquent boys: the culture of the gang. Glencoe, Illinois: Free Press (1955)
HV9069 C63 (Social Work)

Another edition
HV9069 C63 1955a (Main, Social Work, Education, Undergraduate)

Committee on Studies, the Golden Anniversary White House Conference on Children and Youth
Reference papers on children and youth. (Washington?) c1960
HV741 C592 1960 (Education, Social Work)

Congressional Quarterly Service, Washington, D. C.
Urban problems and civil disorder.
Washington, c1967
HV6477 C6 (Main, Undergraduate, Mershon)

Curry, Jesse E
Race tensions and the police. Springfield, Illinois: Thomas (1962)
HV8069 C8

Dukette, Rita
Adoptive resources for Negro children.
New York: Child Welfare League of America, 1959
HV875 D8 (Social Work)

Epstein, Charlotte
Intergroup relations for police officers.
Baltimore: Williams & Wilkins, 1962
HV8141 E6 (Social Work)

Fanshel, David
A study in Negro adoption. New York: Child Welfare League of America, 1957
HV875 F3 (Social Work, Education)

Fisk University, Nashville. Social Science Institute.
God struck me dead. Nashville, Tenn.: Social Science Institute, Fisk University, 1945
H31 F54 no. 2

Racial attitudes. Nashville, Tenn.: Fisk Universities, 1946
H31 F54 no. 3

The social world of the Negro youth.
Nashville: Fisk University, 1946
H31 F54 no. 5

Unwritten history of slavery. Nashville, Tennessee: Fisk University, 1945
H31 F54 no. 1

Microcard edition
E444 F46 1968 (Undergraduate)

Glick, Paul C
American families. New York: Wiley (c1957)
HQ535 G6 (Reference, Architecture, Agriculture, Home Economics, Social Work)

Glueck, Sheldon
Unraveling juvenile delinquency. New York: Commonwealth fund, 1950
HV9069 G5 (Main, Education, Health Center, Agriculture, Social Work)

Another edition
HV9069 G5 1950a (Undergraduate)

Grabill, Wilson H
The fertility of American women. New York: Wiley (c1958)
HB903 F4 G7 (Reference)

Gula, Martin
Quest for equality, the story of how six institutions opened their doors to serve Negro children and their families. (Washington: United States Government Printing Office, 1966)
HV741 A32 no. 441 (Main, Social Work, Education)

Harrington, Michael
The other America: poverty in the United States. New York: Macmillan (1962)
HV91 H3 (Social Work, Home Economics, Commerce, Main, Undergraduate)

Harris, Richard E
Delinquency in our democracy; a study of teen-age behavior among Negroes.... Los Angeles: Wetzel Publishing Company (1954)
HV9104 H3

Henry, Andrew Fred
Suicide and homicide. Glencoe, Illinois: Free Press (c1954)
HV6548 U5 H4 (Education, Social Work)

Hunter, David Romeyn
The slums: challenge and response. (New York) Free Press of Glencoe (1966, c1964)
HV4045 H8 (Main, Home Economics, Social Work)

Julius Rosenwald fund.
Julius Rosenwald fund; a review.... Chicago (1927/1928-
HV97 J8 A3

Kephart, William M
Racial factors and urban law enforcement. Philadelphia: University of Pennsylvania Press (c1957)
HV8138 K4 (Main, Undergraduate, Social Work)

Lake, Isaac Beverly
Discrimination by railroads and other public utilities. Raleigh, N. C.: Edwards & Broughton Company, 1947
HE1843 L19 (Commerce)

Lightfoot, Robert Mitchell
Negro crime in a small urban commun-ity. (Charlottesville) University of Virginia, 1934
AH439 L72

Lohman, Joseph Dean
The police and minority groups.
Chicago (1947)
HV8148 C4 C4 (Main, Social Work)

Lovejoy, Owen Reed
The Negro children of New York....
New York, 1932
AH439 L89

McCormick, Ken
Sprung: the release of Willie Calloway.
New York: St. Martin's Press (1964)
HV6248 C205 M3 (Main, Social Work)

May, Edgar
The wasted Americans; costs of our welfare dilemma. (1st edition) New York: Harper & Row (c1964)
HV91 M37 (Social Work, Home Economics, Undergraduate)

Merton, Robert King
Contemporary social problems. New York: Harcourt, Brace (1961)
HN18 M43 (Main, Social Work)

Another edition
HN18 M43 1966 (Main, Education)

Mid-Century White House Conference on Children and Youth, Washington, D.C., 1950
Personality in the making. (1st edition) New York: Harper (1952)
HV741 M5 1950d (Education, Main, Social Work)

Another edition
HV741 M5 1950a (Education)

Miller, Robert Moats
American Protestantism and social issues, 1919-39. Chapel Hill: University of North Carolina Press (c1958)
HN39 U6 M5

Mississippi black paper.
New York: Random House (1965)
HV8145 M7 M5

Montgomery, Harry Earl
Vital American problems. New York and London: G. P. Putnam's Sons, 1908
HN64 M6

Mundy, Paul William
The Negro boy worker in Washington, D. C. Washington, D. C.: Catholic University of America Press, 1951
HM15 C362 vol. 2

Murchison, Carl Allanmore, ed.
A handbook of social psychology.
Worcester, Mass.: Clarke University Press, 1935
HM251 M96 (Education, Main)

Another edition
HM251 M96 1935a (Architecture)

Murphy, Edgar Gardner
Problems of the present South. New York, London: the Macmillan Company, 1904
AH1606 M97

Murphy, John C
An analysis of the attitudes of American Catholics toward the immigrant and the Negro, 1825-1925. Washington, D. C.: The Catholic University of America Press, 1940
HM15 C36 vol. 1

National Conference of Social Work
Minority groups: segregation and inte-gration. New York: Columbia University Press, 1955
HV95 N3 1955 (Social Work)

National Urban League (for Social Service Among Negroes)
Annual report.
HV3181 N3

Another edition
AH439 A1 N25

New York (City) Interdepartmental Neighborhood Service Center
The poor of Harlem: social functioning of the underclass. New York, 1965, c1966
HN80 N5 A49 (Social Work)

Odum, Howard Washington
Southern regions of the United States.
Chapel Hill: University of North Carolina Press, 1936
AH1606 O27 (Main, Commerce, Education)

Ogden, Frederick D
The poll tax in the South. (University, Alabama) University of Alabama Press, 1958
HJ4931 A13 O4 1958

O'Kelley, H S
**Sanitary conditions among the Negroes
of Athens, Georgia.** (Athens, Georgia:
The University, 1918)
TD25 A86 O4

Personnel Journal, Inc.
**How to recruit minority group college
graduates.** Swarthmore, Pa.: Personnel
Journel, Inc., 1963
HF5549.5 R44 P4 (Education)

Pryor, Thomas M
**Selective processes in a blighted
area....** Ann Arbor, Michigan, 1934
AS30 M62 vol. 3

Postell, William Dosite
**The health of slaves on southern plan-
tations.** Baton Rouge: Louisiana State
University Press (1951)
H31 L88 no. 1

Rainwater, Lee
And the poor get children. Chicago:
Quadrangle Books, 1960
HQ766.5 U5 R3 (Social Work)

Reed, Ruth
Negro illegitimacy in New York City.
New York: Columbia University Press,
1926
JA2 C72 no. 277

Reid, Ira De Augustine
**The Negro immigrant, his background,
characteristics and social adjustment,
1899-1937.** New York: Columbia University Press, London: P. S. King &
Son, Ltd., 1939
JA2 C72 no. 449

Salisbury, Harrison Evans
The shook-up generation. (1st edition)
New York: Harper (c1958)
HV9104 S3 (Browsing Room, Social
Work, Undergraduate)

Sanders, Wiley Britton, ed.
Negro child welfare in North Carolina.
Chapel Hill: University of North Caro-
lina Press, 1933
AH439 S21

Schachter, Stanley
The psychology of affiliation. Stanford:
Stanford University Press, 1959
HM251 S34 (Main, Education, Social
Work)

Scott, Emmett Jay
Negro migration during the war. New
York: Oxford University Press, 1920
HC56 P9 vol. 16 (Main, Commerce)

Shannon, David Allen
The great depression. (Englewood
Cliffs, N.J.) Prentice-Hall (1964,
c1960)
HC106.3 S5 (Main, Commerce)

Shastak, Arthur B, comp.
New perspective on poverty. Englewood, Cliffs, N. J.: Prentice-Hall, Inc.
(1965)
HC110 P6 S5 (Social Work)

Short, James F, Jr.
Group process and gang delinquency.
Chicago: University of Chicago Press
(1965)
HV9104 S48 (Social Work, Education)

**Social and physical condition of Negroes
in cities. Report of an investigation....**
Atlanta, Georgia: Atlanta University
Press, 1897
HT1521 A1 A8 no. 2

Southside Community Committee, Chicago
Bright shadows in Bronzetown. (Chi-
cago, c1949)
HV9106 C4 S6 (Main, Social Work)

Stringfellow, William
**Dissenter in a great society: a Chris-
tian view of America in crisis.** (1st
edition) New York: Holt, Rinehart &
Winston (1966)
HN57 S75

**Supplemental studies for the National
Advisory Commission on Civil Dis-
orders.** Washington: United States
Government Printing Office (1968)
HV6477 S8 1968

Tandy, Elizabeth Carpenter
**Infant and maternal mortality among
Negroes.** Washington: United States
Government Printing Office, 1937
HV741 A32 no. 243 (Main, Commerce,
Education)

Thrasher, Frederic Milton
**The gang; a study of 1,313 gangs in
Chicago.** Chicago: The University of
Chicago Press (c1927)
HV6439 U7 C4 (Agriculture, Under-
graduate)

Another edition
HV6439 U7 C4 1936 (Education, Social Work)

Another edition
HV6439 U7 C4 1936a

Towler, Juby Earl
The police role in racial conflicts.
Springfield, Illinois: C. C. Thomas (1964)
HV8069 T6

U. S. Bureau of Public Assistance
Illegitimacy and its impact on the aid to dependent children program. Washington, 1960
HV700.5 U5 (Main, Social Work)

U. S. Bureau of the Census
....**Fifteenth census of the United States: 1930. Census of agriculture. The Negro farmer in the United States.** Washington: United States Government Printing Office, 1933
HD6305 C7 U5

Negro population in the United States, 1790-1915. New York: Arno Press, 1968
HA205 A3 1918a (Undergraduate)

....**Negro population 1790-1915.** Washington: United States Government Printing Office, 1918
HA205 A3

....**Negroes in the United States.** Washington: United States Government Printing Office, 1904
HA201 1900 A12 no. 8

Negroes in the United States. Washington: United States Government Printing Office, 1915
HA201 1900 A12 no. 129

....**Negroes in the United States, 1920-32.** Washington: United States Government Printing Office, 1935
HA205 A32

....**Sixteenth census of the United States: 1940.** Washington: United States Government Printing Office, 1943
HA201 1940 A407

U. S. Census Office. 12th census, 1900
....**Supplementary analysis and derivative tables.** Twelfth census of the United States. Washington: United States Government Printing Office, 1906
HA201* 1900 E (Main, Social Work)

Vincent, Clark E
Unmarried mothers. (New York) Free Press of Glencoe (1961)
HQ999 U6 V5 (Main, Social Work, Health Center, Home Economics, Agriculture)

Watson, Homer K
Causes of delinquency among fifty Negro boys. Los Angeles, Calif.: University of Southern California (1919)
HV9091 W33

Welfare and Health Council of New York City. Research Dept.
Fact book on youth in New York City. (New York) 1956
HQ796 W48 (Social Work)

White House Conference on Child Health and Protection. Section III: Education and Training. Committee on the Infant and Pre-school Child
The young child in the house. New York, London: D. Appleton-Century (c1936)
HQ769 W585 (Education, Main)

White, Walter Francis
Rope and faggot. New York and London: A. A. Knopf, 1929
HV6457 W58

Wolfgang, Marvin E
Patterns in criminal homicide. Philadelphia: University of Pennsylvania Press (1958)
HV6534 P5 W6 (Main, Social Work)

The sociology of crime and delinquency. New York: Wiley (1962)
HV6028 W65 (Social Work, Education)

Wood, Arthur Evans
....**Trouble cases; a study of the more difficult family problems....** (Detroit, Michigan) Detroit Community Union, 1919
HV99 D4 W8

POLITICS & GOVERNMENT

Aikin, Charles, ed.
The Negro votes. San Francisco:
Chandler Publishing Company (1962)
JK1924 A5

American Civil Liberties Union
Violence in Peekskill. New York
(1949?)
JC599 U52 N7 A6

The Annals of the American Academy of
Political and Social Science. Philadelphia, November, 1928. Entire volume
devoted to "The American Negro"
JA5 A51

Banfield, Edward C
Big city politics; a comparative guide
to the political systems of Atlanta,
Boston, Detroit, El Paso, Los Angeles,
Miami, Philadelphia, St. Louis (and)
Seattle. (New York: Random House,
1965)
JS323 B3

City politics. Cambridge: Harvard University Press and Massachusetts Institute of Technology Press, 1963
JS331 B33 (Architecture, Main, Undergraduate)

Another edition
JS331 B33 1963a

Political influence. Glencoe, Illinois:
Free Press (1962, c1961)
JS708 B3 (Main, Commerce, History
Graduate)

Urban government: a reader. (New
York) Free Press (1961)
JS308 B28

Another edition
JS308 B28 1961a

Barker, Lucius Jefferson
Freedoms, courts, politics: studies in
civil liberties. Englewood Cliffs, N.J.:
Prentice-Hall (1965)
JK1726 B27 (Social Work)

Barnett, Richard
Where the states stand on civil rights.
New York: Sterling (1962)
JC599 U5 B28 (Reference, Social Work)

Berger, Morroe
Equality by statute; legal controls over
group discrimination.New York:
Columbia University Press, 1952
JC594 U5 B4

Equality by statute; the revolution in
civil rights. Revised edition. Garden
City, N.Y.: Doubleday, 1967
JC599 U5 B4 1967

Berman, Daniel M
A bill becomes law: the Civil Rights
Act of 1960. New York: Macmillan
(1962)
JK1096 B4

Another edition
JK1096 B4 1966 (Main, Undergraduate)

Bickel, Alexander M
The least dangerous branch. Indianap-
olis, Indiana: Bobbs-Merrill (c1962)
JK1561 B5

Brackett, Jeffrey Richardson
Notes on the progress of the colored
people of Maryland since the war.
Baltimore: Johns Hopkins University,
1890
JA2 J65 vol. 8

Brant, Irving
The bill of rights: its origin and mean-
ing. Indianapolis: Bobbs-Merrill (1965)
JK168 B7 (Main, Undergraduate)

Brogan, Dennis William
Politics in America. New York: Harper
(c1954)
JK268 B87 1954a (History Graduate,
Undergraduate)

Buck, Pearl (Sydenstricker)
Freedom for all. New York City: The
Post War World Council (1941)
JC545 B92

Bureau of National Affairs. Washington,
D. C.
The Civil Rights Act of 1964. Wash-
ington, D. C. (1964)
JC599 U5 B8 (Reference, Undergrad-
uate, Social Work)

Carmichael, Peter Archibald
The south and segregation. Washing-
ton, D. C.: Public Affairs Press (1965)
JK1781 C3

Civic Federation of New Haven
Living conditions among Negroes in the ninth ward. New Haven, Conn., 1913
JS1195 C5 vol. 14

Congressional Quarterly Service, Washington, D. C.
Revolution in civil rights. 3rd edition, Washington (1967?)
JC599 U5 C59 1967 (Main, Undergraduate, Journalism)

Another edition
JC599 U5 C59 1968 (Reference, Social Work, Journalism, History Graduate)

Cox, Archibald
Civil rights, the Constitution, and the courts. Cambridge: Harvard University Press, 1967
JK1781 C6

Cushman, Robert Eugene
Civil liberties in the United States: a guide to current problems and experience. Ithaca, N.Y.: Cornell University Press (1956)
JC599 U5 C85 (History Graduate, Journalism)

Douglas, William Orville
The anatomy of liberty, the rights of man without force. New York: Pocket Books (1964, c1963)
JC571 D7 1964

Dulles, Foster Rhea
Civil Rights Commission 1957-65.... (East Lansing) Michigan State University Press, 1968
JC599 U5 D8

Dunn, Jacob Piatt
The Negro issue. Indianapolis: Sentinel, 1904
JK1924 D9

Eldredge, Hanford Wentworth
The second American revolution. New York: Morrow, 1964
JC251 E4

Fletcher, John Lockwood
The segregation case and the Supreme Court. (Boston, 1958)
JA2 B6 no. 4

Fox, Early Lee
The American colonization society, 1817-40. Baltimore: Johns Hopkins Press, 1919
JA2 J65 vol. 37

Franklin, Charles Lionel
The Negro labor unionist of New York. New York: Columbia University Press, London: P. S. King & Son, Ltd., 1936
JA2 C72 no. 420

Friedman, Leon, ed.
Southern justice. New York: Pantheon Books (1965)
KB1916 F68 1965 (Undergraduate, Main)

Friese, Philip C
The unconstitutionality of Congressional action. Baltimore: Murphy, 1867
JK1923 F91

Garraty, John A
Quarrels that have shaped the Constitution. New York: Harper (c1964)
JK1561 G3 (Main, Undergraduate)

Gillette, William
Right to vote: politics and the passage of the fifteenth amendment. Baltimore: Johns Hopkins Press, 1965
JK169 15th 1965 G5 (Undergraduate)

Another edition
JA2 J65 vol. 83 no. 1

Gladden, Edward Erwin
The mobility of the Negro. New York: Columbia University Press, London: P. S. King & Son, Ltd., 1931
JA2 C72 no. 342

Gosnell, Harold Foote
Negro politicians. Chicago: The University of Chicago Press (1935)
JK2275 N4 G6

Another edition
JK2275 N4 G6 1967

Greenberg, Jack
Race relations and American law. New York: Columbia University Press, 1959
JK1781 G7 (History Graduate, Social Work)

Greene, Lorenzo Johnston
The Negro in colonial New England, 1620-1776. New York: Columbia University Press, 1942
JA2 C72 no. 494 (Main, Commerce)

Another edition
E445 N5 G7 1942a

Grimes, Alan Pendleton
Equality in America. New York: Oxford University Press, 1964
JC599 U5 G84 (Main, Social Work, Undergraduate)

Griswold, Erwin Nathaniel
Law and lawyers in the United States: the common law under stress. Cambridge: Harvard University Press, 1964
KB2319 G78

Hansen, Marcus Lee
The Atlantic migration, 1607-1860.... Cambridge, Mass.: Harvard University Press, 1940
JV6451 H24

The immigrant in American history. Cambridge, Mass.: Harvard University Press, 1940
JV6451 H25 (Main, History Graduate, Social Work)

Another edition
JV6451 H25 1940a (Undergraduate)

Harris, Robert Jennings
The quest for equality: the constitution, Congress and the Supreme Court. Baton Rouge: Louisiana State University Press (c1960)
JC578 H3

Hart, Albert Bushnell
Negro suffrage. (Atlanta, Georgia: The Niagara Movement, 1906?)
JK1924 H32

Hook, Sidney
The paradoxes of freedom. Berkeley: University of California Press, 1962
JC571 H64 (Main, Undergraduate)

Ingle, Edward
The Negro in the District of Columbia. Baltimore: The Johns Hopkins Press, 1893
JA2 J65 vol. 11

Julian, George Washington
Political recollections, 1840 to 1872. Chicago: Jansen McClurg & Company, 1884
JK2261 J94

Kennedy, John Fitzgerald, President of the United States, 1917-1963
The burden and the glory.... New York: Harper & Row (1964)
J82 D9 1964 (Browsing Room)

Kennedy, Louise Venable
The Negro peasant turns cityward. New York: Columbia University Press, London: P. S. King & Son, Ltd., 1930
JA2 C72 no. 329 (Main, Commerce)

Kilpatrick, James Jackson
The soverign states: notes of a citizen of Virginia. Chicago: Regnery, 1957
JK325 K5 (History Graduate, Undergraduate, Agriculture)

Kiser, Clyde Vernon
Sea island to city. New York: Columbia University Press, London: P. S. King & Son, Ltd., 1932
JA2 C72 no. 368

Konvitz, Milton Riovas, ed.
Aspects of liberty. Ithaca, N.Y.: Cornell University Press (1958)
JC571 C8 K6 (History Graduate)

A century of civil rights. New York: Columbia University Press, 1961
JK1726 K58 (History Graduate, Education)

Krislov, Samuel
The Negro in federal employment: the quest for equal opportunity. Minneapolis: University of Minneapolis Press (1967)
JK723 N4 K7

Kunstler, William Moses
Deep in my heart. New York: Morrow, 1966
KA29 K8 A3

Lane, Robert Edwards
Political life. Glencoe, Illinois: Free Press (c1959)
JA74 L25 (History Graduate)

Another edition
JA74 L25 1959a (Undergraduate)

Lewinson, Paul
The Negro in the white class and party struggle. Austin, Texas (1928)
JK1929 A2 L58

Race, class, and party. London, New York: Oxford University Press, 1932
JK1929 A2 L6

Lewis, Edward Erwin
The mobility of the Negro; a study in the American labor supply. New York: Columbia University Press, London: P. S. King & Son, Ltd., 1931
JA2 C72 no. 342

Lockard, Duane
Toward equal opportunity; a study of
state and local anti-discrimination
laws. New York: Macmillan (1968)
JC599 U5 L55

Logan, Rayford Whittingham
The attitude of the Southern White
press toward Negro suffrage, 1932-
1940. Washington, D. C.: The Foundation Publishers, 1940
JK1929 A2 L8

McClellan, Grant S, editor
Civil rights. New York: H. W. Wilson
Company, 1964
JK1726 M25 (Main, Undergraduate)

Maier, Henry William
Challenge to the cities.... New York:
Random House (1966)
JS1114 A1 M3

Martin, Roscoe Coleman
Metropolis in transition: local government adaptation to changing urban
needs. (Washington, D. C.: Housing
and Home Finance Agency, 1963)
JS422 M3 (Main)

Another edition
JS422 M3 1964 (Architecture)

Miller, Loren
The petitioners: the story of the
Supreme Court of the United States and
the Negro. New York: Pantheon (1966)
JK1561 M5 (Main, Undergraduate)

Moon, Henry Lee
Balance of power: the Negro vote. (1st
edition) Garden City, N.Y.; Doubleday,
1948
JK2275N4 M6 (Main, History Graduate)

Nathans, Elizabeth Studley
Losing the peace: Georgia Republicans
and Reconstruction, 1865-1871. Baton
Rouge: Louisiana State University
Press (c1968)
JK2358 G4 1968

National Association for the Advancement of Colored People
Civil rights in the United States in
1948; a balance sheet of group relations. (Pub. jointly by) National Association for the Advancement of Colored
People (and) American Jewish Congress
(New York, 1948?)
JC599 U5 N3 1948

National Conference on Equal Employment Opportunity, Washington, D. C.,
1962
A time for action; proceedings. (Washington: United States Government
Printing Office, 1963)
JK765 N3 1962

Nowlin, William Felbert
The Negro in American national politics. Boston: The Stratford Company
(c1931)
JK2275 N4 N9

Odum, Howard Washington
Social and mental traits of the Negro;
research into the conditions of the
Negro race in Southern towns, a study
in race traits, tendencies and
prospects. New York: Columbia University, 1910
JA2 C72 vol. 37

Patterson, Haywood
Scottsboro boy. (1st edition) Garden
City, N. Y.: Doubleday, 1950
KA653 P3 (Undergraduate)

Price, Margaret (Walzerm)
The Negro and the ballot in the South.
Atlanta, Georgia: Southern Regional
Council, 1959
JK1929 A2 P7

Porter, Kirk Harold
A history of suffrage in the United
States. Chicago: The University of
Chicago Press. (1918)
JK1846 P84 (History Graduate)

Russell, John Henderson
The free Negro in Virginia, 1619-1865.
Baltimore: Johns Hopkins Press, 1913
JA2 J65 vol. 31

Scarlett, George C
Laws against liberty. New York (c1937)
JC575 S28

Smith, Arthur J
The Negro in the political classes of
the American government. Washington,
D. C. (c1937)
JK2275 N4 S6

South Carolina. Constitutional Conven-
tion, 1868
Proceedings of the constitutional con-
vention of South Carolina. New York:
Arno Press, 1968
JK4225 1868 A4 1968

Spitz, David
Patterns of anti-democratic thought.
New York: Macmillan, 1949
JC481 S6 (Main, History Graduate)

Taper, Bernard
Gomillion versus Lightfoot; the Tuskegee gerrymander case. (1st edition)
New York: McGraw-Hill (1962)
JK1348 A2 Z5 1960

Tatum, Elbert Lee
The changed political thought of the Negro, 1915-1940. New York: Exposition Press (c1951)
JK2275 N4 T3 (History Graduate)

Thomas, Norman C
Rule 9: politics, administration, and civil rights. New York: Random House (1966)
JA37 D6 no. 57

Truman, Harry S., pres. United States, 1884-
Freedom and equality, addresses. Columbia: University of Missouri Press (c1960)
JC599 U5 T7

U. S. Civil Service Commission
Study of minority group employment in the Federal government. (Washington) 1965.
JK765 A523 1965

Another edition
JK765 A523 1966

U. S. Commission on Civil Rights
The 50 states report.... (Washington: United States Government Printing Office, 1961)
JC599 U5 A25 1961 (Reference)

Law enforcement: a report on equal protection in the South. (Washington: United States Government Printing Office) 1965
KB5881 U53 1965

....One nation under God, indivisible, with liberty and justice for all. (Washington: United States Government Printing Office, 1959)
JC599 U5 1959

Political participation. Washington: United States Government Printing Office) 1968
JK1929 A2 U44 1968 (Reference, Undergraduate)

Voting; hearings.... Washington: United States Government Printing Office, 1959
JK1929 A4 U5 1959

Voting in Mississippi; a report. (Washington: United States Government Printing Office) 1965
JK1925 M7 A45 1965 (Main, Reference)

The voting rights act: the first months. (Washington) 1965
JK2164 A2 A45 1965 (Reference)

U. S. Commission on Civil Rights. Mississippi Advisory Committee
Administration of justice in Mississippi. (Washington?) 1963
JC599 U5 A284 1963

U. S. Commission on Civil Rights. North Carolina Advisory Committee
Equal protection of the laws in.... (Washington: United States Government Printing Office, 1962)
JC599 U52 N8 U5 1962

U. S. Dept. of Justice
Prejudice and property, an historic brief against racial covenants. Washington: Public Affairs Press (1948)
JC605 U5

U. S. District Court. Mississippi (Southern District, Jackson Division)
The Evers opinion. (Washington, D. C.: National Putnam Letters Committee, 1964?)
K72 E9 N3

U. S. President's Committee on Civil Right
To secure these rights, report of the President's Committee on Civil Rights. Washington: U. S. Government Printing Office, 1947
JC599 U5 A32 1947

Another edition
JC599 U5 A322 1947 (Main, Undergraduate)

U. S. President's Committee on Government Employment Policy
Report. 1st- 1955/56- Washington: U. S. Government Printing Office)
JK765 A35

Vander, Harry Joseph
The political and economic progress
of the American Negro, 1940-1963.
Dubuque, Iowa: W. C. Brown Book Com-
pany (1968)
JK2275 N4 V3

Virginia. Commission on Constitutional
Government
Voting rights and legal wrongs. (Rich-
mond, 1965)
JK2164 A2 V5 1965

Vose, Clement E
Caucasians only: the Supreme Court,
the NAACP, and the restrictive cov-
enant cases. Berkeley: University of
California Press, 1959
JC605 V6 (Main, Undergraduate)

Warner, William Lloyd
The social systems of American ethnic
groups. New Haven: Yale University
Press, 1945
JC311 W28 (Main, Commerce, Social
Work, Undergraduate)

Watters, Pat
Climbing Jacob's ladder; the arrival of
Negroes in Southern politics. (1st
edition) New York: Harcourt, Brace &
World (1967)
JK1929 A2 W3

Warsoff, Louis A
Equality and the law. New York: Liver-
right (c1938)
JK271 W29

Wilson, James Q
The amateur Democrat. Chicago:
University of Chicago Press (1962)
JK2317 1962 W5 (History Graduate)

Negro politics: the search for leadership. Glencoe, Illinois: Free Press
(1960)
JK1924 W5 (History Graduate)

Woodson, Carter Godwin
Fifty years of Negro citizenship as
qualified by the United States Supreme
Court. Lancaster, Pennsylvania, and
Washington, D. C.? 1921?
JK1781 W89

Wright, James Martin
The free Negro in Maryland, 1634/1860.
New York: Columbia University Press,
1921
JA2 C72 volume 97

EDUCATION

Alexander, Frederick Milton
Education for the needs of the Negro in
Virginia. Washington, D. C.: The South-
ern Education Foundation?, Inc., 1943
LC2802 V8 A3 1943 (Education)

American Association of School Admin-
istrators.
School racial policy. Washington, D. C.
(c1966)
LB3062 A5 (Education)

Anderson, Margaret
The children of the South. New York:
Farrar, Straus & Giroux (1966)
LC2801 A6 (Main, Education, Social
Work)

Armstrong, Byron K
Factors in the formulation of collegiate
programs for Negroes. Ann Arbor, Michigan: Edwards Brothers, Inc. 1939
LC2801 A73

Armstrong, Mary Frances (Morgan)
Hampton and its students. New York:
G. P. Putnam's Sons, 1874
LC2851 H32 A7 (Education)

Ashmore, Harry S
The Negro and the schools. Chapel Hill:
University of North Carolina Press
(1954)
LC2801 A76

Another edition
LC2801 A76 1954a (Education)

Association of Colleges and Secondary
Schools for Negroes
Proceedings of the 2nd-10th annual
meeting.....1935/1943. (n.p., 1938?)
10 Volumes
LC2703 A84 (Education)

Association of Colleges and Secondary
Schools for Negroes. Commission on
Secondary Schools
**Serving Negro schools; a report on the
Secondary School Study.** Atlanta,
Georgia, 1946
LC2771 A7 (Main, Education)

Barrett, Russell H
Integration at Ole Miss. Chicago: Quad-
rangle Books, 1965
LD3413 B3

Baughman, Emmett Earl
Negro and white children. New York:
Academic Press, 1968
LC4092 N8 B3 (Children's Hospital,
Social Work)

Bede, brother
**A study of the development of Negro
education under Catholic auspices in
Maryland and the District of Columbia,**
by Michael Frances Rouse (Brother
Bede, C. F. X.). Baltimore: The Johns
Hopkins Press, 1935
LC2802 M3 B4 1935

Another edition
LB5 J65 number 22

Benson, Charles Scott
**The cheerful prospect; a statement on
the future of American education.....**
Boston: Houghton Mifflin (1965)
LA209.2 B42 (Education)

The economics of public education.
Boston: Houghton Mifflin (1961)
LB2825 B38 (Education, Agriculture,
Commerce)

**Perspectives on the economics of
education....** Boston: Houghton Mifflin
(1963)
LB2824 B4 (Education, Commerce)

The school and the economic system....
Chicago: Science Research Association
(1966)
LB41 B48 (Education)

Bereiter, Carl
**Teaching disadvantaged children in the
preschool.** Englewood Cliffs, N. J.:
Prentice-Hall (1966)
LC4091 B46 (Main, Home Economics,
Education, Children's Hospital)

Berowitz, David Sandler
**Inequality of opportunity in higher ed-
ucation; a study of minority group and
related barriers to college admission.**
Albany: Williams Press, 1948
LA337 B4 (Social Work, Education,
Main)

Berman, Daniel M
**It is so ordered: the Supreme Court
rules on school segregation.** (1st edition) New York: Norton (1966)
LB3062 B4 (Main, Education, Undergraduate)

Bernstein, Abraham Alexander
The education of urban populations.
New York: Random House (1967)
LC5119 B4 (Home Economics, Educa-
tion)

Blaustein, Albert P
**Civil Rights, U. S. A.: public schools;
cities in the North and West, 1963.**
(Washington, 1964)
LA332 C3 B55 (Main, Education)

Desegregation and the law. New Brunswick, N. J.: Rutgers University Press,
1957
LB3062 B45 (Main, Education)

Bloom, Benjamin Samuel
**Compensatory education for cultural
deprivation....** New York: Holt, Rinehart & Winston (1965)
LC4065 B55 1965 (Education)

**Research problems of education and
cultural deprivation.** (Chicago: University of Chicago? 1964?)
LC4065 B555 (Education)

Bond, Horace Mann
**The education of the Negro in the
American social order.** New York: Pren-
tice-Hall, 1934
LC2801 B7 (Education, Main)

Another edition
LC2801 B7 1966 (Main, Undergraduate,
Education)

Negro education in Alabama. Washing-
ton, D. C.: The Association Publishers,
Inc., 1939
LC2802 A2 B7

A study of factors involved in the i-
dentification and encouragement of un-
usual academic talent among under-
privileged populations. (Atlanta: Atlanta University, 1967)
LC2781 B6 (Education)

Bouma, Donald H
The dynamics of school integration.
Grand Rapids: W. B. Eerdmans Publish-
ing Company (1968)
LB3062 B6 (Education)

Boyer, Philip Albert
The adjustment of a school to individ-
ual and community needs. Philadelphia,
Pennyslyvania, 1920
LB2806 B78 (Main, Education)

Brickman, William Wolfgang, editor
The countdown on segregated education
(1st edition) New York: Society for the
Advancement of Education, 1960
LB3062 B7 (Education)

Briggs, William A.
Counseling minority group youth:
developing the experience of equality
through education. (Columbus, Ohio:
Civil Rights Commission) 1962
LB1620.5 B7 (Main, Education, Agriculture)

Brown, Ina Corinne
National survey of the higher education
of Negroes. Washington: U. S. Government Printing Office, 1942
LZ111 A61 number 6 (Main, Commerce)

Brown, William Henry
The education and economic development of the Negro in Virginia. (Charlottesville, Virginia: Surber-Arundale Company, Inc., 1923?)
AH439 B87

Bullock, Henry Allen
A history of Negro education in the
South. Cambridge, Mass.: Harvard
University Press, 1967
LC2801 B9 (Education, Undergraduate)

Burkhead, Jesse
Input and output in large city high
schools.... (1st edition) Syracuse, N. Y.:
Syracuse University Press (1967)
LB2822 B88 (Education)

California. Commission on Equal Oppor-
tunities in Education
Report to the California State Board of
Education. (Sacramento?)
LZ124 H.53 (Education)

Caliver, Ambrose
Availability of education to Negroes in
rural communities. Washington: United
States Government Printing Office,
1936
LZ111 A6 1935 number 12 (Education)

A background study of Negro college
students. Washington: United States
Government Printing Office, 1933
LZ111 A6 1933 number 8 (Main, Education)

Education of Negro leaders; influences
affecting graduate and professional
studies. (Washington) Federal Security
Agency, Office of Education (1949)
LZ111 A6 1948 number 3 (Main, Education, Social Work)

Education of Negro teachers. Washington: U. S. Government Printing Office,
1933
LZ111A6 1933 number 10 pt. 4 (Main,
Education)

The Negro and the emergency in ed-
ucation. (Washington) United States
Department of the Interior, Office of
Education, 1933
LZ111 A62 number 123 (Main, Educa-
tion)

Negro high-school graduates and non-
graduates; relation of their occupational
status to certain school experiences.
Washington: United States Government
Printing Office, 1940
LZ111 A75 number 87 (Main, Education)

A personnel study of Negro college
students; a study of the relations between certain background factors of
Negro college students and their subsequent careers in college. New York:
Teachers College, Columbia University, 1931
LB5 C72 number 484 (Educational)

Rural elementary education among
Negroes under Jeanes supervising
teachers.... Washington: United States
Government Printing Office, 1933
LZ111 A6 1933 number 5 (Main, Ed-
ucation)

Secondary education for Negroes.
Washington: United States Government
Printing Office, 1933
LZ111 A6 1932 number 17 pt. 7 (Main,
Education)

Another edition
LA222 A14 number 7 (Education)

Another edition
LC2801 C15

Supervision of the education of Negroes
as a function of state departments of
education. (Washington: United States
Government Printing Office, 1941)
LZ111 A6 1940 number 6 pt. 11 (Main,
Education)

Vocational education and guidance of
Negroes; report of a survey conducted
by the Office of Education of Negroes...
Washington: United States Government
Printing Office, 1938
LZ111 A6 1937 number 38 (Reference,
Education)

Campbell, Thomas Monroe
The Movable school goes to the Negro
farmer. Tuskegee Institute, Alabama:
Tuskegee Institute Press (c1936)
LC2802 A2 C2 (Education)

Canady, Herman George
Psychology in Negro institutions.
Institute, West Virginia: West Virginia
State College (1939)
LC2801 C3 (Education)

Carmichael, Omer
The Louisville story. (New York)
Simon & Schuster, 1957
LA294 L6 C3 (Main, Education)

Chamber of Commerce of the United
States of America. Task Force on
Economic Growth and Opportunity
The disadvantaged poor: education and
employment. (Washington, D. C., c1966)
LC4091 C44 (Education)

Chapman, Oscar James
A historical study of Negro land-grant
colleges in relationship with their social, economic, political, and educational backgrounds, and a program for
their improvement. (Columbus, Ohio)
1940
AS30 M62 volume 3

Clark, Felton Grandison
The control of state-supported teacher-
training programs for Negroes. New
York: Columbia University, 1934
LB5 C72 number 605 (Education)

Clark, Kenneth Bancroft
Social and economic implications of
integration in the public schools.
(Washington: United States Department
of Labor) 1965
LB3062 C5 (Educational)

Clift, Virgil Alfred, editor
Negro education in America; its ade-
quacy, problems and needs. (1st edition)
New York: Harper (1962)
LC2801 C5 (Main, Education)

Coleman, James Samuel
Equality of educational opportunity.
(Washington: United States Government
Printing Office, 1966)
LB3062 C6 (Reference, Education,
Undergraduate)

Appendix
LB3062 C6 Appendix (Reference,
Education)

Colson, Edna Meade
An analysis of the specific references
to Negroes in selected curricula for
the education of teachers. New York:
Teachers College, Columbia University,
1940
LB5 C72 number 822

Conant, James Bryant
Slums and suburbs; a commentary on
schools in metropolitan areas. New
York: McGraw-Hill (1961)
LC5115 C6 (Main, Education, Browsing Room, Agriculture, Home Economics, Undergraduate)

Conference of Presidents of Negro Land-
Grant Colleges
Proceedings of the...annual conference
of the presidents of Negro land-grant
colleges. (n.p.) 1935-52
LC2781 C78 (Main)

Conference on Adult Education and the
Negro
Findings of the...annual Conference on
Adult Education and the Negro... 1st-
1938- (Hampton? Virginia, 1938-
LC2701 C6 (Education)

Conference on Discriminations in College
Admissions, Chicago, 1949
Discriminations in college admissions.
Washington (1950)
LB5 A54 ser. 1 number 41 (Education)

Conference on Education for Negroes in
Texas
**Proceedings of...conference on educa-
tion for Negroes in Texas...1931-1942.**
(Prairie View, Texas, 1931-1942)
LC2802 T4 C7

Conference on Integration in the New
York City Public Schools, Columbia
University, 1963
**Integrating the urban school; proceed-
ings.** (New York) Columbia University,
1963 (i.e. 1964, c1963)
LC5119 C6 1963 (Main, Education)

Conference on Interinstitutional cooperation in Higher Education, Racine,
Wisconsin, 1967
**Interinstitutional cooperation in higher
education; proceedings of the Conference (on) Interstitutional Cooperation
in Higher Education, Wingspread, Racine, Wisconsin, March 3-4, 1967.** Milwaukee, Wisconsin: Institute of Human
Relations, University of Wisconsin,
1967?)
LB2331.5 C63 1967 (Education)

Conference on "Quality and Equality in
Education", Princeton University, 1966
Proceedings. Princeton: Princeton
University, 1966
LZ106 1966 P7 (Education)

Cook, Lloyd Allen
Intergroup education. New York: Mc-
Graw-Hill, 1954
CB199 C6 (Main, Education)

Cooke, Dennis Hargrove
**The white superintendent and the Ne-
gro schools in North Carolina.** Nash-
ville, Tennessee: George Peabody
College for Teachers, 1930
LC2802 N8 C7

Cooly, Rossa Belle
**School acres, an adventure in rural
education.** New Haven: Yale University Press, London: H. Milford, Oxford University Press, 1930
LC2852 S32 C7

Cooper, Richard Watson
Negro school attendance in Delaware.
Newark, Delaware: University of
Delaware Press, 1923
LC2802 D3 C7

Corson, Oscar Taylor
**Booker T. Washington -- an apprecia-
tion.** (in National Education Association of the United States Journal of
Proceedings and Addresses, 1916.
p. 983-988)
LZ13 N52 1916 (Main, Education)

Cowles, Milly
**Perspectives in the education of dis-
advantaged children; a multi-discipli-
nary approach.** Cleveland: World Publishing Company (1967)
LC4091 C6 (Social Work, Education,
Undergraduate)

Crain, Robert Lee
**The politics of school desegregation;
comparative case studies of community
structure and policy-making.** Chicago:
Aldine Publishing Company (1968)
LB3062 C7 (Education, Architecture)

Cramer, M Richard
**Social factors in educational achieve-
ment and aspirations among Negro
adolescents.** (Chapel Hill: University
of North Carolina) 1966
LC2801 C73 (Education)

Crow, Lester Donald
**Educating the culturally disadvantaged
child; principles and programs.** New
York: D. McKay Company (1966)
LC4091 C7 (Education, Undergraduate)

Dabney, Charles William
Universal education in the South.
Chapel Hill: The University of North
Carolina Press (c1936)
LA205 D3 (Main, Education)

Dabney, Lillian Gertrude
**The history of schools for Negroes in
the District of Columbia, 1807-1947.**
Washington, D. C.: Catholic Univer-
sity of America Press, 1949
LC2802 D65 D3

Damerell, Reginald G
Triumph in a white suburb.... New
York: W. Morrow, 1968
LA333 T4 D3 (Education, Social Work,
Browsing Room)

Daniel, Robert Prentiss
A psychological study of delinquent
and non-delinquent Negro boys. New
York: Teachers College, Columbia
University, 1932
LB5 C72 number 546 (Education)

Daniel, Walter Green
The reading interests and needs of
Negro college freshman regarding so-
cial science materials. New York:
Teachers College, Columbia Univer-
sity, 1942
LB5 C72 number 862 (Education)

Davis, Allison
Social class influences upon learning.
Cambridge: Harvard University Press,
1948
LB1051 D24 (Main, Education, Under-
graduate)

Davis, John Warren
Land-grant colleges for Negroes. In-
stitute, West Virginia: West Virginia
State College (1934)
LC2781 D37 (Main, Education)

Problems in the collegiate education
of Negroes. Institute, West Virginia,
1937
LC2801 D26 (Main, Education)

Davis, William Riley
The development and present status of
Negro education in east Texas. New
York: Teachers College, Columbia
University, 1934
LB5 C72 number 626 (Education)

Day, Richard E
Civil rights, U. S. A.; public schools,
southern states, 1963: North Carolina.
Staff report submitted to the U. S.
Commission on Civil Rights. (Wash-
ington? 1963?)
LA340 D3

Dentler, Robert A
The urban R's; race relations as the
problem in urban education. New York:
Praeger (1967)
LC5131 D4 (Main, Education)

Derbigny, Irving Anthony
General education in the Negro college.
Stanford: Stanford University Press.
(1947)
LC2781 D4 (Education)

Detroit. Citizens Advisory Committee on
School Needs
Findings and recommendations (a-
bridged) of the city-wide Citizens Ad-
visory Committee on School Needs.
(Detroit) 1958
LZ163 D6 G517 1958 (Education)

Detweiler, Frederick German
The Negro press in the United States.
Chicago: The University of Chicago
Press (1922)
L155 D48

Deutsch, Martin
The disadvantaged child; selected
papers of Martin Deutsch and associates. New York: Basic Books (1967)
LC4065 D4 (Main, Undergraduate,
Education, Social Work, Home Economics)

Minority groups and class status as related to social and personality factors
in scholastic achievement. (Ithaca,
New York) Society for Applied Anthro-
pology (c1960)
LC203 D4 (Main, Education)

Developing programs for the educationally
disadvantaged. A. Harry Passow, editor
New York: Teachers College Press,
Columbia University (1968)
LC4065 D43 (Education)

Dickerman, George Sherwood
Common sense in Negro public
schools. n.p. (1909)
LC2761 D55

Disadvantaged child. (Jerome Hellmuth,
ed. Seattle: B. Straub & J. Hellmuth,
1967-
LC4091 D5 (Education)

Education Conference on Problems of
Segregation and Desegregation of
Public Schools
Conference before the U. S. Commis-
sion on Civil Rights. (1st)- 1959-
(Washington)
LZ111 G5 C6 (Main, Education, Social
Work)

Education Conference on Problems of
Segregation and Desegregation of
Public Schools, 4th, Washington, D. C.,
1962
Synopsis of conference before the
U. S. Commission on Civil Rights:
Problems of segregation and desegre-
gation of public schools; staff report.
(Washington, 1964)
LZ112 H73 1962 (Main, Education)

Educational Policies Commission
Education and the disadvantaged American. (Washington, 1962)
LC4091 E3 (Main, Education)

Egerton, John
Higher education for "high risk" students. Atlanta (Southern Education Foundation) 1968
LC4091 E34 (Education)

Embree, Edwin Rogers
Education for all the people: divided we fall. Chicago, 1936
LC2801 E53 (Education)

Equality of educational opportunity; a radio discussion by Robert Redfield, George Stoddard, and Louis Wirth.
697th broadcast in cooperation with the National Broadcasting Company (Chicago) 1947
LB3062 E6

Fantini, Mario D
The disadvantaged: challenge to education. New York: Harper & Row (1968)
LC4091 F33 (Education, Home Economics)

Favrot, Leo Mortimer
A study of county training schools for Negroes in the South. Charlottesville, Virginia, 1923
LC2801 F27

Fichter, Joseph Henry
Graduates of predominantly Negro colleges: class of 1964. (Washington: United States Government Printing Office, 1967)
LC2781 F5 1964 (Education)

Fleming, Harold C
What's happening in school integration? (1st edition. New York: Public Affairs Committee, 1956)
LB3062 F5 (Main, Education)

Forten, Charlotte L
Journal. New York: Dryden Press (c1953)
LA2317 F6 A3

Frost, Joe L., editor
The disadvantaged child; issues and innovations. Boston: Houghton Mifflin (1966)
LC4091 F7 (Education, Home Economics, Social Work)

Fuchs, Estelle
Pickets at the gates. New York: Free Press (1966)
LA209.2 F8 (Education)

Galloway, Oscar Fitzgerald
Higher education for Negroes in Kentucky. Lexington, Kentucky: The University of Kentucky (1932)
LC2802 K4 G2 (Education)

Gates, Robbins L
The making of massive resistance; Virginia's politics of public school desegregation, 1954-1956. Chapel Hill: University of North Carolina Press (1964)
LA379 G3

Giles, Hermann Harry
The integrated classroom. New York: Basic Books (c1959)
LB3062 G5 (Education)

Gittell, Marilyn
Educating an urban population. Beverly Hills, California: Sag Publishing (1967)
LC5131 G5 (Education)

Goldman, Freda H., editor
Educational imperative: the Negro in the changing South. (Chicago) Center for the Study of Liberal Education for Adults (c1963)
LC5201 N6 no. 37 (Main, Education)

Goldwin, Robert Allen
The case of the lively ghost. Chicago: American Foundation for Political Education (1958, c1956)
LB3062 G6 (Education)

Gordon, Edmund W
Compensatory education for the disadvantaged; programs and practices, preschool through college. New York: College Entrance Examination Board, 1966
LC4091 G6 (Education, Undergraduate, Children's Hospital)

Gore, George William
In-service professional improvement of Negro public school teachers in Tennessee. New York: Teachers College, Columbia University, 1940
LB5 C72 no. 786 (Education)

Gowan, John Curtis, editor
The disadvantaged and potential drop-out: compensatory education programs...
Springfield, Illinois: C. C. Thomas (1966)
LC4091 G65 (Education)

Grambs, Jean Dresden
Education in a transition community.
(New York, National Conference of Christians and Jews, 1955?)
LB3062 G7 (Education)

A guide to school integration. 1st edition. New York: Public Affairs Committee, c1957
LB3062 G72 (Main, Education)

Intergroup education; methods and materials. Englewood Cliffs, N. J.: Prentice-Hall (1968)
CB199 G72 (Education)

Gray, Susan Walton
Before first grade.... New York: Teachers College Press, 1966
LB1140 G7 (Education, Children's Hospital)

Gray, William Herbert
Needs of Negro high school graduates.
Philadelphia, 1945
LC2802 L8 G7

Green, Robert Lee
The educational status of children in a district without public schools. East Lansing: Bureau of Educational Research, College of Education, Michigan State University, 1964
LA380 P74 G7 (Education)

Greene, Harry Washington
Holders of doctorates among American Negroes. Boston: Meador Publishing Company (1946)
LC2781 G79 (Education, Main)

Greene, Mary Frances
The schoolchildren growing up in the slums. New York: Pantheon Books (c1965)
LC5133 N4 G7 (Education)

Another edition
LC5133 N4 G7 1965a (Education)

Group for the Advancement of Psychiatry. Committee on Social Issues
Emotional aspects of school desegragation; a report by psychiatrists. (New York: Group for the Advancement of Psychiatry, 1960)
LB3062 G7517 (Education)

Gurin, Patricia
Motivation and aspiration in the Negro college. Ann Arbor, Michigan: University of Michigan, 1966
LC2781 G85 (Education)

Hamlin, Ruth
Schools for young disadvantaged children. New York: Teachers College Press, Columbia University, 1967
LC4091 H3 (Education, Home Economics)

Hampton, Virginia Normal and Agricultural Institute
22 years' work of the Hampton Normal and Agricultural Institute at Hampton, Virginia. Hampton: Normal School Press, 1893
LC2851 H23 1893

Harlan, Louis R
Separate and unequal. Chapel Hill: University of North Carolina Press (c1958)
LC2801 H28 (Main, Education)

Harris, Irving D
Emotional blocks to learning; a study of the reasons for failure in school. (New York) Free Press of Glencoe (1961)
LB1073 H3 (Education, Home Economics)

Harris, Marquis LaFayette
The voice in the wilderness. Boston: Christopher (c1941)
LC2801 H3

Harris, Ruth Miriam
Teachers' social knowledge and its relation to pupils' responses. New York: Teachers College, Columbia University, 1941
LB5 C72 no. 816 (Education)

Havighurst, Robert James
The public schools of Chicago....
Chicago: The Board of Education of the City of Chicago, 1964
LB2823 H38 (Education)

Hayes, Rutherford Birchard, President
U. S. 1822-1993
Teach the freeman. (Baton Rouge)
Louisiana State University Press
(c1959)
LC2707 J6 H3 (Main, Education)

Henton, Comradge L
**Relationship between selfconcepts of
Negro elementary school children and
their academic achievement, intelligence,
interests, and manifest anxiety.** Baton
Rouge, Louisiana: Department of
Psychology, Southern University (1964?)
LB1117 H35 (Education)

Hill, Henry Harrington
Public funds for private schools?
Nashville, Tennessee: Center for
Southern Education Studies, George
Peabody College for Teachers (1962?)
LC89 H53 (Education)

Hill, Herbert
**Citizen's guide to desegregation; a
study of social and legal change in
American life.** Boston: Beacon Press
(c1955)
LB3062 H5 (Main, Agriculture)

Holmes, Dwight Oliver Wendell
The evolution of the Negro college.
New York: Teachers College, Columbia
University, 1934
LB5 C72 no. 609 (Main, Education)

Howard University, Washington, D. C.
**The inauguration of J. Stanley Durkee,
A. M., Ph. D., as president of Howard
University, Nov. 12, 1912, and the
readjustment and reconstruction con-
gress, Nov. 13, 1919?** Washington, D. C.:
Howard University (1919?)
LC2852 W3 H8

Humphrey, Hubert Horatio, editor
Integration vs. segregation. New York:
Crowell (1964)
LB3062 H8 1964a (Main, Education)

**School desegregation: documents and
commentaries.** New York: Crowell
(1964)
LB3062 H8 1964

Indianapolis Freeman
A word for the southern people. (Normal,
Alabama: A. & M. College Printing,
n. d.)
LC2801 I39

Integrated education.
vol. 1- (no. 1-
Jan. 1963-
Chicago: Integrated Education
Associates
LB3062 A115 (Education)

**Learning together; a book on inte-
grated education.** Chicago: Integrated
Education Associates, 1964
LB3062 I5 (Education)

Jaffe, Abram J
Negro higher education in the 1960's
New York: Praeger (1968)
LC2781 J3 (Education, Undergraduate)

The John F. Slater Fund
Proceedings and reports.... 1886-
New York, 1881-19——
LC2707 J6

**...Reference list of southern colored
schools.** (Lynchburg, Virginia: J. P.
Bell Company, Inc., printers) 1918
LC2801 J648

John F. Slater fund for the education of
freedmen, New York
**A suggested course of study for county
training schools for Negroes in the
South.** (Lynchburg, Virginia: J. P.
Bell) 1917
LC2801 J65

Johnson, Charles Spurgeon
The Negro college graduate. Chapel
Hill, The University of North Carolina
Press, 1938
LC2781 J66

Johnson, Miley Kimball
**School conditions in Clarke County,
Georgia, with special reference to
Negroes.** (Athens, Georgia, The
University, 1916)
LC2803 A8 J6

Johnson, Ozie Harold
Price of freedom. (Houston? Texas)
c1954
LC2802 T4 J6

Joint Committee of the National Educa-
tion Association and the American
Teachers Association
**Study of the status of the education of
Negroes.** Montgomery, Alabama: Ameri-
can Teachers Association, 1954
LC2801 J67 (Education)

Jones, Lance George Edward
The Jeanes teacher in the United
States, 1908-1933.... Chapel Hill:
the University of North Carolina Press,
1937
LC2707 N3 J7

Jones, Laurence Clifton
Piney woods and its story. New York:
Fleming H. Revell (c1922)
LC2852 B72 J7

Jones, M A
Founder's day address, by Dr. M.
Ashbie Jones of Atlanta, Georgia,
delivered in the Institute Chapel at
Tuskegee Normal and Industrial In-
stitute, Tuesday, April 12, 1921.
(Tuskegee: Students of the Tuskegee
Normal and Industrial Institute, 1921)
AH395 W3 J7

Jones, Thomas Jesse
...Recent progress in Negro education.
Washington: Government Printing Office,
1919
LZ111 A6 1919 no. 27 (Reference,
Education)

The Journal of Negro education vol. 1-
April 1932- Washington, D. C.: The
College of Education, Howard Uni-
versity
LC2701 J86 (Main, Education)

Keach, Everett Thompson, comp.
Education and social crisis... New
York: Wiley (1967)
LC4091 K4 (Education, Social Work,
Home Economics)

Kendall, Robert
White teacher in a black school. New
York: Devin-Adair (1964)
LC2803 L6 K4 (Browsing Room)

Kennedy, Wallace A
A normative sample of intelligence and
achievement of Negro elementary
school children in the Southeastern
United States. (Layfayette, Ind.) Child
Development Publishers of the Society
for Research in Child Development
(1963)
LB1103 S6 vol. 28 no. 6 (Education)

The standardization of the 1960 re-
vision of the Stanford-Binet intelli-
gence scale on Negro elementary
school children in the Southeastern
United States. Tallahassee: Florida
State University, Human Development
Clinic, 1961
LB1131 K34 (Education)

Kentucky State College for Negroes,
Frankfort, Kentucky
Ten year report of Kentucky State
College, 1929-1939. Frankfort, Ken-
tucky: Kentucky State College (1939)
LC2802 K4 K3

Kerber, August F., editor
The schools and the urban crisis; a
book of readings. New York: Holt,
Rinehart and Winston (1965)
LC5131 K4 (Agriculture, Education)

Klingel, E Harold
Methods employed to reduce racial
imbalance in schools; a study of
approaches to the problem of de facto
segregation. Columbus: Ohio Civil
Rights Commission (1966 or 7)
LB3062 K53 (Education)

Klopf, Gordon John
Teacher education in a social context;
a study of the preparation of school personnel for working with disadvantaged
children and youth. New York: Published
for Bank Street College of Education
by Mental Health Materials Center (1967)
LC4091 K55 (Education, Home Economics)

Knapp, Robert B
Social integration in urban communi-
ties; a guide for educational planning.
New York: Bureau of Publications,
Teachers College, Columbia Univer-
sity, 1960
LB3062 K55 (Education, Social Work)

Knox, Ellis O
Democracy and the District of Columbia
public schools; a study of recently in-
tegrated public schools. Washington:
Judd & Detweiler, 1957
LA255 K6 (Education)

Kohl, Herbert R
36 Children. (New York) New American
Library (1967)
LC2803 H3 K6 (Education)

Kontos, Peter G
Teaching urban youth; a source book for urban education. New York: Wiley (1967)
LC5131 K6 (Education, Home Economics)

Kozol, Jonathan
Death at an early age.... Boston: Houghton Mifflin, 1967
LC2803 B7 K6 (Browsing Room, Education, Social Work)

Kvaraceus, William Clement
Poverty, education, and race relations; studies and proposals. Boston: Allyn and Bacon (1967)
LC2801 P6 (Education, Social Work)

Lamont, Hammond
Negro self-help. (Tuskegee, Alabama: Tuskegge Institute Press, n. d.)
LC2851 T9 L23

Leavell, Ullin Whitney
Philanthropy in negro education. Nashville, Tennessee: George Peabody College for Teachers, 1930
LC2801 L43

Another edition
LC2801 L43 1930a (Education)

Lee, Alfred McClung
Fraternities without brotherhood; a study of prejudice on the American campus. Boston: Beacon Press (c1955)
LJ51 L4

Leupp, Francis Ellington
Negro self-uplifting. (Tuskegee, Alabama, 1902)
LC2851 T9 L6

Lieberman, Myron
The future of public education. (Chicago) University of Chicago Press 1960
LA216 L6 (Education)

Long, Hollis Moody
Public secondary education for negroes in North Carolina. New York: Columbia University, 1932
LB5 C72 no. 529 (Education)

Loretan, Joseph O
Teaching the disadvantaged; new curriculum approaches. New York: Teachers College Press, Columbia University (1966)
LC5131 L6 (Education)

Louisville, Kentucky. University
A century of municipal higher education; a collection of address.... Chicago: Lincoln Printing Company (1937?)
LD3131 L42 C3 (Main, Education)

Lovejoy, Elijah
Attention in discrimination learning; a point of view and a theory. San Francisco: Holden Day (1968)
LB1059 L6 (Education, Mershon)

McAllister, Jane Ellen
The training of negro teachers in Louisiana. New York: Teachers College, Columbia University, 1929
LB5 C72 no. 364 (Education)

McGuiston, Fred
Graduate instruction for Negroes in the United States. Nashville, Tennessee: George Peabody College for Teachers, 1939
LC2781 M13 (Main, Education)

McGeoch, Dorothy M
Learning to teach in urban schools. New York: Teachers College Press, Columbia University (1966, c1965)
LC5131 M3 (Education, Home Economics)

McGinnis, Frederick Alphonso
The education of Negroes in Ohio. Wilberforce, Ohio, 1962
LC2802 O5 M3 (Reference, Education)

A history and interpretation of Wilberforce University, Wilberforce Ohio. (Blanchester, Ohio: printed at the Brown Publishing Company) 1941
LC2851 W77 M2

McGrath, Earl James
The predominantly Negro colleges and universities in transition. (New York) Columbia University (1965)
LC2801 M13 (Education, Undergraduate)

McGraw, Myrtle Byram
...A comparative study of a group of
southern white and Negro infants.
Worcester, Mass.: Clark University
1931
LB1101 G32 vol. 10 no. 1

Mack, Raymond W
Our children's burden; a study of desegregation in nine American communities. New York: Random House (1968)
LB3062 M26 (Education, Main)

McKinney, Theophilus Elisha, editor
Higher education among Negroes;
addresses.... Charlotte, North Carolina: Johnson C. Smith University
(c1932)
LC2801 M15

Maryland, Morgan State College, Baltimore
The Morgan State College program, an
adventure in higher education... Baltimore: Morgan State College Press 1964
LC2851 M83 A2 (Education)

Maslow, Will
School segregation, Northern style.
1st edition New York: Public Affairs
Committee, 1961
LB3062 M3 (Main, Education, Social
Work)

Mayo, Amory Dwight
...Southern women in the recent educational movement in the South.
Washington: Government Printing Office,
1892
LZ111 A64 1892 no. 1 (Main, Education)

Another edition
LA205 M47 (Education)

Meece, Leonard Ephraim
... Negro education in Kentucky, a
comparative study of white and Negro
education on the elementary and
secondary school levels. (Lexington,
Kentucky, 1938)
LC2802 K4 M4 (Education, Main)

Meredith, James Howard
Three years in Mississippi. Blooming-
ton: Indiana University Press (1966)
LD3412.9 M4 A3 (Main, Undergraduate)

Michael, W E
The age of error. 1st edition. New
York: Vantage Press (1957)
LB3062 M45

Miller, Arthur Selwyn
Racial discrimination and private ed-
ucation; a legal analysis. Chapel Hill:
University of North Carolina Press
(c1957)
LB3062 M5 (Main, Education)

Miller, Harry L
Education for the disadvantaged;
current issues and research. New York:
Free Press (1967)
LC4091 M45 (Education, Home Eco-
nomics)

Education in the metropolis. New York:
Free Press (1967)
LC5115 M5 (Education)

Miller, Kelly
National responsibility for education of
of the colored people.... (In National
Education Association of the United
States Address and proceedings, 1918,
pp. 555-567.)
LZ13 N52 1918 (Main, Education)

Mose, Ashriel I
A study of the nature of guidance and
counseling services among Negro high
schools in South Carolina. Orangeburg,
South Carolina: School of Education,
South Carolina State College, 1962
LC2802 S6 M6 (Education)

Muse, Benjamin
Virginia's massive resistance. Bloomington: Indiana University Press
(1961)
LA379 M94 (Main, Undergraduate)

National Association of Intergroup Re-
lations Officials. Commission on
School Integration
Public school segregation and integra-
tion in the North. Analysis and pro-
posals by the Commission on School
Integration. (Washington, D. C.)
National Association of Intergroup
Relations Officials, 1963
LB3062 N27 (Main, Education, Social
Work, Reference)

National conference on fundamental
problems in the education of the
Negroes, Washington, D. C. 1934
...Fundamentals in the education of
Negroes. Washington: Government
Printing Office, 1935
LZ111 A6 1935 no. 6 (Reference,
Education)

National Council of Teachers of
English. Task Force on Teaching
English to the Disadvantaged.
Language programs for the disadvan-
taged. (Chicago) National Council of
Teachers of English (c1965)
LC4091 N33 (Education)

National Education Association of the
United States. National Commission on
Professional Rights and Responsibilities
Report of Task Force survey of teacher
displacement in seventeen states.
1965
LB2843 N4 N3 (Education)

National NEA-PR&R Conference on
Civil and Human Rights in Education
(Proceedings. 1st)- 1964- Washington, D. C.: National Education Association, National Commission on Professional Rights and Responsibilities.
LC2703 N3 (Education)

National Scholarship Service and Fund
for Negro Students, 1950-
Report.
LC2801 N3

Neely, Alvin J
The first six years of the new principal of Tuskegee Institute.... (Tuskegee, Alabama) Tuskegee Institute
(1922)
CT275 M9 N37

The Negro educational review. vol 1-
1950- New York: Published by the
National Teachers' Research Association.
LC2701 N4

Newbold, Nathan Carter, editor
Five North Carolina Negro educators.
Chapel Hill: The University of North
Carolina Press, 1939
LC2802 N8 N5

New York (State) University. Bureau of
Guidance
Developing work-study programs for
potential drop outs: a manual. STEP;
the school to employment programs.
Albany, 1965
LB1029 C6 N45 1965 (Education)

New York (State) University. Commis-
sioner's Advisory Committee on Human
Relations and Community Tensions
Desegregating the public schools of
New York City.... Columbia University
(New York) 1964
LA339 N5 N45 1964 (Education)

Noar, Gertrude
The teacher and integration. Washington: Student National Education Association (1966)
LB3062 N58 (Education)

Noble, Jeanne L
The Negro woman's college education.
New York: Teachers College, Colum-
bia University, 1956
LC1605 N6 (Education)

Noble, Stuart Grayson
Forty years of the public schools in
Mississippi, with a special reference
to the education of the negro. New
York: Columbia University, 1918
LB5 C72 no. 94 (Main, Education)

Norfleet, Marvin Brooks
Forced school integration in the United
States of America. New York: Carlton
Press, 1961
LB3062 N6 (Education)

Norman, Loyal Vernon
A slice of Arkansas school admini-
stration. Philadelphia: Dorrance (1965)
LA242 S4 N6 (Education)

North Carolina. Governor's commission
for the study of problems in the education of Negroes in North Carolina
Report of the Governor's commission
for the study of problems in the education of Negroes in Raleigh, North
Carolina. (Raleigh, North Carolina:
1935)
LC2802 N8 A4 (Education)

North Carolina. University. Institute of
Government
The school segregation decision....
Chapel Hill (1954)
LB3062 N66 (Main, Education)

Ohio. Civil Rights Commission
Legal trends in de facto segregation:
the meaning for Ohio's public schools.
Columbus, 1962
LB3062 O35 1962 (Main, Education)

Racial imbalance in the public schools.
Columbus, 1965
LA346 A28 1965 (Reference)

Passow, A Harry, comp.
Education of the disadvantaged; a book
of readings. New York: Holt, Rinehart
& Winston (1967)
LC4065 P3 (Education, Social Work)

Peltason, Jack Walter
Fifty-eight lonely men.... (1st edition)
New York: Harcourt, Brace & World
(1961)
LB3062 P37

Phelps-Stokes Fund
Educational adaptions; report of ten
years' work of the Phelps-Stokes
Fund, 1910-1920, by Thomas Jesse
Jones. New York: Phelps-Stokes Fund
(1920)
LC243 P53

Twenty year report on the Phelps-
Stokes Fund, 1911-1931.... New York:
The Phelps-Stokes Fund, 1932
LC243 P53 D5

Phi Delta Kappa. Commission on the
Study of Educational Policies and
Programs in Relation to Desegregation
Action patterns in school desegrega-
tion. Bloomington, Indiana: Phi Delta
Kappa (1959)
LB3062 P4

Pierce, Truman Mitchell
White and Negro schools in the South.
Englewood Cliffs, N. J.: Prentice-Hall,
1955
LA212 P5 (Education, Main)

Plaüt, Richard L
Blueprint for talent searching: Ameri-
ca's hidden manpower. (New York)
National Scholarship Service and Fund
for Negro Students (1957)
LB2338 P56

Powledge, Fred
To change a child: a report on the
Institute for Developmental Studies.
Chicago: Quadrangle Books (1967)
LC4069 P6 (Education, Social Work)

Price, Joseph St. Clair
The Negro elementary school teacher
in West Virginia. Institute, W. Va.:
The West Virginia Collegiate Institute
(1924)
LB1776 P94 (Main, Education)

The quality of inequality: urban and
suburban public schools. (Chicago)
The University of Chicago, Center for
Policy Study (1968)
LA210 Q3 (Education)

The quarterly review of higher educa-
tion among Negroes. vol. 1- Jan. 1933-
Charlotte, N. C.: Johnson C. Smith
University
LC2701 Q8

Range, Willard
The rise and progress of Negro col-
leges in Georgia, 1865-1949. Athens:
University of Georgia Press (1951)
LC2802 G4 R3

Record, Wilson, editor
Little Rock, U. S. A. San Francisco:
Chandler Publishing Company (1962)
LA242 L5 R4

Redclay, Edward Edgeworth
County training schools and public
secondary education for Negroes in
the South. Washington, D. C.: The
John F. Slater Fund, 1935
LC2801 R32 (Education)

Regional Conference on Special Pro-
grams for Preparation of In-service
Teachers for Admission to Graduate
Study, Atlanta University, 1965
The conference report. (Atlanta? At-
lanta University?) 1966
LB1731 R4 1965 (Education)

The Relationship of Education to Self-
concept in Negro Children and Youth,
Tufts University, 1963
Negro self-concept: implications for
school and citizenship.... Medford,
Mass.: Tufts University, 1964
LC2703 R4 1963 (Education)

Another edition
LC2703 R4 1963a

Research Seminar on Racial and Other
Issues Affecting School Administra-
tion in the Great Cities of America,
Northwestern University, 1965
Research Seminar on Racial and Other
Issues Affecting School Administra-
tion in the Great Cities of America.
Evanston, Illinois: Northwestern Uni-
versity, 1966
LB2819 R47 1965 (Education)

Riessman, Frank
The culturally deprived child and his
education. (1st edition) New York:
Harper (1962)
LC4069 S6 R5 (Main, Education, Social
Work, Home Economics, Undergraduate)

Riley, Donald Alan
Discrimination learning. Boston: Allyn
& Bacon (1968)
LB1059 R5 (Education)

Roberts, Joan I, Comp.
**School children in the urban slum;
readings in social science research.**
New York: Free Press (1967)
LC5101 R6 (Education)

Roche, Richard Joseph
**Catholic colleges and the Negro stu-
dent.** Washington, D. C.: Catholic University of America Press, 1948
HM15 C36 vol. 28

Rockefeller Foundation
**The long road to college: a summer of
opportunity.** New York, 1965
LC2801* R6

Rose, Arnold Marshall
De facto school segregation. (New
York) National Conference of Chris-
tians and Jews (1964)
LB3062 R6

Sarratt, Reed
**The ordeal of desegregation; the first
decade.** (1st edition) New York: Harper
& Row (1966)
LC2801 S2

Scarborough, William Saunders
**What should be the standard of the
university, college, normal school,
teacher training and secondary schools.**
(Durham, North Carolina, 1916)
LC2801 S28

Schrag, Peter
Voices in the classroom. Boston:
Beacon Press (1965)
LA216 S3 (Education)

Schreiber, Daniel, editor
The school dropout. Washington, D. C.:
National Education Association. (1964)
LC143 S34 (Education, Home Econom-
ics, Social Work)

Schroeder, Oliver, editor
**De facto segregation and civil rights;
struggle for legal and social security.**
Buffalo, N. Y.: W. S. Hein (1965)
LB3062 S37 (Education)

Scott, Emmett Jay
The Tuskegee Negro conferences.
(Tuskegee, Alabama: Tuskegee Insti-
tute, 1904)
LC2851 T9 S4

Scott, John Irving E
Negro students and their colleges.
Boston: Meador Publishing Company,
(1949)
LZ901 S48

Segregation and the schools. (1st edition, New York: Public Affairs Committee, 1954)
LC2801 S4 (Main, Education, Social
Work)

Sexton, Patricia Cayo
Education and income.... New York:
The Viking Press, 1961
LA210 S45 (Education, Main)

Another edition
LA210 S45 1961a (Home Economics)

Smith, Fred Tredwell
**An experiment in modifying attitudes
toward the Negro.** New York: Teachers
College, Columbia University, 1943
LB5 C72 no. 887 (Education)

Smith, Robert Collins
They closed their schools. Chapel
Hill: University of North Carolina
Press (1965)
LA380 P74 S6 (Education)

Southern Education Foundation, Inc.
**A brief review of the growth and im-
provement of education for Negroes in
Florida, 1927-1962.** (by) D. E.
Williams. Atlanta, Georgia (1963)
LC2802 F5 S6 (Education)

Report. (Atlanta?)
LC2707 S6

Southern Education Report. vol 1-
July/Aug. 1965- (Nashville: Southern
Education Reporting Service)
LZ11 S713 (Education)

Southern Education Reporting Service
**Southern schools: progress and
problems.** Nashville, Tennessee (c1959)
LA201 S6 (Education)

With all deliberate speed.... (1st edition) New York: Harper (c1957)
LB3062 S6 (History Graduate)

The Southern workman. vol. 50-68
Jan. 1921-July 1939 Hampton, Va.:
Hampton Institute Press
LC2701 S72 (Commerce)

Spurlock, Clark
Education and the Supreme Court.
Urbana: University of Illinois.Press,
1955
LB2523 S6 (Education)

Steele, Algernon Odell
Shifts in the religious beliefs and
attitudes of students in two Presby-
terian colleges. Chicago, 1945
LB3609 S8

Stember, Charles Herbert
Education and attitude change: the
effect of schooling on prejudice
against minority groups. (1st edition)
New York: Institute of Human Relations, 1961
LC189 S74 (Main, Education)

Sterling, Dorothy
Tender warriors. New York: Hill &
Wang (c1958)
LB3062 S7

Stoff, Sheldon
The two-way street.... Indianapolis:
David-Stewart Publishing Company
(1967)
LB3062 S75 (Education)

Storen, Helen Frances
The disadvantaged early adolescent;
more effective teaching. New York:
McGraw-Hill (1968)
LC4091 S7 (Home Economics, Educa-
tion)

Stowell, Jay Samuel
Methodist adventures in Negro education. New York, Cincinnati: The Methodist book concern (c1922)
LC577 S7

Strom, Robert D
The inner-city classroom; teacher be-
haviors. Columbus, Ohio: C. E. Merrill
Books (1966)
LC5131 S8 (Education, Home
Economics)

Teaching in the slum school. Columbus, Ohio: C. E. Merrill Books (1965)
LC5115 S8 (Education)

Suchman, Edward Allen
Desegregation: some propositions and
research suggestions. New York: Anti-
defamation League of B'nai B'rith
(c1958)
LB3062 S85 (Social Work)

Sullivan, Neil Vincent
Bound for freedom: an educator's ad-
ventures in Prince Edward County,
Virginia. (1st edition) Boston: Little,
Brown (1965)
LA380 P74 S8 (Main, Undergraduate)

Swanson, Bert E
School integration controversies in
New York City; a pilot study. Bronx-
ville, N.Y.: Sarah Lawrence College,
1965
LB3062 S93 (Education)

The struggle for equality.... New York:
Hobbs, Dorman (1966)
LA339 N5 S9 (Education)

Swanson, Ernst Werner
Public education in the south today
and tomorrow. Chapel Hill: University
of North Carolina Press (c1955)
LA210 S8 (Main, Education)

Swint, Henry Lee
The northern teacher in the South,
1862-1870. Nashville, Tennessee:
Vanderbilt University Press, 1941
LC2801 S97

Taba, Hilda
Teaching strategies for the culturally
disadvantaged. Chicago: Rand McNally
(1968, 1966)
LC4069 T3 (Education, Home
Economics)

Tallahassee. Lincoln High School
The evolution of Susan Prim. Talla-
hassee, Florida, c1944
LC2803 T3 T3 (Education)

Texas. Dept. of Education
Negro education in Texas....State De-
partment of Education, Austin. (Austin,
Texas, 1926)
LC2802 T4 A3 (Education)

Another edition
LC2802 T4 A3 1931 (Education)

Another edition
LC2802 T4 A3 1935 (Education)

School plant improvement. Austin, 1937
LB3218 T4 A5 1937 (Education)

Thomas, Robert Murray
Social differences in the classrooms.
New York: D. McKay Co. (1965)
LC191 T47 (Education)

Thomason, John Furman
History and experience or the Supreme
Court? Rock Hill, South Carolina, 1956
LB3062 T4

Thurmond, Sarah
A comparison of the intelligence and
achievement of twelve-year old Negro
Children in the rural schools of Clarke
County, Georgia. (Athens, Georgia,
1933)
AH439 T53

Tillman, Nathaniel, editor
Summaries of research projects, 1947-
1952, Atlanta University Center and
Associated Colleges. Atlanta, 1953
AS36 A85

Tipton, James H
Community in crisis ... New York:
Bureau of Publications, Teachers
College, Columbia University, 1953
LB3062 T5 (Education, Main)

Trillin, Calvin
An education in Georgia ... New York:
The Viking Press (1964)
LB3062 T7 (Browsing Room, Education,
Undergraduate)

Tuskegee Institute
The new South and higher education ...
Tuskegee, Alabama: Tuskegee Insti-
tute, 1954
LA228 T8 (Education, Social Work)

Tuskegee Normal and Industrial Institute. Extension Department.
The Negro rural school and its relation
to the community. Tuskegee, Alabama:
Extension Department, Tuskegee Institute, 1915
LC2771 T96

U. S. Bureau of Education
... Negro education. Washington: United
States Government Printing Office,
1917 2 vols.
LC2801 U64 (Main, Education)

Another edition
LZ111 A6 1916 no. 38-39 (Education,
Reference)

U. S. Commission on Civil Rights
Civil rights U.S.A.: public schools,
cities in the North and West, 1962;
staff reports. (Washington: United
States Government Printing Office,
1962)
LB3062 U4 C5 1962 (Main, Education)

Civil rights U.S.A.: public schools,
Southern states, 1962; staff reports.
(Washington: United States Government
Printing Office, 1962)
LA209.2 A44 1962 (Main, Education)

Education; conference before the U. S.
Commission on Civil Rights. Confer-
ence held in Nashville, Tennessee,
March 5-6, 1959. (Washington, 1959)
LZ111 C5 1959

Equal protection of the laws in public
higher education, 1960. (Washington,
1961)
LB3062 U4 E7 1960 (Main, Education)

Hearing(s) held in Boston, Mass.,
October 4-5, 1966. (Washington: United
States Government Printing Office,
1967)
LB3062 U5 B6 1966

Hearing(s) held in Rochester, New
York, September 16-17, 1966. Washing-
ton: United States Government Printing
Office (1967)
LB3062 U5 R6 1966

Public education; staff report. (Wash-
ington: United States Government
Printing Office) 1963-
LB3062 A2 U5 (Main, Education)

Racial isolation in the public schools;
a report. Washington: United States
Government Printing Office (1967)
LB3062 U4 R4 1967 (Reference, Education, Undergraduate, Social Work)

Southern school desegregation, 1966-
67; a report. (Washington) 1967
LB3062 U4 S6 1966-67 (Education)

U. S. Commission on Civil Rights.
Louisiana State Advisory Committee
The New Orleans school crisis; report.
(Washington: United States Government
Printing Office, 1961)
LA297 N4 U5 1961

Survey of school desegregation in the
Southern and border states, 1965-66; a
report. (Washington: United States
Government Printing Office) 1966
LB3062 U4 S8 1965-66 (Education)

U. S. Commission on Civil Rights.
Massachusetts Advisory Committee
Report on racial imbalance in the
Boston public schools, by the Massa-
chusetts State Advisory Committee to
the U. S. Commission on Civil Rights.
(Washington: United States Government
Printing Office) 1965
LA306 B7 U5 1965 (Education)

U. S. Congress. House. Committee on
Education and Labor
Integration in public education pro-
grams. Report of the Subcommittee on
Integration in Federally Assisted
Public Education Programs. Washing-
ton: United States Government Printing
Office, 1962
LB3062 U53 1962 (Main, Education)

U. S. National Student Association
Steps toward equality. Philadelphia:
International Commission, United
States National Student Association,
1961
LB3062 U56 (Education)

U. S. Office of Education
Disadvantaged children series. no. 1-
1965-
LC4091 A26 (Education, Reference)

Equality of educational opportunity.
(Washington: United States Government
Printing Office, 1966)
LB3062 C617 (Reference, Education)

National survey of the higher education of Negroes.... Washington: United
States Government Printing Office,
1942-43
LZ111 A61 no. 6 (Main, Education)

Negro farm families can feed them-
selves. Washington: United States
Government Printing Office, 1942
LC1045 A283 no. 8

Postwar education of Negroes ....
Washington: Federal Security Agency,
United States Office of Education,
(1945)
LC2801 A5 1945

Survey of Negro colleges and universities. Washington: United States Government Printing Office, 1929
LZ111 A6 1928 no. 7 (Main, Education)

Statistics of the education of Negroes,
1925/1926- Washington: United
States Government Printing Office,
1928-
LZ111 A6 1925-26, 1932–1935-36
(Main, Education)

Another edition
LZ111 A75 1927-1928 (Main, Education)

Another edition
LZ111 A62 1945-46 (Main, Education)

U. S. Office of Education. Equal Edu-
cational Opportunities Program
Assurances of compliance for public
school systems. list no. AS-1-
June 1, 1965 (Washington)
LB3062 A2 U6

Status of compliance, public school
districts, 17 Southern and border
states, report. no. 1-   1967-
(Washington)
LB3062 A2 U64

Washington, Booker T
Negro education and the nation. (In the
National Education Association of the
United States, Journal of Proceedings
and Addresses, 1908, p. 87-93)
LZ13 N52 1908 (Main, Education)

Washington, Booker Taliaferro
The successful training of the Negro.
New York: Doubleday, Page & Co.,
1903
LC2851 T9 W37

Webster, Staten W., editor
The disadvantaged learner: knowing,
understanding, educating .... San
Francisco: Chandler Publishing Com-
pany (1966)
LC4091 W4 (Undergraduate, Education,
Main, Social Work)

Another edition
LC4091 W4 1966a (Education)

Weinberg, Meyer
Desegregation research, an appraisal.
Bloomington, Indiana: Phi Delta Kappa,
1968
LB3062 W38 (Education)

Integrated education, a reader.
Beverly Hills, California: Glencoe
Press (1968)
LB3062 W39 (Education)

Race and place. (Washington: United
States Government Printing Office,
1967, i. e. 1968)
LB3062 W4 (Education)

Wesley, Charles Harris
The history of Alpha Phi Alpha: a
development in Negro college life.
Washington, D. C.: The Foundation
Publishers, 1939
LJ121 A55 W5 1939

Another edition
LJ121 A55 W5 1942

West Virginia. Department of Education
Biennial report of the state super-
visor of Negro schools... 1924/26-
(Charleston, West Virginia, 1926)-
LZ214 B4

Wiggins, Samuel Paul
Higher education in the South. Berke-
ley, California: McCutchan Publishing
Corp. (1966)
LA226 W6 (Main, Education)

Wilkerson, Doxey Alphonso
Special problems of Negro education.
Washington: United States Government
Printing Office, 1939
LZ111 B35 no. 12 (Main, Education,
Social Work)

Williams, Robin Murphy, editor
School in transition.... Chapel Hill:
University of North Carolina Press
(c1954)
LB3062 W5 (Education, Main)

Williams, William Taylor Burwell
Duplication of schools for Negro youth.
(Lynchburg, Virginia: U. P. Bell Com-
pany, Printers) 1914
LC2707 W72

Report on Negro universities and colleges. (Baltimore?) 1922
LC2801 W72

Wilmington, Deleware. Public Schools
An adventure in human relations.
Wilmington: Wilmington Public Ele-
mentary Schools (1962-63) v. 2-3
LZ133 W7 A55 1960 (Education)

Wilson, Charles H
Education for Negroes in Mississippi
since 1910. Boston: Meador (1947)
LC2802 M7 W7 (Education)

Woodson, Carter Godwin
...Early Negro education in West Vir-
ginia. Institute, West Virginia: The West
Virginia Collegiate Institute, 1921
LC2802 W4 W8

The education of the Negro prior to
1861. New York and London: G. P.
Putnam's Sons, 1915
LC2741 W89

Another edition
LC2741 W89 1919a (Undergraduate)

Work Conference on Curriculum and
Teaching in Depressed Urban Areas,
Columbia University, 1962
Education in depressed areas: (papers)
York: Bureau of Publishers, Teachers
College, Columbia University, 1963
LC5105 W6 1962 (Education, Social
Work, Home Economics)

Workshop on Catholic College Integra-
tion, Catholic University of America,
1949
Integration in Catholic Colleges and
Universities... Ed. by Roy J. Deferrari.
Washington, D. C.: Catholic University
Press, 1950
LC487 W6 1949 (Education)

Worth, Stephen W
Public education and the equal pro-
tection clause of the Fourteenth
Amendment. Wichita, Kansas, 1955
AS36 W63 no. 3

Wright, Harry K
Civil rights U. S. A.: public schools,
Southern States, 1963, Texas. Staff
report submitted to the United States
Commission on Civil Rights (Wash-
ington? 1964)
LA370 W7 (Main, Education)

Wright, Mrs. Marion Manola (Thompson)
The education of Negroes in New
Jersey. New York: Teachers College,
Columbia University, 1941
LB5 C72 no. 815 (Education)

Wright, Richard Robert, jr.
Self-help in Negro education. Cheyney,
Pennsylvania: Committee of 12 for the
Advancement of the Interests of the
Negro Race. (1908?)
LC2801 W95

MUSIC & MUSICIANS

Allen, William Francis
Slave songs of the United States. New
York: P. Smith, 1929
M1670 A42 1929

Anderson, Marian
**My Lord, what a morning; an auto-
biography.** New York: Viking Press,
1956
ML420 A6 A3 1956a (Main, Music)

Armstrong, Louis
Satchmo: my life in New Orleans. New
York: Prentice-Hall (c1954)
ML419 A7 A3 (Browsing Room)

Swing that music.... London, New York
(etc.) Longmans, Green & Company,
1937 (c1936)
ML3561 J3 A7 S8

Bailey, Pearl
The raw pearl. (1st edition) New York:
Harcourt, Brace & World (1968)
ML420 B123 A3 (Browsing Room, Mus-
ic)

Blesh, Rudi
Shining trumpets, a history of jazz. New
York: A. A. Knopf, 1946
ML3561 J3 B64 (Browsing Room, Music)

**They all played ragtime, the true story
of American music.** (1st edition) New
York: Knopf, 1950
ML3561 J3 B643 (Music)

Brown University. Library
Series of old American songs. Pro-
vidence, R. I.: Brown University
Library, 1936
M1628 B88 (Main, Music)

Burlin, Mrs. Natalie (Curtis)
Hampton series Negro folksongs. New
York, Boston: G. Schirmer (c1918-19)
M1670 B96

Carawan, Guy
**We shall overcome! Songs of the South-
ern Freedom Movement.** New York:
Oak (1963)
M1629 C2 W4

Chambers, Henry Alban
The treasury of Negro spirituals. New
York: Emerson Books (1963, c1959)
M1670 C4 T7 1959a

Chapman, Maria (Weston)
**Songs of the free, and hymns of
Christian freedom...** Boston: I. Knapp,
1836
E449 C45

Charters, Samuel Barclay
**The bluesmen; the story and the
music of the men who made the blues.**
New York: Oak Publishers (1967)
ML3561 J3 C4 B5 (Music)

The country blues. New York: Holt
Rinehart & Winston (1959)
ML3561 J3 C4 C6

**Jazz: New Orleans, 1885-1957; an in-
dex to the Negro musicians of New
Orleans.** Belleville, New Jersey:
W. C. Allen, c1958
ML3561 J3 C4 J3

Coleman, Satis Narrona (Barton)
Songs of American folks. New York:
The John Day Company (1942)
M1629 C69 (Music, Main)

Courlander, Harold
Negro folk music, U. S. A. New York:
Columbia University Press, 1963
ML3556 C6 N4 (Main, Music)

Negro songs from Alabama. New York:
Published with the assistance of the
Wenner - Gren Foundation for Anthro-
pological Research, c1960
M1670 C6 N4 (Main, Music)

Daly, John Jay
A song in her heart. Philadelphia:
Winston (c1951)
ML410 B627 D3

Dankworth, Avril
**Jazz: an introduction to its musical
basis.** London, New York (etc) Oxford
University Press, 1968
ML3561 J3 D3 J3 (Music)

Dann, Hollis Ellsworth
Fifty-eight spirituals for choral use.
Boston: C. C. Birchard & Company
(c1924)
M1670 D18 (Music)

Dennison, Tim
  The American Negro and his amazing music. (1st edition) New York: Vantage Press (1963)
  ML3556 D4 A5

Dett, Robert Nathaniel
  The Dett collections of Negro spirituals. Chicago: Hall & McCreary Company (1936)
  M1670 D48

  Religious folk-songs of the Negro as sung at Hampton Institute. Hampton, Virginia: Hampton Institute Press, 1927
  M1670 H23 1927 (Music)

Dixon, Christa
  Wesen und Wandel geistlicher Volkslieder. Wuppertal: Jugenddienst-Verlag (1967)
  ML3556 D5 W4 1967 (Music)

Dixon, Robert Malcom Ward
  Blues and gospel records, 1902-1942. (n. p., 1963?)
  ML156.2 D5 B5

Down beat
  v. 1- 1934 Chicago: Maher Publishers
  ML1 D6 (Music)

The encyclopedia of Jazz.
  1955- New York: Horizon Press
  ML3561 J3 F3 (Reference)

Erlich, Lillian
  What jazz is all about. New York: J. Messner (1964, c1962)
  ML3561 J3 E7 W5 (Music)

Esquire's...jazz book.
  1944- New York: A. S. Barnes & Company (etc, etc.) 1943- . Annual
  ML3561* J3 A1 E8

Ewen, David
  Panorama of American popular music... Englewood Cliffs, N. J.: Prentice-Hall (c1959, c1957)
  ML2811 E8 P3 (Reference, Music)

Feather, Leonard G
  The book of jazz, from then till now; a guide to the entire field. (rev. and up-to-date ed.) New York: Horizon Press (1965)
  ML3561 J3 F38 B6 1965 (Reference, Music)

The encyclopedia of jazz in the sixties...
  New York: Horizon Press (1966)
  ML105 F38 E5 (Reference, Music)

Fenner, Thomas P
  Religious folk songs of the Negro as sung on the plantations (New edition) Hampton, Virginia: The Institute Press, 1916
  M1670 H23

Fisher, Miles Mark
  Negro slave songs in the United States. Ithaca: Cornell University Press, 1953
  M1670 F5 N4

Fisher, William Arms
  Seventy Negro spirituals. Boston: Oliver Ditson Company, New York: C. H. Ditson & Company (c1926)
  M1670* F53 (Main, Music)

Fletcher, Tom
  100 years of the Negro in show business. (1st edition) New York: Burdge (1954)
  ML3561 N4 F5

Gilbert, Douglas
  Lost chords... Garden City, N. J., New York: Doubleday, Doran & Company Inc., 1942
  ML2811 G4 L8

Goffin, Robert
  ...Jazz, from the Congo to the Metropolitan... Garden City, New Jersey, New York: Doubleday, Doran & Co., inc., 1944
  ML3561 J3 G6 J3

Gold, Robert S
  A jazz lexicon. (1st edition) New York: A. A. Knopf, 1964
  ML3561 J3 G64 J3 (Reference)

Goldberg, Isaac
  Tin pan alley... New York: The John Day Company, 1930
  ML3551 G62 T5

Goodell, Walter
  Famous spirituals (male voices). Chicago: Hall & McCreary Company (c1934)
  M1670 G64 (Music)

Graham, Shirley
  Paul Robeson, citizen of the world... New York: J. Messner, inc. (1946)
  ML420 R6 G7

Grisson, Mary Allen
The Negro sings a new heaven.
Chapel Hill: University of North Carolina Press, 1930
M1670 G8 N3

Grossman, William Leonard
The heart of jazz.... New York: New York University Press, 1956
ML3561 J3 G7 (Music)

Handy, William Christopher
Father of the blues. Edited by Arna W. Bontemps. New York: Macmillan, 1941
ML410 H25 A3 (Main, Music)

Negro authors and composers of the United States. New York: Handy brothers music co., inc. (1938?)
ML3556 H23

Hare, Mrs. Maud (Cuney)
Negro musicians and their music. Washington, D. C.: Associated (c1936)
ML3556 H27 N3 (Main, Music)

Hayes, Roland
My songs; Aframerican religious folk songs. (1st edition) Boston: Little, Brown, 1948
M1670 H3 M9 (Main, Music)

Helm, Mac Kinley
Angel Mo' and her son, Roland Hayes... Boston: Little, Brown & Company,1942
ML420 H42 H4 (Main, Music)

Hentoff, Nat
Jazz; new perspectives on the history of jazz.... New York: Rinehart (c1959)
ML3561 J3 H4 J3 (Music)

The jazz life. New York: Dial Press, 1963
ML3561 J3 H4 J4 (Browsing Room)

Hobson, Wilder
American jazz.... New York: W. W. Norton & Company, inc. (c1939)
ML3561 J3 H56 A5

Hodeir, André
Jazz: its evolution and essence. Translated by David Noakes. New York: Grove Press (1956)
ML3561 J3 H61

Horne, Lena
Lena. Garden City, New York: Doubleday, 1965
ML420 H6 A3 (Browsing Room)

Hoyt, Edwin Palmer
Paul Robeson, the American Othello (1st edition) Cleveland: World Publishing Company (1967)
ML420 R6 H6

Jackson, George Pullen
White and Negro spirituals, their life span and kinship. New York: J. J. Augustin (c1943)
ML3551 J135 (Main, Music)

Jazz & pop.
vol. 1- Oct. 1962- New York: Jazz Press, Inc.
MLi J3 (Music)

Jazz review.
vol. 1-3, vol. 9
Nov. 1958 - Oct. 1960 New York
ML3561 J3 A1 J3 (Music)

Jazz review.
(A selection of notes and essays... London) Jazz Music Books (1945)
ML3561 J3 J3

Jazz panorama, from the pages of Jazz review. (New York) Crowell-Collier Press (1962)
ML3561 J3 J33

Johns, Altona (Trent) arr.
Play songs of the Deep South. Washington, D. C.: The Associated Publishers, inc. (1944)
M1629 J65 P7

Johnson, Guy Bentan
John Henry: tracking down a Negro legend. Chapel Hill: University of North Carolina Press, 1929
ML3556 J7 J7

Johnson, James Weldon
The book of American Negro spirituals. New York: The Viking Press, 1929
M1670 J67

The books of American Negro spirituals, including the Book of American Negro spirituals and the Second book of Negro spirituals. New York: The Viking Press, 1940
ML670 J673 (Music, Main)

Johnson, John Rosamond
Rolling along in song. New York: The Viking Press, 1937
M1670 J66 R7 (Main, Music)

Jones, Le Roi
Black music. New York: W. Morrow,
1967
ML3556 J73 B5 (Main, Music, Browsing Room)

Blues people: Negro music in white
America. New York: Morrow, 1963
ML3556 J73 B55 (Main, Music)

Keil, Charles
Urban blues. Chicago: University of
Chicago Press (1966)
ML3556 K447 (Main, Architecture)

Kennedy, Robert Emmet
Mellows; a chronicle of unknown sing-
ers. New York: A. & C. Boni (c1925)
M1670* K36 (Music, Main)

More Mellows. New York: Dodd, Mead &
Company, 1931
M1670 K362

Krehbiel, Henry Edward
Afro-American folk songs.... New
York & London: G. Schirmer (c1914)
ML3556 K7 A4 (Music)

Another edition
ML3556 K7 A4 1962

Landeck, Beatrice
Echoes of Africa in folk songs of the
Americans. New York: D. McKay Co.
(1961)
M1680 L3 E3 (Main, Music)

Leonard, Neil
Jazz and the white Americans.
(Chicago) University of Chicago Press
(1962)
ML3561 J3 L4 J3 (Main, Music)

Locke, Alain LeRoy
The Negro and his music. Washington,
D. C.: The Associates in Negro Folk
Education, 1936
ML3556 L81 (Main, Music)

Logan, William Augustus
Road to heaven; twenty-eight Negro
spirituals. University, Alabama: University of Alabama Press, 1955
M1670 L6 R6

Lomax, Alan
Mister Jelly Roll. (1st edition) New
York: Sloan & Pearce, 1950
ML410 M82 L6

Another edition
ML410 M82 L6 1956 (Music)

Lomax, John Avery
Negro folk songs as sung by Lead
Belly. New York: The Macmillan Co.,
1936
M1670 L83 (Main, Music)

Longstreet, Stephen
The real jazz, old and new. (Baton
Rouge) Louisana State University
Press (c1956)
ML356 J3 L6 (Browsing Room, Music)

McRae, Barry
The jazz cataclysm. South Brunswick,
New York: A. S. Barnes (1967)
ML3561 J3 M3 (Music)

Marsh, J B T
The story of the Jubilee singers.
(Rev. ed.) New York: S. W. Green's
son, 1883
M1670 M36

Another edition
M1670 M36 1885

Metfessel, Milton Franklin
Phonophotography in folk music;
American Negro songs in new no-
tation. Chapel Hill: The University
of North Carolina Press, 1928
ML3556 M59

Mezzrow, Milton
Really the blues. New York: Random
House (1946)
ML419 M6 A3 (Music)

Minstrel songs, old and new.
Boston: O. Ditson, c1882
M1365* M5

Morgan, Alun
Modern jazz; a survey of developments
since 1939. London: V. Gallancz,
1957 (1956)
ML3561 J3 M6 (Music)

Nathan, Hans
Dan Emmett and the rise of early
Negro minstrelsy. (1st edition) Norman:
University of Oklahoma Press (1962)
ML410 E5 N3 (Main, Music)

Nelson, Rose K.
The Negro's contribution to music in
America. New York: Service bureau for
intercultural education, 1941
ML3556 N42 N4 (Main, Social Work)

Niles, John Jacob
Seven Negro exaltations. New York:
G. Schirmer, Inc. (1929)
M1670* N69 (Music)

Singing soldiers. New York, London:
C. Scribner's sons, 1927
M1629 N69

Odum, Howard Washington
**The Negro and his songs; a study of
typical Negro songs in the South.**
Chapel Hill: The University of North
Carolina Press, 1925
ML3556 O27 (Main, Music)

Negro workaday songs. Chapel Hill:
The University of North Carolina
Press, London: H. Milford, Oxford
University Press, 1926
ML3556 O28

Oliver, Paul
**Blues fill this morning; the meaning of
the blues.** London: Cassell (1960)
ML3561 J3 O4 B5

Osgood, Henry Osborne
So this is jazz. Boston: Little, Brown,
and Company, 1926
ML3561 O82 (Main, Music)

Ostransky, Leroy
The anatomy of jazz. Seattle: Univer-
sity of Washington Press, 1960
ML3561 J3 O8 (Music)

Otis, Johnny
Listen to the lambs. (1st edition) New
York: W. W. Norton (1968)
ML419 O85 A3

Panassié, Hugues
Dictionary of jazz. London: Cassell
(1954)
ML3561 J3 P3 D51 (Reference)

Guide to jazz. Boston: Houghton,
Mifflin, 1956
ML3561 J3 P3 D51 1956 (Music)

Parrish, Mrs. Lydia (Austin) comp.
**Slave songs of the Georgia Sea
Islands.** New York: Creative Age
Press, inc., 1942
M1670 P26 S6 (Main, Music)

Paskman, Daily
**"Gentlemen, be seated!" A parade
of the old-time minstrels.** New York:
Doubleday, Doran & Company, inc.,
1928
M1365 P28 (Main, Music)

Patterson, Lindsay, comp.
The Negro in music and art. (1st
edition) New York: Publishers Co.
(1967)
ML3556 P3 N4

Pike, Gustavus D
**The singing campaign for ten thou-
sand pounds; or The Jubilee singers
in Great Britain.** (Revised edition)
New York: American Missionary
Society, 1875
ML400 P63

Pleasants, Henry
Death of a music? London: V. Gallancz,
1961
ML197 P5 D4 (Music)

Progressive book co.
**Songs and spirituals of Negro com-
position; also patriotic songs, songs
of colleges and college fraternities &
sororities.** Chicago: Progressive Book
Company (c1928)
M1670 P96

Pyke, Launcelot Allen
Jazz, 1920-1927: an analytical study.
(Iowa City, Iowa, 1962)
Film 1396 (Music)

Raim, Walter, editor
The Josh White song book. Chicago:
Quandrangle Books (1963)
M1629* R27 J6 (Browsing Room)

Ramsey, Frederic
Been here and gone. New Brunswick,
New Jersey: Rutgers University Press
(c1960)
ML3556 R3 B4 (Browsing Room)

Jazzmen. New York: Harcourt, Brace
(1947, c1939)
ML3561 J3 R3 J3 (Browsing Room)

Reisner, Robert George, comp.
**The literature of jazz, a preliminary
bibliography.** New York: New York
Public Library, 1954
ML128 J3 R4 (Music)

The literature of jazz, a selective
bibliography. (2nd edition, revised &
enlarged) New York: New York Public
Library, 1959
ML128 J3 R4 1959 (Reference)

Revett, Marion S
A minstrel town. (1st edition) New
York: Pageant Press (c1955)
ML3556 R4 M5

Rose, Al
New Orleans jazz; a family album.
Baton Rouge: Louisiana State Univer-
sity Press (1967)
ML3561 J3 R6 (Music)

Rust, Brian A L
Jazz records: A-Z; 1897-1931. (2nd
edition,Hatch End, Middlesex, England,
1962, c1961)
ML156.4 J3 R8 1962 (Reference)
Index (Reference)

Jazz records: A-Z; 1932-1942. (Hatch
End, Middlesex, England, 1965)
ML156.4 J3 R82 (Reference)

Scarborough, Dorothy
On the trail of Negro folksongs. Cam-
bridge: Harvard University Press, 1925
M1670 S28 (Main, Music)

Schuller, Gunther
The history of jazz. New York: Oxford
University Press, 1968-
ML3561 J3 S3 H5 (Music)

Shapiro, Nat, ed.
Hear me talkin' to ya; the story of
jazz by the men who made it. New
York: Rinehart (1955)
ML3561 J3 S4 (Music)

Shaw, Arnold
Belafonte, an unauthorized biography.
(1st edition) Philadelphia: Chilton
Company, Book Division (1960)
ML420 B4 S4 (Browsing Room)

Shirley, Kay, ed.
The book of the blues. New York:
Leeds Music Corporation (1963)
M1629* S55 B6

Smith, Charles Edward
The jazz record book. New York:
Smith & Durrell, 1942
ML156 S64 J4

Smith, Willie
Music on my mind; the memoirs of an
American pianist.... (1st edition)
Garden City, New York: Doubleday,
1964
ML417 S6 A3 (Browsing Room)

Spaeth, Sigmund Gottifried
A history of popular music in America.
New York: Random House (1948)
ML2811 S7 (Music)

Stearns, Marshall Winslow
The story of jazz. New York: Oxford
University Press, 1966
ML3561 J3 S8 (Main, Music)

Stock, Dennis
Jazz Street. (1st edition) Garden City,
New York: Doubleday, 1960
ML3561 J3 S84 (Browsing Room)

Talley, Thomas Washington
Negro folk rhymes, wise and otherwise.
New York: The Macmillan Company,
1922
ML3556 T14

Thomas, William Henry
Some current folk-songs of the Negro.
(Austin, Texas) Folk-Lore Society of
Texas (1936)
M1670 T46

Ulanov, Barry
A handbook of jazz. New York: Viking
Press, 1957
ML3561 J3 U38

A history of jazz in America. New
York: Viking Press, 1952
ML3561 J3 U4 1962 (Main, Music)

Vehanen, Kosti
Marian Anderson, a portrait .... New
York, London: Whittlesey House,
McGraw-Hill Book Company, Inc.
(c1941)
ML420 A6 V4 (Main, Music)

Waters, Ethel
His eye is on the sparrow; an auto-
biography .... Garden City, New York:
Doubleday, 1951
ML420 W3 A3 (Browsing Room)

Another edition
ML420 W3 A3 195-

Wheeler, Mary
Steamboatin' days. Baton Rouge:
Louisiana State University Press, 1944
M1670 W56 (Music, Main)

White, Clarence Cameron
Forty Negro spirituals. Philadelphia:
T. Presser Company, c1927
M1670* W58

White, Newman Ivey
American Negro folk songs. Cambridge
University Press, 1928
ML3556 W58

Williams, Martin T., ed.
**The art of jazz; essays on the nature
and development of jazz.** New York:
Oxford University Press, 1959
ML3561 J3 W5 (Music)

Jazz masters of New Orleans. New
York: Macmillan Company (1967)
ML3561 J3 W5195 (Music)

Where's the melody? New York: Pantheon Books (1966)
ML3561 J3 W52

Wilson, John Steuart
Jazz: the transition years, 1940-1960.
New York: Appleton-Century-Crofts
(1966)
ML3561 J3 W56 (Music)

Work, John Wesley
**American Negro songs; a comprehen-
sive collection of 230 folk songs,
religious and secular.** New York:
Howell, Soskin & Company (c1940)
M1670 W92 A5 (Music, Main)

**American Negro songs; a comprehen-
sive collection of religious and secular
folk songs, for mixed voices.** Philadelphia: Theodore Presser Company,
1948
M1670 W92 A5 1948 (Music)

Folk song of the American Negro.
Nashville, Tennessee: Press of Fisk
University (c1915)
ML3556 W92 (Main, Music)

Jubilee: SATB. New York: Holt, Rinehart & Winston (1962)
M1670 W92 J8

ART

Crite, Allan Rohan
Three spirituals from earth to heaven.
Cambridge: Harvard University Press,
1948
N8150 C7

Dover, Cedric
American Negro art. London: Studio
(1960)
N6538 N5 D6

Eickemeyer, Rudolph
Down South. New York: R. H. Russell,
1900
NE2670* E35

Hirschfeld, Albert
Harlem as seen by Hirschfeld. New
York: The Hyperion Press (c1941)
NC1429* H66

Kemble, Edward Windsor
Coontown's 400. New York: Life Pub-
lishing Company, 1899
NC1429 K38

Kemble's pickaninnies. New York:
R. H. Russell, London: John Lane
1901
NC1429 K4

Locke, Alain LeRoy
**The Negro in art; a pictorial record of
the Negro artist and of the Negro theme
in art....** Washington, D. C.: Associates
in Negro Folk Education, 1940
N6538* N5 L8

Porter, James Amos
Modern Negro art.... New York: The
Dryden Press, 1943
N6538 N5 P6

Rodman, Selden
Horace Pippin, a Negro painter in America. New York: Quadrangle Press, 1947
ND237* P5 R6

United States Committee for the First World Festival of Negro Arts
Dix artistes nègres des États-Unis.... (New York: Distributed by October House, 1966)
N6538 N5 U51

LITERATURE

Adams, Francis Colburn
Manuel Pereira; or, The sovereign rule of South Carolina. Washington: Buell & Blanchard, 1853
PS1003 A62 M2 (Rare Book Collection)

Uncle Tom at home. A review of the reviews and repudiators of Uncle Tom's cabin by Mrs. Stowe .... Philadelphia: W. P. Hazard, 1853
PS2954 U518 A3

Adams, Edward Clarkson Leverett
Congaree sketches; scenes from Negro life in the swamps of the Congaree. Chapel Hill: University of North Carolina Press, 1927
PS647 N6 A4

Nigger to nigger. New York, London: C. Scribner's Sons, 1928
PS3501 D2177 N5 1928

Adoff, Arnold, comp.
I am the darker brother; an anthology of modern poems by Negro Americans. New York: Macmillan (1968)
PS591 N4 A3 (Main, Browsing Room)

Aloisi, Enzo
Negro bufon. Buenos Aires: Ediciones del Carro de Tespis (1960)
PQ7797 A4 N4 1960

Atkins, Russell
Phenomena. Wilberforce, Ohio: The Free Lance Poets and Prose Workshop, Wilberforce University Press, 1961,
PS3501 T48 P4 1961

Baldwin, James
The amen corner; a play. New York: Dial Press, 1968
PS3552 A48 A8

Another country. New York: Dial Press, 1962
PS3503 A553 A7 1962 (Browsing Room, Rare Book Collection)

Another edition
PS3503 A553 A7 1963

Another edition
PS3503 A553 A7 1967 (Undergraduate)

Blues for Mister Charlie. New York: Dial Press, 1964
PS3503 A553 B5 1964a (Browsing Room, Undergraduate)

Giovanni's room. New York: Dial Press (1963, c1956)
PS3503 A553 G5 1963

Another edition
Precat A28795

Go tell it on the mountain. (1st edition) New York: Knopf, 1953
PS3503 A553 G6 (Browsing Room)

Going to meet the man. New York: Dial Press, 1965
PS3503 A553 G64

Tell me how long the train's been gone; a novel. New York: Dial Press, 1968
PS3503 A553 T4 (Browsing Room)

Another edition
(Apply Rare Book Collection)

Barton, Rebecca Chalmers
Race consciousness and the American Negro .... Copenhagen: A. Busck, 1934
PS374 N4 B3

Basshe, Emmanuel Jo
Earth. New York: The Macaulay Company (c1927)
EL140 B319 Ea

Bekker, Meri Iosifovna
Progressionaia negritianskaia literatura .... Leningrad, Sovetskiia p'satel', 1957
PS153 N5 B4

Black Orpheus
Black Orpheus; an anthology of African and Afro-American prose .... (Ikeja) Longmans of Nigeria (1964)
PL8010 B4

Bond, Frederick Weldon
The Negro and the drama .... Washington, D. C.: Association Publishers, Inc. (c1940)
PS338 N4 B7

Bone, Robert A
The Negro novel in America. (Revised edition) New Haven: Yale University Press (1968, c1965)
PS153 N5 B6 1965

Bontemps, Arna Wendell, editor
American Negro poetry. New York: Hill & Wang (1964, c1963)
PS591 N4 B67

Golden slippers, an anthology of Negro poetry for young readers. New York, London: Harper and Brothers (c1941)
PS591 N4 B7

Boston Commercial Bulletin
Negro minstrelsy. (Boston, n.d.)
PN3195 B75

Boston Minstrelsy
Morris and Wilson's troupe, with Lou Morris as banjoist. (n.p., n.d.)
PN3195 B74

Botkin, Benjamin Albert
Black magic: a pictorial history of the Negro in American entertainment. Englewood Cliffs, New Jersey: Prentice-Hall (1967)
PN2286 H8

Brackett, Jeffrey Richardson
The Negro in Maryland .... Baltimore: Johns Hopkins University, 1889
JA2 J65 ex vol. 6

Braithwaite, Edward Ricardo
The golden treasury of magazine verse .... Boston: Small, Maynard & Company (c1918)
PS614 B7

Our lady's choir, a contemporary anthology of verse by Catholic sisters .... Boston: B. Humphries, Inc., 1931
PS591 C3 B7

Braithwaite, William Stanley Beaumont
The bewitched parsonage; the story of the Brontes. New York: Coward-McCann (1950)
PR4168 B7

The book of Elizabethan verse. (2nd edition) Boston: H. B. Turner & Company, 1907
PR1217 B8 1907

The book of modern British verse. Boston: Small, Maynard & Company (c1919)
PR1225 B7

The book of restoration verse .... New York: Brentano's, 1910
PR1213 B6

The poetic year for 1916, a critical anthology .... Boston: Small, Maynard & Company (c1917)
PN1271 B8

Brawley, Benjamin Griffith, editor
Early Negro American writers. Chapel Hill: The University of North Carolina Press, 1935
EL110 B82

Paul Laurence Dunbar, poet of his people. Chapel Hill: The University of North Carolina Press, 1936
PS1557 B7

Bronz, Stephen H
Roots of Negro racial consciousness; the 1920's: three Harlem Renaissance authors ... New York: Libra (1964)
PS508 N3 B85

Brooks, Gwendolyn
Selected poems. (1st edition) New York: Harper & Row (1963)
PS3503 R7164 A6 1963 (Browsing Room)

Brooks, Maxwell Roy
The Negro press re-examined....
Boston: Christopher Publishing House
(c1959)
PN4888 N4 B7 (Main, Journalism)

Brooks, Stella (Brewer)
Joel Chandler Harris, folklorist. Athens:
University of Georgia Press (1950)
PS1817 F6 B7

Brown, Sterling Allen
The Negro caravan. New York: Dryden
Press (c1941)
PS508 N3 B87 (Main, English Depart-
ment)

The Negro in American fiction. Washington, D. C.: The Associates in Negro
folk education, 1937
PS374 N4 B8

Negro poetry and drama. Washington,
D. C.: Associates in Negro Folk
Education, 1937
PS153 N5 B7

Butcher, Charles Philip
**George W. Cable: the Northhampton
years.** New York: Columbia University
Press, 1959
PS1246 B8

Another edition
PS1246 B82 (Main, English.Graduate)

**The cabin boy's story: a semi-nautical
romance founded on fact.** New York:
Garrett & Company (c1854)
PS991 A7 P5 1854

Cable, George Washington
Gideon's band. New York: C.
Scribner's Sons, 1914
EL140 C115 Gi

The Grandissimes. New York: Scribner's Sons, 1899
EL140 C115 Gr

Another edition
(Apply Rare Book Collection)

Another edition
PS1244 G7 1919

Another edition
EL140 C115 GR2

John March, southerner. New York: C.
Scribner's Sons, 1894
PS1244 J6 1894 (Rare Book Collection)

Another edition
(Apply Rare Book Collection)

Another edition
EL140 C115 J

Old Creole days. New York: C. Scrib-
ner's Sons, 1879
PS1244 O4 (Main, Rare Book
Collection)

Another edition
PS1244 O4 1897

Another edition
PS1244 O4 1900

Another edition
EL140 C115 O

"Posson Jone" and Pere Raphael...
New York: C. Scribner's Sons, 1909
PS1244 P6 1909

Strange true stories of Louisiana. New
York: Scribner's, 1889
EL140 C115 S

Calverton, Victor Francis
**Anthology of American Negro litera-
ture.** New York: The Modern Library
(c1929)
EL110 C16

Campbell, Roald Fay
**The organization and control of Ameri-
can schools.** Columbus, Ohio: C. E.
Merrill Books (1965)
LB2806.5 C3 (Education, Agriculture)

Carter, Hodding
First person rural. (1st edition) Garden
City, New York: Doubleday, 1963
PN4874 C3 A25 (Browsing Room)

The winds of fear. New York: Farrar &
Rinehart (1944)
PS3505 A78 W7 (Main, Social Work)

Chandler, Elizabeth Margaret
Essays, philanthropic and moral.
Philadelphia: L. Howell, 1836
PS1289 C45 P7 1836 (Rare Book
Collection)

**The poetical works of Elizabeth Mar-
garet Chandler.** Philadelphia: L.
Howell, 1836
PS1289 C45 P7 1836 (Rare Book
Collection)

Chappell, Louis Watson
John Henry, a folk-lore study. Jena:
Frommannsche verlag, W. Biedermann,
1933
PS461 J6 C5

Charters, Samuel Barclay
The poetry of the blues. New York:
Oak Publishers (1963)
PS591 N4 C45

Chase, Lucien Bonaparte
English serfdom and American slavery;
or, Ourselves — as others see us. New
York: H. Lang & Brothers (c1854)
PS1292 C39 E5 1854 (Rare Book
Collection)

Chesnutt, Charles Waddell
The colonel's dream. New York:
Doubleday, Page & Company, 1905
EL140 C535 CO

Another edition
PS1292 C6 C6 1927

The conjure woman. Boston and New
York: Houghton, Mifflin & Company,
1899
PS1292 C6 C6 1899

The marrow of tradition. Boston and
New York: Houghton & Mifflin Com-
pany, 1901
EL140 C535 M

The wife of his youth and other stories
of the color line. Boston and New
York: Houghton, Mifflin Company,
1899
EL140 C535 Wi

Chesnutt, Helen M
Charles Waddell Chesnutt, pioneer of
the color line. Chapel Hill: University
of North Carolina Press (1952)
PS1292 C6 Z8 C4

Child, Mrs. Lydia Maria (Francis)
A romance of the republic. Boston:
Ticknor & Fields, 1867
EL140 C5354 Ro

Clarke, John Henrik, ed.
American Negro short stories. (1st edi-
tion) New York: Hill & Wang (1966)
PZ1 C62 A7

Clurman, Harold
The fervent years .... New York: Knopf,
1945
PN2297 G8 C6

Coffin, Charles Carleton
Caleb Krinkle, a story of American
life. Boston: Lee & Shepard, New
York: Lee, Shepard & Dillingham, 1875
PS1357 C345 C3 1874 (Rare Book
Collection)

Another edition
PS1357 C345 C3 1875 (Main, Rare Book
Collection)

Another edition
Published as Dan of Milbrook ....
Precat AO6230

Cohen, Inez (Lopez)
Our darktown press. New York, London:
D. Appleton & Company, 1932
PN6231 N5 C6

Conference of Negro Writers, 1st. New
York, 1959
The American Negro writer and his
roots; selected papers. New York:
American Society of African Culture,
1960
PS153 N5 C6 1959

Corrothers, James David
The Black cat club .... New York:
Funk & Wagnalls Company, 1902
PN6161 C8

Cotter, Joseph Seamon
Links of friendship .... Louisville,
Kentucky: The Bradley & Gilbert Com-
pany, 1898
Micro card PS1449

Cowan, Michael H
Twentieth century interpretations of
the sound and the fury; a collection of
critical essays. Englewood Cliffs, New
Jersey: Prentice-Hall (1968)
PS3511 A86 S6517 C6 (English
Graduate)

Crump, Paul
Burn, killer, burn! Chicago: Johnson
(1962)
PS3553 R8 B8 1962a (Browsing Room)

Cullen, Countee
The ballad of the brown girl, an old
ballad retold. New York and London:
Harper & Brothers, 1927
PS3505 U287 B3 1927 (Main, Rare
Book Collection)

The Black Christ and other poems.
New York: Harper, 1929
PS3505 U287 B5 1929a

Caroling dusk, anthology of verse by
Negro poets. (1st edition) New York
and London: Harper & Brothers (C1927)
PS591 N4 C9

Another edition
PS591 N4 C9 1927a

Color. New York and London: Harper
& Brothers, 1925
PS3505 U287 C6 1925 (Rare Book
Collection)

Another edition
PS3505 U287 C6 1925a

Copper sun. New York: Harper, 1927
PS3505 U287 C65 1927a

On these I stand; an anthology of the
best poems of Countee Cullen. New
York and London: Harper & Brothers
(1947)
PS3505 U287 A6 1947

Cunningham, Virginia
Paul Laurence Dunbar and his song.
New York: Dodd-Mead & Company,
1947
EL140 D899 C8

Davis, Christopher
First family. New York: Avon Book
Division, The Hearst Corporation
(c1961)
PS3554 A8 F5 1961a

Davis, Daniel Webster
'Weh down souf, and other poems.
Cleveland: The Helman-Taylor Com-
pany, 1897
PS1514 D59 W4 1897

Davis, Ossie
Purlie Victorious; a comedy in three
acts. New York: S. French (c1961)
PS3507 A7444 P8 1961

Davis, Sammy
Yes I can .... New York: Farrar,
Straus & Giroux (1965)
PN2287 D27 A3 (Browsing Room)

Day, Charles H
Fun in black: or, sketches of minstrel
life .... New York: R. M. DeWitt (c1874)
PN3195 B87

Dickinson, Donald C
A bio-bibliography of Langston Hughes,
1902-1967. (Hamden, Conn.) Archon
Books, 1967
PS3515 U274 Z8 D5 1967

Dionne, Jack
"Cullud" fun. (3rd edition, Houston,
Texas, c1932)
PN6231 N5 D5 1932

Dixie, Edward F
Dixey's essence of burnt cork. Phila-
delphia: A. Winch (c1859)
PN4305 N6 D6

Dixon, Thomas
The clansman, an historical romance
of the Ku Klux Klan. New York:
Grosset & Dunlap (1905)
PS3507 I93 C5

Another edition
PS3507 I93 C5 1903

The leopard's spots; a romance of the
white man's burden, 1865-1900. New
York: Doubleday, Page and Company,
1902
PS3507 I93 L4 1902

Dodson, Owen
Powerful long ladder. New York:
Farrar, Straus & Company, Inc., 1946
English Department Library

Downer, Alan Seymour
American drama and its critics: a
collection of critical essays. Chicago:
University of Chicago Press (1965)
PS351 D59

Dreer, Herman
American literature by Negro authors.
New York: Macmillan, 1950
PS508 N3 D7

Drew, Elizabeth A
Discovering drama. New York: W. W.
Norton & Company, Inc. (c1937)
PN1655 D77

Duberman, Martin B
In white America, a documentary play.
Boston: Houghton Mifflin, 1964
PS3554 U25 I5 1964

Dubois, William Edward Burghardt
Dark princess, a romance. New York:
Harcourt, Brace and Company (c1928)
PS3507 U234 D3 1928

Mansart builds a school. New York:
Mainstream Publishers, 1959
PS3507 U234 M3 1959

The ordeal of Mansart. New York:
Mainstream Publishers, 1957
PS3507 U234 O7 1957

The quest of the silver fleece.
Chicago: A. C. McClurg & Company,
1911
E1140 D816 Q

Worlds of color. New York: Mainstream
Publishers, 1961
PS3507 U234 W6 1961

Dunbar, Paul Laurence
Best stories of Paul Laurence Dunbar.
New York: Dodd, Mead & Company,
1938
EL140 D899 Be

Candle-lightin' time. New York: Dodd,
Mead & Company, 1901
PS1556 C3 1901 (Rare Book
Collection)

The complete poems of Paul Laurence
Dunbar.... New York: Dodd, Mead &
Company, 1915 (c1913)
PS1556 A1 1915

Another edition
PS1556 A1 1918

Another edition
PS1556 A1 1934

The fanatics. New York: Dodd, Mead
& Company, 1901
PS1556 F2

Folks from Dixie. New York: Dodd,
Mead & Company, 1898
EL140 D899 Fo

The heart of Happy Hollow. New York:
Dodd, Mead & Company, 1904
EL140 D899 He

Howdy, honey, howdy. New York: Dodd,
Mead & Company, 1905
EL140 D899 Ho

In old plantation days. New York:
Dodd, Mead & Company, 1903
EL140 D899 In

Joggin' erlong. New York: Dodd Mead
& Company, 1906
EL140 D899 Jo

Paul Laurence

The life and works of Paul Laurence
Dunbar .... (Naperville, Illinois: J. L.
Nichols, c1907)
PS1556 A2 W5 1907

Another edition
PS1556 A2 W5 1907a (Main, Undergraduate)

Li'l gal. New York: Dodd, Mead &
Company, 1904
EL140 D899 Li

Little brown baby. New York: Dodd,
Mead & Company, 1947 (c1940)
PZ8,3 D89 L7 (Education)

The love of Landry. New York: Dodd,
Mead & Company, 1900
EL140 D899 Lo

Lyrics of love and laughter. New York:
Dodd, Mead & Company, 1903
EL140 D899 Ly

Lyrics of lowly life. New York: Dodd,
Mead & Company, 1898
EL140 D899 Lyr

Lyrics of sunshine and shadows. New
York: Dodd, Mead & Company, 1905
PS1556 L9 1905

Lyrics of the hearthside. New York:
Dodd Mead & Company, 1899
EL140 D899 Lyri

Majors and minors: poems. (Toledo:
Hadley & Hadley, c1895)
PS1556 M3 1895

Oak and ivy. Dayton, Ohio: Press of
United Brethren Publishing House,
1893
PS1556 O3 1893 (Rare Book Collection)

Poems of cabin and field. New York:
Dodd Mead & Company, 1899
EL140 D899 Ps

The sport of the gods. New York: Dodd,
Mead & Company, 1902
EL140 D899 Sp

The strength of Gideon, and other
stories. New York: Dodd, Mead & Company, 1900.
EL140 D899 Str

Another edition
(Apply Rare Book Collection)

The Uncalled; a novel. New York:
Dodd, Mead & Company, 1898
PS1556 U5 1898 (Main, Rare Book
Collection)

When Malindy sings. New York: Dodd,
Mead & Company, 1904
EL140 D899 Wh

Durham, Philip
Down these mean streets a man must
go; Raymond Chandler's Knight.
Chapel Hill: University of North
Carolina Press (1963)
PS3505 H3224 Z8 D8

Dykes, Eva Beatrice
The Negro in English romantic thought;
or a study of sympathy for the
oppressed. Washington, D. C.: The
Associated Publishers, Inc., 1942
PR447 D99

East, P. D.
The magnolia jungle .... New York:
Simon & Schuster, 1960
PN4874 E3 A3 (Main, Browsing Room)

Eckman, Fern Marja
The furious passage of James Baldwin.
New York: M. Evans; distributed in
association with Lippincott, Philadel-
phia (c1966)
PS3503 A553 Z8 E4

Edmonds, Randolph
Six plays for a Negro theater. Boston:
Walker H. Baker Company (c1934)
PS3509 D56 S6

Egri, Lajos
The art of dramatic writing; its basis
in the creative interpretation of human
motives. New York: Simon & Schuster,
1946
PN1661 E3 (Main, Undergraduate)

Eleazer, Robert Burns
Singers in the dawn, a brief anthology
of American Negro poetry. Atlanta,
Georgia: Conference on Education &
Race Relations (1937)
PS591 N4 E3

Another edition
PS591 N4 E3 1943

Ellison, Ralph
Invisible man. New York: Random
House (c1952)
PS3509 L6 I5 1952 (Undergraduate)

Another edition
PS3509 L6 I5 1952a

Shadow and act. New York: Random
House (1964)
PS153 N4 E4 1964 (Browsing Room)

Emanuel, James A
Dark symphony: Negro literature in
America. New York: Free Press (c1968)
PS508 N3 E4 (Main, Browsing Room)

Langston Hughes. New York: Twayne
Publishing (1967)
PS3515 U274 Z8 E4 (Main, Under-
graduate, English Graduate)

Esslin, Martin
The theatre of the absurd. (1st edition)
New York: Doubleday & Company,
1961
PN1861 E8 (Main, Browsing Room,
Foreign Language Graduate)

Another edition
PN1861 E8 1961a

Another edition
PN1861 E813 1964

Fair, Ronald L
Many thousand gone; an American
fable. (1st edition) New York: Harcourt, Brace & World (c1965)
PS3556 A4 M3 (Browsing Room)

Fast, Howard Melvin
Freedom road. New York: Duell (1944)
EL140 F252 Fr

Another edition
PS3511 A745 1944a

Another edition
PS3511 A745 F4 1944b

Another edition
PS3511 A745 F4 1945 (Undergraduate)

Faulkner, William
Go down Moses, and other stories.
New York: Random House (1942)
PS3511 A86 G6 (Undergraduate, Rare
Book Collection)

Another edition
PS3511 A86 G6 1942

Another edition
PS3511 A86 G6 1955

Intruder in the dust. New York: Random
House (c1948)
PS3511 A86 I5 1948 (Browsing Room,
Rare Book Collection, Undergraduate)

Another edition
PS3511 A86 I5 1948a (Main, Undergraduate)

Another edition
PS3511 A86 I5 1960

The sound and the fury. New York: J.
Cape & H. Smith (c1929)
PS3511 A86 S65 1929 (Main, Rare Book
Collection)

Another edition
PS3511 A86 S65 1931 (Rare Book
Collection)

Another edition
PS3511 A86 S65

Another edition
PS3511 A86 S65 1946a

Another edition
PS3511 A86 S65 1957 (Undergraduate)

Another edition
PS3511 A86 S65 1961

...The unvanquished. New York:
Random House (1938)
PS3511 A86 U5 (Browsing Room, Rare
Book Collection, Undergraduate)

Another edition
PS3511 A86 U5 1965 (Undergraduate)

Federal Theatre Project
Federal theatre plays.... New York:
Random House (c1938)
PS634 F29 (Main, Education)

Another edition
PS634 F28

Feibleman, Peter S
A place without twilight. Cleveland:
World Publishing Company (c1958)
PS3553 E4 P5 1958 (Browsing Room)

Ferguson, Blanche E
**Countee Cullen and the Negro
renaissance.** New York: Dodd, Mead
& Company (1966)
PS3505 U287 Z8 F4

Field, Marshall
**The Negro press and the issues of
democracy.** (Chicago: American Council on Race Relations, 1944?)
PN4888 N4 F5 (Social Work)

Fields, Mrs. Annie (Adams)
**Life and letters of Harriet Beecher
Stowe.** Boston and New York: Hough-
ton, Mifflin 1899
EL140 S892 F4

Fisher, Rudolph
The walls of Jericho. New York &
London: A. A. Knopf, 1928
EL140 F535 Wa

Flanagan, Mrs. Hallie (Ferguson)
Arena .... New York: Duell, Sloan, and
Pearce (c1940)
PN2266 F58

Flanders, Mrs. G M
The ebony idol. New York: Appleton &
Company, 1860
EL140 F584 Eb

Ford, Nick Aaron
**The contemporary Negro novel, a study
in race relations.** Boston: Meador Publishing Company, 1936
PS374 N4 F6

Ford, Jesse Hill
The feast of Saint Barnabas. Boston:
Little, Brown and Company (1968)
PS3556 O74 F4 (Browsing Room)

Freuchen, Peter
The legend of Daniel Williams.
New York: Messner (c1956)
PT8175 F65 L4 1956a (Undergraduate)

Another edition
PT8175 F65 L4 1958

Gaines, Ernest J
Bloodline.... New York: Dial Press,
1968
PS3557 A3 B5 (Browsing Room)

Of love and dust. New York: Dial
Press, 1967
PS3557 A3 O3 (Browsing Room)

Gilbertson, Mrs. Catherine (Peebles)
Harriet Beecher Stowe. New York,
London: D. Appleton-Century Company,
Inc., 1937
EL140 S892 G4

Gilmore, James Roberts
Among the pines: or, South in seces-
sion time. By Edmund Kirke (pseud.)
6th edition, New York: J. R. Gilmore,
1862
PS1744 G68 A8 1862

Another edition
PS1744 G68 A8 1862a (Rare Book
Collection)

Another edition
PS1744 G68 A8 1863 (Rare Book
Collection)

My southern friends .... By Edmund
Kirke (pseud.) New York: Carleton,
1863
PS1744 G68 M8 1863 (Rare Book
Collection)

Another edition
PS1744 G68 M8 1864 (Rare Book
Collection)

Closter, Hugh Morris
Negro voices in American fiction.
Chapel Hill: The University of North
Carolina Press, 1948
PS374 N4 G5

Another edition
PS374 N4 G5 1948a

Gordon, Armistead Churchill
Befo' de war; echoes in Negro dialect.
New York: C. Scribner's Sons, 1888
PS3513 O65 B4

Another edition
PS3513 O65 B4 1891

Graham, Lorenz B
North Town. New York: Crowell (1965)
PS3557 R3 N6 (Education)

Grayson, William John
The hireling and the slave.... 2nd edi-
tion, Charleston: John Russell, 1855
PS1764 G238 H6

Green, Mrs. Elizabeth Atkinson (Lay)
The Negro in contemporary American
literature; an outline for individual and
group study. Chapel Hill: The University of North Carolina Press, 1928
LC6301 N86 vol. 7 no. 14

Another edition
PS153 N5 G7 1928a (Reference)

Green, Paul
Dramatic heritage. New York: Samuel
French (c1953)
PN2021 G7

Gregory, Dick
Nigger; an autobiography. (1st edition)
New York: Dutton, 1964
PN2287 G68 A3 (Browsing Room)

Griffin, John Howard
The devil rides outside. Fort Worth
(Texas) Smiths, Inc., 1952
PS3513 R673 D4 1952a

The John Howard Griffin reader.
Boston: Houghton, Mifflin, 1968
(c1967)
PS3557 R53 A6 1968

Gross, Seymour Lee, ed.
Images of the Negro in American litera-
ture. Chicago: University of Chicago
Press (1966)
PS173 N4 G7 (Main, Undergraduate)

Guthrie, Alfred Bertram
The blue hens' chick; a life in context.
(1st edition) New York: McGraw-Hill
(1965)
PS3513 U84 Z5 (Browsing Room,
Journalism)

Hansberry, Lorraine
The sign in Sidney Brustein's window,
a drama in three acts. New York:
Random House (1965)
PS3515 A526 S5 1965

A raisin in the sun; a drama in three
acts. New York: Random House (c1959)
PS3513 A526 R3 1959a (Main, Browsing
Room)

Harper, Frances Ellen (Watkins)
Poems on miscellaneous subjects.
Boston: J. B. Yerrinton & Son, printers,
1855
PS1799 H58 P6 1855

Harris, Joel Chandler
Mingo, and other sketches in black and
white. Boston: J. R. Osgood & Company (1884)
EL140 H314 Mi

Another edition
PS1805 M66 (Rare Book Collection)

Another edition
EL140 H314 Mi2

Another edition
Precat AOO294

Another edition
(Apply Rare Book Collection)

Uncle Remus and his friends. Boston &
New York: Houghton, Mifflin & Company (c1892)

Another edition
PS1808 1920

**Uncle Remus, his songs and his say-
ings.** New & revised edition. New
York: D. Appleton & Company, 1901
(c1895)
PS1809 A1 1901

Another edition
PS1809 A1 1886

Another edition
PS1809 A1 1899

Another edition
PS1809 A1 1921 (Education)

Another edition
PS1809 A1 195- (Education)

Haverly, Jack
Negro minstrels .... Chicago: F. J.
Drake & Company (c1902)
PN4305 N6 H3 (Rare Book Collection)

Hawkins, Walter Everette
Chords and discords. Boston: R. G.
Badger (c1920)
PS3515 A894 C5 1920

Hayden, Robert Earl, comp.
**Kaleidoscope; poems by American
Negro poets.** New York: Harcourt,
Brace & World (1968, c1967)
PS591 N4 H3

Selected poems. (1st edition) New
York: October House (1966)
PS3515 A918 A6

Henderson, Elliot Blaine
Plantation echoes .... Columbus, Ohio:
Press of F. J. Heer, 1904
PS3515 E434 P5 1904

Another edition
PS3513 E434 P5 1905

Hercules, Frank
Where the hummingbird flies. (1st edi-
tion) New York: Harcourt, Brace (1961)
PS3515 E6 W4

Heyward, Mrs. Dorothy Hartzell (Kuhns)
Mamba's daughters; a play. New York,
Toronto: Farrar & Rinehart, Inc. (c1939)
EL140 H622 Ma

Heyward, Du Bose
Brass ankle, a play in three acts. New
York: Farrar & Rinehart (c1931)
PS3515 E98 B7 1931

Mamba's daughters. Garden City, N.Y.:
Doubleday, Doran & Company, 1929
PS3515 E98 M3 1929

Another edition
PS3515 E98 M3 1929a

Porgy. New York: George H. Doran
Company (c1925)
PS3515 E98 P6 1925

Another edition
PS3515 E98 P6 1925a (Rare Book
Collection)

Another edition
EL140 H623 Po

Another edition
EL38 W39

Another edition
PN6112 T3 7

Star spangled virgin. New York: Farrar
& Rinehart (c1939)
EL140 H623 St

Hill, Herbert
**Anger, and beyond: the Negro writer in
the United States.** New York: Harper
& Row (c1966)
PS153 N5 H5

**Soon, one morning: new writing by
American Negroes, 1940-1962.** New
York: Knopf, 1963
PS508 N3 H5

Hill, Leslie Pinckney
The wings of oppression. Boston: The
Stratford Company, 1921
PS3515 I486 W5 1921

Himes, Chester B
The big gold dream. (New York) Berkley Publishing Corporation (1966,
c1960)
PS3515 I714 B5 1966

Cast the first stone, a novel. New York:
Coward-McCann (c1952)
PS3515 I714 C3 1952a

Cotton comes to Harlem. (1st American
edition) New York: Putnam (1965)
PS3515 I714 C6 1965 (Main, Browsing
Room)

The crazy kill. (New York) Berkley
Publishing Corporation (1966, c1959)
PS3515 I714 C7 1966

Dare-dare. (Run man run) Traduit de
l'americain par Pierre Verrier. (Paris)
Gallimard (1959)
PS3515 I714 R812 1959

... If he hollers let him go. Garden
City, N. Y.: Doubleday, Doran &
Company, Inc., 1945
PS3515 I714 I3

Lonely crusade. (1st edition) New
York: A. A. Knopf, 1947
PS3515 I714 L6

The heat's on. New York: Putnam
(c1966)
PS3515 I714 H4 1966a

Pinktoes. Paris: Olympia Press (1961)
PSI714 P5 1961 (Rare Book Collection)

Another edition
PS3515 I714 P5 1965

The primitive. (New York) New American Library (1955)
PS3515 I714 P7 1955a

A rage in Harlem. (New York: Avon
Books, c1965)
PS3515 I714 R3 1965

The real cool killers. (New York)
Berkley Publishing Corporation (1966,
c1959)
PS3515 I714 R4 1966

Run man run. New York: Putnam (1966)
PS3515 I714 R8 1966

Third generation. (New York) New
American Library (1964, c1954)
PS3515 I714 T4 1964

Homburger, Lilias
The Negro-African languages. (First
English translation) London: Routledge
& Kegan Paul (1949)
PL8005 H761

Howard, James H
Bond and free; a true tale of slave
times. Harrisburg (Pa.) E. K. Meyers,
Printer, 1886
PS2014 H15 B7 (Rare Book Collection)

Howells, William Dean, ed.
Southern lights and shadows .... New
York and London: Harper & Brothers
(c1907)
PZ1 H8495

Hughes, Langston
Ask your mama: 12 moods for jazz.
(1st edition) New York: Knopf, 1961
PS3515 U274 A8 (Browsing Room)

The best short stories by Negro writers; an anthology from 1899 to the
present. 1st edition. Boston: Little,
Brown (1967)
PZ1 H89 B4 (Main, Browsing Room)

Black magic. Englewood Cliffs, N. J.:
Prentice-Hall (1967)
PN2286 H8

The book of Negro humor. New York:
Dodd, Mead (1966)
PN6231 N5 H8

Five plays. Bloomington: Indiana
University Press (1963)
PS3515 U274 A19 1963 (Browsing
Room)

The Langston Hughes reader. New
York: G. Braziller (1965, c1958)
PS3515 U274 A6 1965 (Browsing Room)

New Negro poets U. S. A. Bloomington,
Indiana: Indiana University Press
(1966, c1964)
PS591 N4 H8 (Main, Browsing Room)

Poems from Black Africa .... Bloomington, Indiana: Indiana University Press
(1963)
PL8013 E5 H8 (Undergraduate)

The poetry of the Negro, 1746-1949.
(1st edition) Garden City, New York:
Doubleday, 1949
PN6109.7 H8 (Main, Education)

The poetry of the Negro, 1946-1949.
1st edition. Garden City, New York:
Doubleday, 1949
PN6109.7 H8

Selected poems. (1st edition) New York: Knopf, 1959
PS3515 U274 A6 1959

Another edition
PS3515 U274 A6 1969 (Undergraduate)

Simple stakes a claim. New York: Rinehart (1957)
PS3515 U274 S53 1957 (Browsing Room)

Simple's Uncle Sam. (1st edition) New York: Hill & Wang (1965)
PS3515 U274 S56 (Browsing Room)

Hunter, Evan
Blackboard jungle, a novel. New York: Simon and Schuster, 1954
PS3515 U592 B5 1954a (Browsing Room)

Insua, Alberto
El negro que tenia el alma blanca. (7 edition) Madrid Renacimiento (c1922)
PQ6617 N96 N38 1922

Isaacs, Mrs. Edith Juliet (Rich)
The Negro in the American theatre. New York: Theatre Art Books, 1947
PN2286 I8

Izzo, Carlo, ed.
Nuovissima poesia americana e negra, con testo a fronte, 1949-1953. (Parma) Guanda (1953)
PS614 I9 1953

Johnson, James Weldon
The autobiography of an excoloured man. Garden City, New York: Garden City Publishing Company (c1927)
PS3519 O2625 A8 1927

Another edition
EL140 J674 Au

Another edition
PS3519 O2625 A8 1948

The book of American Negro poetry. New York: Harcourt, Brace (c1922)
PS591 N4 J6

Johnson, Samuel
Dr. Johnson, his life in letters. Selected and edited by David Littlejohn. Englewood Cliffs, New Jersey: Prentice-Hall (1965)
PR3533 A22 1965

Johnston, Johanna
Runaway to heaven; the story of Harriet Beecher Stowe. (1st edition) Garden City, New York: Doubleday, 1963
PS2956 J6

Jones, LeRoi
Black fire; an anthology of Afro-American writing. New York: Morrow, 1968
PS508 N3 J6 (Browsing Room)

The dead lecturer; poems. New York: Grove Press (1964)
PS3519 O565 D4 (Browsing Room)

Dutchman and The slave, two plays. New York: William Morrow & Company, 1964
PS3519 O565 D8 1964 (Main, Rare Book Collection, Browsing Room)

The moderns; an anthology of new writings in America. New York: Corinth Books, 1963
PS536 J6 (Browsing Room)

Preface to a twenty volume suicide note; (poems). New York: Totem Press in association with Corinth Books (1961)
PS3519 O565 P7 1961

The system of Dante's hell; (a novel) New York: Grove Press (1965)
PS3519 O565 S9 1965

Tales. New York: Grove Press (1967)
PS3519 O565 T3 (Browsing Room)

Another edition
PS3519 O565 T3 1968 (Undergraduate)

Kelley, William Melvin
A different drummer. Garden City, N.Y.: Doubleday, 1962
PS3561 E4 D5 1962 (Browsing Room)

Dem. (1st edition) Garden City, New York: Doubleday, 1967
PS3561 E4 D4 (Browsing Room)

Kerlin, Robert Thomas
Negro poets and their poems. Washington, D. C.: Associated Publishers, Inc. (c1923)
PS591 N4 K4

Theocritus in English literature.... Lynchburg, Virginia; J. P. Bell Company (Inc.) Printers. 1910
PA4444 K4

Kingsbury, Susan Myra
Newspapers and the news, an objective
measurement of ethical and unethical
behavior by representative newspapers.
New York: G. P. Putnam's Sons, 1937
PN4756 K55 (Main, Journalism)

(Lanusse, Armand) comp.
Creole voices .... Washington, D. C.:
The Associated Publishers, 1945
PQ3937 L8 L32

Lewis, Wyndham
Paleface; the philosophy of the 'melting pot.' London: Chatto & Windus,
1929
PR6023 E97 P3 1929

Linton, William James
Poetry of America; selections from one
hundred American poets from 1776 to
1876. London: G. Bell, 1878
PS586 L7

Littlejohn, David
Black on white: a critical survey of
writing by American Negroes. New
York: Grossman, 1966
PS153 N5 L5

Locke, Alain LeRoy
Plays of Negro life; a source-book of
native American drama. New York,
London: Harper & Brothers, 1927
PS627 N4 L6 (Social Work)

Loggins, Vernon
The negro author, his development in
America. New York: Columbia Univer-
sity Press, 1931
PS153 N5 L6 1931a

McCullough, Norman Verrle
The Negro in English literature, a
critical introduction. Ilfracombe (Eng.)
A. H. Stockwell (1962)
PR151 N4 M3

McKay, Claude
Harlem shadows. New York: Harcourt,
Brace & Company (c1922)
EL140 M149

Home to Harlem. New York and London:
Harper & Brothers, 1928
PS3525 A24785 H6 1928

A long way from home. New York: L.
Furman, Inc. (c1937)
EL140 M149 A2

Selected poems. New York: Bookman
Associates, 1953
PS3525 A24785 A6 1953

Magidoff, Robert
Negry poiut. Soiuza russkikh revoliut-
sioniykh robotnikov iskusstva im.
Maksima Gor'kogo v S. A. S. Sh., New
York, 1934
PS619 R8 M3

Margolies, Edward
Native sons; a critical study of
twentieth-century Negro American
authors. (1st edition) Philadelphia:
Lippincott (1968)
PS153 N5 M3

Marshall, Herbert
Ira Aldridge, the Negro tragedian.
London: Rockliff (1958)
PN2598 A5 M3

Mays, Benjamin Elijah
The Negro's God, as reflected in his
literature. New York: Russell &
Russell (1968)
PS153 N5 M35 1938a (Undergraduate)

Means, Eldred Kurtz
Further E. K. Means ...: New York and
London: G. P. Putnam's Sons (c1921)
PS3525 E22 F8 1921

More E. K. Means .... New York and
London: G. P. Putnam's Sons, 1919
PS3525 E22 M6 1919

Melone, Thomas
De la négritude dans la litterature
négro-africaine. Paris: Presence
africaine (1962)
PQ3980 M4

Miller, Warren
The cool world, a novel. Boston:
Little, Brown (c1959)
PS3525 I567 C6

The siege of Harlem. (1st edition)
New York: McGraw-Hill (1964)
PS3525 I567 S5 (Browsing Room)

Mira de Amescua, Antonio
... Comedia famosa. El negro del mejor
amo. (Madrid, 1653)
PQ6413 M7 N3 1653

Mitchell, Loften
Black drama; the story of the American
Negro in the theatre. (1st edition) New
York: Hawthorne Books (1967)
PS338 N4 M5 (Main, Browsing Room)

Morán López, Fernando
Nacion y alienación en la literatura
negro-africaina. (Madrid: Taurus Ediciones, 1964)
PL8010 M64

Morand, Paul
... Black magic. London: W. Heinemann
Ltd. (1929)
PQ2625 O67 M21 M

Morton, Lena Beatrice
Negro poetry in America. Boston: The
Stratford Company, 1925
EL123 M88

Motley, Willard
... Knock on any door. New York and
London: D. Appleton-Century Company,
Inc. (1947)
PS3525 O84 K7 1947a (Main, Rare
Book Collection, Undergraduate)

Another edition
PS3525 O84 K7 1950a (Social Work)

Another edition
PS3525 O84 K7 1958

Let no man write my epitaph. New
York: Random House (c1958)
PS3525 O84 L4 1958 (Browsing Room,
Undergraduate, Social Work)

Let noon be fair, a novel. New York:
Putnam (c1966)
PS3525 O84 L42 1966

We fished all night. New York: Appleton-Century Crofts (1951)
PS3525 O84 W4 1951 (Main, Undergraduate)

Murphy, Beatrice M
Ebony rhythm. New York: Exposition
Press (c1948)
PS591 N4 M8

Nathan, George Jean
Passing judgments. New York: Knopf,
1935
PN2266 N265 (Main, Journalism)

Testament of a critic. New York:
Knopf, 1931
EL140 N274 Te

Nelson, John Herbert
The Negro character in American literature. Lawrence, Kansas: University
of Kansas Press, 1926
AS36 K3 vol. 4 no. 1

Nelson, Truman John
The sin of the prophet. Boston: Little,
Brown, 1952
PS3527 E449 S5 1952a

Nilson, Charles H
Faulkner and the Negro. Boulder: Uni-
versity of Colorado Press, 1962
P25 C7 no. 8

Odum, Howard Washington
Wings on my feet; black Ulysses at the
wars. Indianapolis: The Bobbs-Merrill
Company (c1929)
PS3529 D8 W5 1929

Olivari, Nicolás
Un negro y un fósforo; cuentos.
Buenos Aires: T. Rocamora (1959)
PQ7797 O47 N4 1959

Olsen, Otto H
Carpetbagger's crusade: the life of
Albion Winegar Tourgee. Baltimore:
Johns Hopkins Press, 1965
PS3088 O5

Onstott, Kyle
Mandingo. Richmond: Denlinger (c1957)
PS3529 N75 M3 1957

Another edition
PS3529 N75 M3 19572 (Undergraduate)

Ottley, Roi
The lonely warrior: the life and times
of Robert S. Abbott. Chicago: H.
Regnery Company, 1955
PN4874 A23 O8

Parrish, Anne
A clouded star. (1st edition) New York:
Harper (1948)
PS3531 A695 C6 (Education)

Patok, Chaim
The chosen, a novel. New York: Simon
& Schuster (1967)
PS3566 O7 C5 (Browsing Room)

Another edition
PS3566 O7 C5 1967a

Patterson, Lindsay, comp.
Anthology of the American Negro in
the theatre. (1st edition) New York:
Publishers Company (1967)
PN2226 P3

Penn, Irvine Garland
The Afro-American press and its editors .... Springfield, Mass.: Willey & Company, 1891
PN4888 N4 P4

Petry, Ann (Lane)
Country place. Boston: Houghton Mifflin Company, 1947
PS3531 E933 C6

Harriet Tubman, conductor on the Underground Railroad. New York: Crowell (c1955)
PS3531 E933 H3 1955a (Education)

... The street. Boston: Houghton Mifflin Company (c1946)
PS3531 E933 S8 (Main, Undergraduate)

Tituba of Salem Village. New York: Crowell (1964)
PZ7 P44 T5 (Education)

Pitcher, Oliver
Dust of silence. New York: Troubador Press (c1958)
PS3531 I86 D8 1958

Powell, Herbert Preston
Gentlemen, be seated, a complete minstrel .... New York, Los Angeles: S. French, London: S. French, Ltd. (c1934)
PN4305 N6 P78

Minstrel maids and men .... New York, Los Angeles: S. French, Inc., London: S. French, Ltd., c1934
PN4305 N6 P79

The world's best book of minstrelsy. Philadelphia: The Penn Publishing Company, 1926
PN4305 N6 P8 (Social Work)

Reach, James
The darktown follies .... New York, Los Angeles, Calif.: S. French, London: S. French Ltd., c1936
PN4305 N6 R28

Redding, Jay Saunders
Stranger and alone. (1st edition) New York: Harcourt, Brace (c1950)
PS3535 E175 S7

To make a poet black. College Park, Maryland: McGrath Publishing Company (1968 c1939)
PS153 N5 R4 1939a

Reynolds, Harry
Minstrel memories .... London: A. Rivers, Ltd. (1928)
PN2582 N4 R4

Richardson, Willis
Plays and pageants from the life of the Negro. Washington, D. C.: The Associated Publishers, Inc. (c1930)
PS627 N4 R5

Rogers, Lettie (Hamlett)
Birthright. New York: Simon & Schuster, 1957
PS3535 O415 B5 1957

Rollins, Charlemae Hill
Famous American Negro poets. New York: Dodd, Mead, & Company (1965)
PS153 N5 R6

Rowe, George Clinton
Thoughts in verse.... Charleston, S. C.: Kahrs, Stolze & Welch, printers, 1887
PS2735 R75 T4 1887

Russell, Beth Duvall
On earth as it is. Boston: Christopher Publishing House (1963)
PS3535 U667 O5 1963

Sandle, Floyd L
The Negro in the American educational theatre: an organizational development, 1911-1964. 1st edition (Grambling? La.) 1964
PN3182 S3

Schuyler, George Samuel
Black and conservative; the autobiography of George S. Schuyler. New Rochelle, New York: Arlington House (1966)
PN4874 S36 A3

Simpson, George Eaton
The Negro in the Philadelphia press. Philadelphia: University of Pennsylvania Press, 1936
PN4899 P456

Another edition
PN4899 P4 S6 1936a

Smith, Lillian Eugenia
Killers of the dream. (1st edition) New York: W. W. Norton (1949)
PS3537 M653 K5 (Main, Social Work, Undergraduate)

Smith, William L G
Life at the South: or, "Uncle Tom's cabin" as it is ... Buffalo: George H. Derby & Company, 1852
PS2878 S358 L7 (Rare Book Collection)

Sontag, Susan
Against interpretation, and other essays. New York: Farrar, Strauss & Giroux (1966)
PN771 S64 1966 (Main, Undergraduate)

Sorrentino, Gilbert
Black and white. New York: Totem Press (1964)
PS3569 O7 B5 1964

Spivak, John Louis
Georgia nigger. New York: Brewer, Warren & Putnam, 1932
PS3537 P8 G4 1932

Stowe, Harriet Elizabeth (Beecher)
The annotated Uncle Tom's cabin. New York: P. S. Ereksson (1964)
PS2954 U5 1964 (Main, Undergraduate)

The key to Uncle Tom's cabin. New York: Arno Press, 1968
PS2954 U518 S7 1854a (Undergraduate)

Uncle Tom's cabin: or, Negro life in the slave states of America. (author's edition) London: T. Bosworth, 1852
PS2954 U5 1852

Styron, William
The confessions of Nat Turner. New York: Random House (1967)
PS3537 T98 C6 (Main, Undergraduate, Browsing Room)

Swift, Hildegarde (Hoyt)
North Star shining, a pictorial history of the American Negro. New York: W. Morrow & Company (1947)
PS3537 W658 N6

The railroad to freedom; a story of the Civil War.... New York: Harcourt, Brace & Company (1939, c1932)
PZ7 S978 R3 (Main, Education)

Tolson, Melvin Beaunorus
Harlem gallery. New York: Twayne. (1965- vol. I-
PS3539 O334 H3 1965

Libretto for the Republic of Liberia. New York: Twayne Publishing (1953)
PS3539 O334 L5 1953

Toomer, Jean
Cane. New York: Boni & Liveright (c1923)
EL140 T672

Townsend, George Alfred
Tales of the Chesapeake. New York: American News Company, 1880
PS3089 T4 T3 (Rare Book Collection)

Turner, Darwin T., ed.
Images of the Negro in America. Boston: D. C. Heath (1965)
PS508 N3 T8

Turner, Lorenzo Dow
Anti-slavery sentiment in American literature prior to 1865. Washington, D. C.: Association for the Study of Negro Life and History, Inc. (c1929)
PS169 S47 T8 1929

Another edition
PS169 S47 T8 1929a

U. S. Library of Congress. Gertrude Clarke Whittall Poetry and Literature Fund
The writer's experience (lectures by) Ralph Ellison and Karl Shapiro. Washington: United States Government Printing Office, 1964
PN149 U5 1964

Visscher, William Lightfoot
Blue grass ballads, and other verse. New York: H. M. Caldwell (c1900)
PS3543 I87 B5 1900a

Walker, Margaret
For my people. New Haven: Yale University Press (1945, c1942)
PS3545 A417 F6

Waring, Robert
As we see it. Washington, D. C.: Press of C. F. Sudwarth, 1910
PS3149 W4 A7 1910

Watkins, Ann,
Taken at the flood; the human drama as seen by modern American novelists. New York and London: Harper & Brothers (1946)
PZ1 W33 T13

itkins, Sylvester C, ed.
Anthology of American Negro literature.
New York: The Modern Library (1944)
PS508 N3 W3 (Main, Undergraduate)

Watts Writers' Workshop
From the ashes; voices of Watts. (New
York) New American Library (1967)
PS508 N3 W33 (Browsing Room, Social
Work)

Weatherby, William J
Out of hiding. (1st edition in the U.S.A.)
Garden City, New York: Doubleday,
1967 (c1966)
PR 6073 E2 O8 1967

Weeden, Miss Howard
Old voices .... New York: Doubleday,
Page & Company, 1904
PS3545 E38 O5 1904

Wheatley, Phillis (afterwards, Phillis
Peters)
**The poems of Phillis Wheatley, as they
were originally published in London,
1773.** Philadelphia: Republished by
R. R. & C. C. Wright, 1909
PS866 W5 P6 1909

**The poems of Phillis Wheatley, edited
by Julian D. Mason, Jr.** Chapel Hill:
University of North Carolina Press,
1966
PS866 W5 1966

**Poems on various subjects, religious
and moral ...** London: Printed for A.
Bell, bookseller, Algate, and sold by
Messers. Cox and Berry, King-street,
Boston. mdcclxxiii.
EL140 W56 1773 (Rare Book Collection)

White, Newman Ivey, ed.
**An anthology of verse by American
Negroes.** Durham, North Carolina:
Trinity College Press, 1924
EL116 W58

Whitman, Albery Allson
Not a man, and yet a man. Springfield,
Ohio: Republic Printing Company, 1877
PS3187 W2 N6 1877 (Rare Book
Collection)

Williams, John Alfred
Beyond the angry Black. (2nd edition)
New York: Cooper Square Publishing,
1966
PS509 N4 W5 1966 (Browsing Room)

The man who cried I am; a novel. (1st
edition) Boston: Little, Brown (1967)
PS3573 I28 M3 (Browsing Room)

Sissie. New York: Farrar, Straus, and
Cudahy (1963)
PS3573 I28 S5

Williamson, Joanne S
The glorious conspiracy. New York:
Knopf (1964, c1961)
PZ7 W728 G5 1964 (Education)

**William Styron's Nat Turner; ten Black
writers respond.** Edited by John Henrik
Clarke. Boston: Beacon Press (1968)
PS3537 T98 C618 W5

Woodson, J H Harmon
Negro orators and their orations. Washington, D. C.: The Associated Publishers, Inc., 1925
PS663 N4 W6

Woodson, Leroy Henry
**American Negro slavery in the works of
Friedrich Struberg, Friedrich Gerstäcker
and Otto Ruppius.** Washington: Catholic
University of America Press, 1949
PT35 C3 no. 22

Wright, Charles Stevenson
The messenger. New York: Farrar,
Straus and Cudahy (1963)
PS3573 R5 M4 (Browsing Room)

Wright, Richard
**Black boy, a record of childhood and
youth.** (1st edition) New York: Harper
(c1945)
PS3545 R86 Z5 (Home Economics)

Another edition
PS3545 R86 Z5 1945a (Main)

Another edition
PS3545 R86 Z5 1945b

Another edition
PS3545 R86 Z5 1945c (Main, Undergraduate)

Another edition
PS3545 R86 Z5 1950 (Browsing Room)

Eight men. (1st edition) Cleveland:
World Publishing Company (c1961)
PS3545 R86 E3 (Browsing Room)

Lawd today. New York: Walker (1963)
PS3545 R86 L3 1963a (Browsing Room)

The long dream, a novel. Garden City,
New York: Doubleday, 1958
PS3545 R86 L6 1958 (Browsing Room)

Native son. New York and London:
Harper & Brothers, 1940
PS3545 R86 N29 (Main, Undergraduate)

Another edition
PS3545 R86 N29 1940a (Undergraduate)

Another edition
PS3545 R86 N29 1940b (Main, Rare
Book Collection)

**Native son (the biography of a young
American) a play in ten scenes.** New
York and London: Harper & Brothers
(c1941)
PS3545 R86 N3

Negerjongen. Leiden: A. W. Sijtholf,
1947
PS3545 R86 Z516 D8 1947 (Rare Book
Collection)

The outsider (1st edition) New York:
Harper (1953)
PS3545 R86 O8 (Browsing Room,
Undergraduate)

Another edition
PS3545 R86 U5 1938a (Rare Book
Collection)

Uncle Tom's children, four novellas.
New York: Harper & Brothers, 1938
PS3545 R86 U5

Yerby, Frank
Benton's row. New York: Dial Press,
1954
PS3547 E7 B4 1954

Captain rebel. New York: Dial Press
(1956)
PS3547 E7 C3 1956

The devil's daughter. New York: Dial
Press, 1953
PS3547 E7 D4 1953

Floodtide. New York: Dial Press,
1950
PS3547 E7 F5 1950

The foxes of Harrow. New York: Dial
Press, 1946
PS3547 E7 F6 1946a (Browsing Room)

The golden hawk. New York: Dial
Press, 1948
PS3547 E7 G6 1948a

Another edition
PS3547 E7 G6 1951

Jarrett's jade, a novel. New York: Dial
Press, 1959
PS3547 E7 J3 1959a

Pride's castle. New York: Dial Press,
1949
PS3547 E7 P7 1949 (Browsing Room)

The Saracen blade, a novel. New York:
Dial Press, 1952
PS3547 E7 S3 1952

The serpent and the staff. New York:
Dial Press, 1958
PS3547 E7 S4 1958

BIOLOGY – RACE

Les Afro-Américaines. Dakar: IFAN,
1952 (i.e. 1953)
Q89 I55 no. 27

Boyd, William Clouser
Genetics and the races of man.... (1st
edition) Boston: Little, Brown, 1950
QH431 B7 (Botany & Zoology, Main,
Education)

Croly, David Goodman
**Miscegenation; the theory of the blend-
ing of the races, applied to the Ameri-
can white man and Negro....** New York:
H. Dexter, Hamilton & Company, 1864
HT1581 C94

Davis, Allison W
   Father of the Man: how your child gets
   his personality. Boston: Houghton
   Mifflin, 1947
   HQ772 D26 (Social Work, Main,
   Education)

Dobzhansky, Theodosius Grigorievich
   Heredity and the nature of man. (1st
   edition) New York: Harcourt, Brace &
   World (1964)
   QH431 D632 (Main, Botany & Zoology)

   Another edition
   QH431 D632 1964a

   Mankind evolving; the evolution of the
   human species. New Haven: Yale
   University Press, 1962
   QH368 D6 (Botany & Zoology, Main,
   Orton, Education, Undergraduate)

Dubois, William Edward Burghardt
   The health and physique of the Negro
   American. Atlanta, Georgia: The
   Atlanta University Press, 1906
   HT1521 A1 A8 no. 11

Fuller, John L
   Behavior genetics. New York: Wiley
   (c1960)
   QH431 F88 (Agriculture, Education,
   Botany & Zoology)

Gates, Reginald Ruggles
   Pedigrees of Negro families. Philadel-
   phia: Blakiston Company, 1949
   QH431 G3 (Main, Botany & Zoology)

Haller, Mark Hughlin
   Eugenics, hereditarian attitudes in
   American thought. New Brunswick,
   New Jersey: Rutgers University Press
   (1963)
   HQ753 H29

Herskovits, Melville Jean
   The American Negro: a study in racial
   crossing. New York: A. A. Knopf, 1928
   E185.89 A5 H4 (Social Work, Main)

   The anthropometry of the American
   Negro. New York: Columbia University
   Press, 1930
   E51 C7 vol. 11

Jones, Fred Nowell
   The explanations of physical phenom-
   ena given by white and Negro children.
   Baltimore, Maryland: William &
   Wilkins, c1945
   QL750 C73 vol. 18 no. 5 (Education)

Lewis, Julian Herman
   The biology of the Negro. Chicago: The
   University of Chicago Press (1942)
   GN57 N4 L6 (Main, Health Center)

Peterson, Joseph
   The comparative abilities of white and
   Negro children. (Baltimore: Williams &
   Wilkins Company, c1923)
   QL750 C73 v. 1, no. 5

Reuter, Edward Byron
   Race mixture; studies in intermarriage
   and miscegenation.... New York:
   Whittlesey House, McGraw-Hill Book
   Company, Inc., 1931
   GN237 R44 (Main, Botany & Zoology,
   Social Work)

Shapiro, Harry Lionel
   Race mixture. Paris: UNESCO (1953)
   GN237 S46

Smith, Samuel Stanhope
   An essay on the causes of the variety
   of complexion and figure in the human
   species. Cambridge: Harvard University
   Press, 1965
   GN353 S6 1965

Another edition
GN353 S6 1810 (Rare Book Collection)

Another edition
GN353 S6 1788 (Rare Book Collection)

Zimmermann, Arnold Albert
   Melanoblasts and melanocytes in fetal
   Negro skin. Urbana: University of
   Illinois Press, 1959
   QM484 Z5 (Health Center)

MEDICINE

Association of American Medical Colleges. Committee on the Resurvey of Preprofessional Education in the Liberal Arts College
Preparation for medical education, a restudy. New York: Blakiston Division, McGraw Hill (1961)
R745 A845 (Health Center)

Commission on Chronic Illness
Chronic illness in the United States. Cambridge: Published for the Commonwealth Fund by Harvard University Press, 1956-59. 4 vols.
RA407.3 C65 vol. 4 (Health Center)

Corwin, Edward Henry Lewinski
Opportunities for the medical education of Negroes. New York: C. Scribner's Sons, 1936
RA982 N5 H28

Dummett, Clifton Orrin, ed.
The growth and development of the Negro in dentistry in the United States. (Chicago?) National Dental Association (c1952)
E185.82 D8 (Health Center, Main)

Faris, Robert E Lee
Mental disorders in urban areas. Chicago: University of Chicago Press (c1939)
RC445 I28 F3
Another edition
RC445 I28 F3 1939a (Health Center, Social Work)

Fein, Rashi
Economics of mental illness. New York: Basic Books (c1958)
RC455 F4 (Social Work, Health Center)

Group for the Advancement of Psychiatry
Psychiatric aspects of school desegregation. New York, 1957
RC326 G7 no. 37 (Social Work, Health Center)

Hilleboe, Herman Ertresvaag
Preventive medicine. Philadelphia: Saunders, 1959
RA425 H6 (Health Center)

Another edition
RA425 H6 1965 (Health Center, Physical Education-Women, Pharmacy)

Hollingshead, August de Belmont
Social class and mental illness; a community study. New York: Wiley (c1958)
RC455 H6 (Main, Agriculture, Education, Health Center, Social Work, Undergraduate)

Joint Health Education Committee, Nashville
Rural Negro health; a report on a five-year experiment in health education in Tennessee. Nashville, Tennessee: Julius Rosenwald Fund, 1937
RA420 J74

Julius Rosenwald Fund
Negro hospitals. Chicago: Julius Rosenwald Fund, 1931
RA981 A45 J9

Lichello, Robert
Pioneer in blood plasma; Dr. Charles Richard Drew. New York: J. Messner (1968)
R154 D75 L5 (Health Center)

Malzberg, Benjamin
Migration and mental disease.... New York: Social Science Research Council, 1956
RC445 N68 M3 (Health Center)

Morais, Herbert Montfort
The history of the Negro in medicine. (1st edition) New York: Publishers Company, (1967)
R695 M6

Mossell, Sadie Tanner
A study of the Negro tuberculosis problem in Philadelphia. Philadelphia: Henry Phipps Institute, 1923
RC313 A57 M9

Negro health survey, Pittsburgh
Tuberculosis and the Negro in Pittsburgh. (Pittsburgh) Tuberculosis league of Pittsburgh, 1934
RC313 A57 N4

New York Association for Improving the Conditions of the Poor
Health work for mothers and children in a colored community. New York: Association for Improving the Conditions of the Poor (c1924)
RA448 N5 N55

Parker, Seymour
**Mental illness in the urban Negro
community.** New York: Free Press,
(c1966)
RC451.5 N4 P3 (Education, Social
Work)

Pasamanick, Benjamin, ed.
Social aspects of psychiatry ....
(Washington, D. C.:) American Psy-
chiatric Association, 1958
RC458 P3 (Social Work, Health
Center)

Peyton, Thomas Roy
Quest for dignity .... Los Angeles:
W. F. Lewis (1950)
R154 P4 A3

Another edition
R154 P4 A3 1963 (Social Work)

Reitzes, Dietrich Carl
Negroes and medicine. Cambridge:
Published for the Commonwealth Fund
by Harvard University Press, 1958
E185.82 R4 (Health Center, Main)

Riese, Hertha (Pataky)
**Heal the hurt child; an approach
through educational therapy with
special reference to the extremely
deprived Negro child.** Chicago: University of Chicago Press (1962)
RJ499 R5 (Health Center, Social Work,
Education)

Staupers, Mabel Keaton
No time for prejudice.... New York:
Macmillan (1961)
RT83.5 S7 (Health Center)

Studies on tuberculosis.... Baltimore:
The Johns Hopkins Press, 1941
RC315 J3 S9 (Health Center, Micro-
biology)

**Tuberculosis in white and Negro chil-
dren.** Cambridge: Published for the
Commonwealth Fund by Harvard University Press, 1958
RC312.6 C4 T8 (Health Center)

U. S. Public Health Service
**National Negro health week... the 11th
annual observance....** Washington:
United States Government Printing
Office, 1925-
RA431 U5

Wilson, Ernest B
The water supply of the Negro....
(Athens, Georgia, 1931)
RA592 G3 W7

AGRICULTURE

Bontemps, Arna Wendell
The story of George Washington Carver.
New York: Grosset & Dunlap (1954)
S417 C33 B6

Conference of state supervisors and
Negro teacher trainers in agricultural
education
**Regional conference of state super-
visors and Negro teacher trainers in
agricultural education.** Memphis,
Tennessee, 1928
S533 C74 1928

Elliot, Lawrence
**George Washington Carver, the man
who overcame.** Englewood Cliffs, New
Jersey: Prentice-Hall (1966)
S417 C33 E4

Evans, James A
**Extension work among Negroes con-
ducted by Negro agents, 1923.** Wash-
ington: (United States Government
Printing Office) 1925
S21 A812 no. 355

Graham, Shirley
   Dr. George Washington Carver, scientist. New York: Messner (1946, c1944)
   S417 C33 G7

Martin, Oscar Baker
   A decade of Negro extension work 1914-1924. (Washington: United States Government Printing Office, 1926)
   S21 A814 no. 72

Mercier, William Benjamin
   Extension work among Negroes, 1920. Washington: United States Government Printing Office, 1921
   S21 A812 no. 190

Scarborough, William Saunders
   Tenancy and ownership among Negro farmers in Southampton County, Virginia. Washington (United States Government Printing Office) 1926
   S21 A8 no. 1404

Wilkerson, Doxey Alphonso
   Agricultural extension services among Negroes in the South.... The Conference of Presidents of Negro Land-grant Colleges (1942)
   S533 W68

Williams, Louis Albion
   In memory of George Washington Carver (a funeral sermon). Cleveland, Ohio: The American Weave Magazine (1944)
   S417 C33 W5

VOCATIONAL TRAINING

Avedon, Richard
   Nothing personal. (New York: Atheneum, 1964)
   TR680* A89 (Browsing Room)

Berean manual training and industrial school, Philadelphia
   ... Annual conference. 3d-   1902 Philadelphia: n.p. (1903)-
   T171 B48

Carver, George Washington
   How to dry fruits and vegetables... (Tuskegee, Alabama: Tuskegee Institute) 1917
   TX609 C33

Lembezat, Bertrand
   Eve noire. Neuchatel: Editions Ides et Calendes (1952)
   TR675 L4

National Manpower Council
   Improving the work skills of the nation.. New York: Columbia University Press, 1955
   T73 N35 1955 (Main, Education)

Oliver, John William
   History of American technology. New York: Ronald Press Company (c1956)
   T21 O4 (History Graduate, Education, Architecture, Engineering-Metal, Mechanical-Engineering)

U. S. Federal Board for Vocational Education
   A study of home-economics education in teacher-training institutions for Negroes. Washington: United States Government Printing Office, 1923
   LC1045 A28 no. 79 (Main, Education)

   Vocational education in agriculture for Negroes. Washington: United States Government Printing Office, 1926
   LC1045 A28 no. 111 (Main, Education)

Washington, Ella Mae (Barnett)
   Color in dress for dark-skinned people. (Langstan? Oklahoma) c1949
   TT507 W3 1949

MILITARY

Lee, Irvin H
Negro Medal of Honor men. New York:
Dodd, Mead (1967)
UB433 L4 (Main, Undergraduate)

Lee, Ulysees Grant
The employment of Negro troops. Wash-
ington: Office of the Chief of Military
History, United States Army, 1966
D7669 U47 L37 (Main, Undergraduate)

Paynter, John Henry
Joining the Navy. Hartford: American,
1895
G440 P3

U. S. President's Committee on Equality
of Treatment and Opportunity in the
Armed Services
Freedom to serve. Washington: United
States Government Printing Office,
1950
UB412 A4 1950

BIBLIOGRAPHY

American Library Association. Library
Extension Board
Library service to Negroes. Chicago:
Committee on library extension, Ameri-
can Library Association, 1929
Z716 A514

Atlanta University. Library
Graduate theses of Atlanta University.
1931- . Compiled by Gaynelle Barksdale, reference librarian. Atlanta, 1944-
Z5055 U5 A75

Brooks, Alexander D
Civil rights and liberties in the United
States, an annotated bibliography ....
New York: Civil Liberties Educational
Foundation, c1962
Z7164 L6 B7 (Reference)

Brown, Warren
Check-list of Negro newspapers in the
United States (1827-1946). Jefferson
City, Missouri: Lincoln University,
School of Journalism, 1946
Z6944 N39 B8

Conference on the Library and Graduate
Instruction, Atlanta University, 1944
Conference on the library and graduate
instruction held under the auspices of
Atlanta University, June 14-20, 1944.
Atlanta, Georgia: Atlanta University
(1944)
Z675 U5 C75

Conference on the Role of the Library in
Improving Education in the South,
Atlanta University, 1965
The role of the library in improving
education in the South; papers, edited
with an introduction by Hallie Beachem
Brooks. Atlanta: Atlanta University,
School of Libraries Service, 1965
Z673 A1 C6 1965

Culturally disadvantaged; a bibliography
and key word out-of-context (KWOC)
index. (by) Robert S. Booth (and others)
Detroit: Wayne State University Press,
1967
Z5814 C52 C8 (Social Work)

Dodds, Barbara
Negro literature for high school stu-
dents. (Champaign, Illinois) National
Council of Teachers of English (1968)
Z1361 N39 D6

DuBois, William Edward Burghardt
A select bibliography of the Negro
America. Atlanta, Georgia: The
Atlanta University Press, 1905
HT1521 A1 A8 no. 10

Dumond, Dwight Lowell
A bibliography of antislavery in
America. Ann Arbor: University of
Michigan Press (1961)
Z1249 S6 D8

Ellis, Ethel M Vaughan
The American Negro: a selected check-
list of books. Washington, D. C.:
Negro Collection, Howard University
Library, 1968
Z1361 N39 E4

Fisk University, Nashville. Library
A list of manuscripts, published works
and related items in the Charles
Waddell Chesnutt collection of the
Erastus Milo Memorial Library. (Pre-
pared by Mildred Freeney and Mary T.
Henry. Nashville, 1954)
Z8166 F5

A select, classified, and briefly annotated list of two hundred fifty books by
or about the Negro, published during
the past ten years. 1939
Z1361 N39 G8

Foreman, Paul Breck
The Negro in the United States: a
bibliography. Stillwater (1947)
Z1361 N39 F6

Gleason, Eliza Valeria (Atkins)
The government and administration of
public library service to Negroes in
the South. Chicago, 1943
Z711.9 G45

The southern Negro and the public
library. Chicago: University of Chicago Press (1941)
Z711.9 G5 (Education)

Guzman, Jessie Parkhurst
Civil rights and the Negro, a list of
references relating to present day dis-
cussions. (Revised) Tuskegee Institute, Alabama: Tuskegee Institute.
Department of Records & Research,
1950
Z1361 N39 G87 1950

George Washington Carver, a classified bibliography. (Tuskegee Institute,
Alabama) Tuskegee Institute, Department of Records & Research, 1953
(i.e. 1954)
Z8150.7 G8 (Reference)

Haywood, Charles
A bibliography of North American folk-
lore and folksong. New York: Green-
berg (1951)
Z5981 H3 (Main, Music, English
Graduate)

Another edition
Z5981 H3 1961 (Reference, Music)

International Research Associates
Access to public libraries. Chicago:
American Library Association, 1963
Z711.9 I5

Index to selected periodicals received
in the Hallie Q Brown Library. 1950-
1959- Boston: G. K. Hall & Co.
Z1361 N39 I5 (Reference)

John, Janheinz
A bibliography of neo-African litera-
ture from Africa, America, and the
Carribean. New York: F. A. Praeger
(1965)
Z3508 L5 J31 (Reference)

Johnson, Preston Clarence
The education of Negroes in Virginia;
an annotated bibliography .... (n.p.,
1944)
Z1361 N39 J6

Koblitz, Minnie W
The Negro in schoolroom literature;
resource materials for the teacher of
kindergarten through the sixth grade.
(New York: Center for Urban Education,
1967?)
Z1037 K6 (Education)

Locke, Alain LeRoy
A decade of Negro self-expression.
(Charlottesville, Virginia) 1928
Z6514 N5 L8

Merriam, Alan P
A bibliography of jazz. Philadelphia:
American Folklore Society, 1954
ML128 J3 M4 (Music)

Miller, Elizabeth
The Negro in America: a bibliography...
Cambridge, Mass.: Harvard University
Press, 1966
Z1361 N39 M5

National Association for the Advancement of Colored People. Education
Department
Integrated school books; a descriptive
bibliography of 399 pre-school and
elementary school texts and story
books. New York: National Association
for the Advancement of Colored People
Special Contribution Fund, 1967
Z5814 D5 N3 (Education)

National Council of the Churches of
Christ in the United States of America.
Division of Christian Education
**Negro heritage resource guide; a biblio-
graphy of the Negro in contemporary
America.** (New York: Council Press,
c1967)
Z1361 N39 N16

National Urban League (for social service
among Negroes) Department of Research
Selected bibliography on the Negro.
Supplement to the 3rd edition, 1942
Z1361 N39 N2 1940 Supplement

The Negro in print. vol. 1- May 1965-
Washington: Negro Bibliographic Re-
search Center
Z1361 N39 N524 (Reference)

The Negro; a list of significant books,
1st- edition. New York: New York
Public Library, 1935
Z1361 N39 N5

New Jersey Library Association. Bibliography Committee
**New Jersey and the Negro; a biblio-
graphy, 1715 - 1966.** (Trenton) 1967
Z1361 N39 N526

New York (City) Public Library. Schom-
burg Collection of Negro Literature
**Dictionary catalog of the Schomburg
Collection of Negro literature and
history.** Boston: G. K. Hall, 1962.
9 vols.
Z1361* N39 N53 (Reference)
Supplement 1. 2 vols.

Porter, Dorothy (Burnett)
**North American Negro poets; a biblio-
graphical checklist of their writings,
1760-1944.** Hattiesburg, Miss.: The
Book Farm, 1945
Z1361 N39 P8

Pride, Armistead Scott
**Negro newspapers on microfilm: a
select list.** Washington, D. C.: Photo-
duplication Service, The Library of
Congress, 1953
Z6944 N39 P7

Reid, Ira De Augustine
**Negro youth, their social and economic
backgrounds; a selected bibliography
of unpublished studies, 1900-1938.**
Washington, D. C.: The American
Youth Commission of the American
Council on Education (c1939)
Z1361 N39 R35 (Education)

Rollins, Charlemae Hill
**We build together, a reader's guide to
Negro life and literature for elementary
and high school use ....** Chicago: The
National-Council of Teachers of
English (1941?)
Z1361 N39 R7 (Education)

Another edition
Z1361 N39 R7 1948 (Education)

Another edition
Z1361 N39 R7 1967 (Education)

Ross, Frank Alexander
A bibliography of Negro migration.
New York: Columbia University Press,
1934
Z1361 N39 R8 (History Graduate)

Russell Sage Foundation, New York.
Library
**Negro housing in towns and cities,
1927-1937.** New York: Russell Sage
Foundation (1937)
Z881 R96 no. 146

Rutgers University, New Brunswick,
N. J. Library
**The Negro and New Jersey; a check-
list of books, pamphlets, official
publications, broadsides, and disserta-
tions, 1754-1964, in the Rutgers University Library.** New Brunswick, 1965
Z1361 N39 R83

Salk, Erwin A
A layman's guide to Negro history....
Chicago: Quadrangle Books, 1966
Z1361 N39 S3

Another edition
Z1361 N39 S3 1967 (Reference, Undergraduate)

Spangler, Earl
**Bibliography of Negro history; selected
and annotated entries, general and
Minnesota.** Minneapolis: Ross and
Haines, 1963
Z1361 N39 S6 (History Graduate)

Thompson, Edgar Tristram
**Race and region, a descriptive biblio-
graphy compiled with special reference
to the relations between whites and
Negroes in the United States.** Chapel
Hill: University of North Carolina
Press, 1949
Z1361 N39 T48 (Reference)

Tuskegee Institute. Department of
Records and Research
**A selected list of references relating
to the elementary, secondary and higher education of Negroes, 1949 to June,
1955.** (Tuskegee, Institute, Ala.) 1955
Z1361 N39 T8 (Reference)

**A selected list of references relating
to the Negro teacher, 1949 to June,
1955.** (Tuskegee Institute, Ala.) 1955
Z1361 N39 T83

U. S. Library of Congress. Division of
Bibliography
**Fourteenth and fifteenth amendments
and Negro suffrage.**
Z1361 N39 U6

**Select list of references on the Negro
question.**
Z1361 N39 U61

Another edition
Z1361 N39 U62

Voorhoeve, Jan
**Bibliographie du negro-anglais du
Surinam.** 's - Gravenhage, M. Nijhoff,
1963
Z1808 L5 V6

Weinberg, Meyer
School integration. Chicago: Integrated
Education Associates, 1967
Z5814 D5 W4 (Education, Reference,
Social Work)

Another edition
Z5814 D5 W4 1967a (Education)

Welsch, Erwin K
**The Negro in the United States: a re-
search guide.** Bloomington, Indiana:
Indiana University Press, 1964
Z1361 N39 W37

Another edition
Z1361 N39 W37 1965 (Main, Reference,
Undergraduate)

Whiteman, Maxwell
**A century of fiction by American
Negroes, 1853-1952.** Philadelphia:
Saifer, 1955
Z1361 N39 W4 (Reference)

Another edition
Z1361 N39 W4 1955a

Wilberforce University, Wilberforce,
Ohio. Library
**The Levi Jenkins Coppin collection at
Carnegie Library, Wilberforce Univer-
sity, Wilberforce, Ohio.** Compiled by
Casper LeRoy Jordon. Wilberforce,
Ohio: Wilberforce University, 1957
Z1361 N39 W5

Work, Monroe Nathan
**A bibliography of the Negro in Africa
and America.** New York: Wilson, 1928
Z1361 N39 W9 (Reference)

RECENTLY ACQUIRED

Abramson, Doris E
Negro playwrights in the American theatre, 1925-1959. New York: Columbia University Press, 1969

Allen, James Egert
The Negro in New York. (1st edition) New York: Exposition Press, 1964

Aptheker, Herbert
The Negro today. New York: Marzani & Munsell, 1962

Barrett, William Edmund
Lilies of the field. (1st edition) Garden City, New York: Doubleday, 1962
Precat A30633

Bayley, David M
Minorities and the police; confrontation in America. New York: Free Press, 1968

Bayton, James A
Tension in the cities: three programs for survival. Philadelphia (etc.) Chilton Book Company (1969)

Bedau, Hugo Adam
Civil disobedience theory and practice. New York: Pegasus (c1969)

Bell, Inge Powell
CORE and the strategy of nonviolence. New York: Random House (1968)

Berstein, Barton J
Twentieth century America: recent interpretations.... New York: Harcourt, Brace & World, Inc. (1969)

Black protest pamphlets; a compendium. New York: Arno Press, 1969
Precat A33063

Blair, Lewis Harvie
A southern prophecy. Boston: Little, Brown, 1964
Precat A29076

Bledsoe, Thomas
Or we'll all hang separately: the High-lander idea. Boston: Beacon Press (c1969)

Bloch, Charles J
The states rights: the law of the land. Atlanta, Georgia: Harrison, 1958
Precat A26970

Botkin, Benjamin Albert
Lay my burden down: a folk history of slavery. Chicago: University of Chicago Press, 1945
Precat A28697

Bradford, Amory
Oakland's not for burning. New York: McKay, 1968

Bryant, Lawrence C, ed.
Negro law-makers in the South Carolina Legislature, 1868-1902. Orangeburg, South Carolina: South Carolina State College, School of Graduate Studies, 1968

Brewer, John Mason
Worser days and bitter times. Chicago: Quadrangle, 1965
Precat A29525

Burgess, Alan
The word for love. New York: E. P. Dutton & Company, Inc., 1968

Business leadership and the Negro crisis. Edited by Eli Ginzberg. New York: McGraw-Hill (1968)

Clayton, Edward T
Martin Luther King: the peaceful warrior. Englewood Cliffs: Prentice-Hall, 1964

Cleage, Albert B
The black messiah. New York: Sheed, 1968

Cook, Mercer
The militant black writer in Africa and the United States. Madison: University of Wisconsin Press, 1969

Cotter, Joseph Seamon
Caleb, the degenerate. New York: Harrison, 1940
Precat AO8202

Coulter, E Merton
Negro legislators in Georgia during the Reconstruction period. Athens: Georgia Historical Society, 1968

Decker, Sunny
An empty spoon. New York: Harper &
Row, Publishers (c1969)

Dialogue on violence. (Edited by George
Vickers) Indianapolis: Bobbs-Merrill
Company, Inc. (1968)

Dixon, Thomas
The black hood. New York: D. Apple-
ton & Company, 1924
Precat AO9557

Dodson, Owen
Boy at the window, a novel. New York:
Farrar, Straus & Young (1951)
Precat AO4226

Dubois, William Edward Burghardt
John Brown. New York: International
Publishers (1962)
Precat A29928

In battle for peace. New York: Masses
and Mainstream, 1952
Precat A13620

Eisenstadt, Murray
The Negro in American life. New York
& Los Angeles: Oxford Book Company
(c1968)

Etzkowitz, Henry
Ghetto crisis: riots or reconciliation?
Boston: Little, Brown & Company
(c1969)

Fauset, Jessie Redmon
The Chinaberry tree. New York:
Frederick A. Stokes Company, 1931
Precat AO7367

Feur, Lewis S
The conflict of generations: the character and significance of student
movements. New York: Basic Books
(c1969)

Flipper, Henry O
The colored cadet at West Point. New
York: H. Lee, 1878 (Reprint by John-
son, 1969)

Foote, John Taintor
Alister Jones. New York: Appleton,
1927 (c1913)
Precat A13102

Four fugitive slave narratives .... Reading, Mass.: Addison-Wesley Publishing
Company (c1969)

Freed, Leonard
Black in white America. New York:
Grossman Publishing (1968?)

Gillard, Rev. John Thomas
Colored Catholics in the United States.
Baltimore, Maryland: The Josephite
Press, 1941
Precat A30918

Gittell, Marilyn
The politics of urban education. New
York: Praeger, 1969

Gittings, James A
Life without living: people of the inner
city. Philadelphia: Westminster Press,
1966
Precat X129 (Social Work)

Glock, Charles Y, comp.
Prejudice U. S. A. New York:
Praeger (1969)

Goode, Kenneth G
From Africa to the United States and
then ... a concise Afro-American
history. (Glenview, Illinois) Scott,
Foresman & Company (c1969)

Graduate opportunities for black students, 1969-1970. Edited by Julie
Paynter. Chicago: Graduate opportunities for Black Students, 1969

Graham, Shirley
The story of Phillis Wheatley. New
York: Messner, 1949
Precat A30692

Gurin, Gerald
Inner-city Negro youth in a job training
project: a study of factors related to
attrition and job success. Final report
to the Manpower Administration, U. S.
Dept. of Health, Education and Welfare. Ann Arbor: Institute for Social
Research, the University of Michigan,
1968

Handlin, Oscar
Booker T. Washington and the Negro's
place in American life. Boston: Little
Brown, 1955
Precat A25511

Hansberry, Lorraine
The movement: documentary of a struggle for equality. New York: Simon & Schuster, 1964
Precat A30699

Harris, M A
A Negro tour of Manhattan. New York: Greenwood Press, 1968

Harris, Marvin
Patterns of race in the Americas. New York: Walker & Company, 1964

Harrison, Delores
We shall live in peace: the teachings of Martin Luther King. (1st edition) New York: Hawthorne Books (1968)

Harvard Educational Review
Equal educational opportunity. Cambridge: Harvard University Press, 1969

Helper, Rose
Racial policies and practices of real estate brokers. Minneapolis: University of Minnesota Press (c1969)

Henson, Matthew A
A black explorer at the North Pole: an autobiographical report.... New York: Walker & Company, 1969

Heyer, Robert
Am I a racist? Glen Rock, New Jersey: Paulist Press, New York: Association Press (1969)

Hicks, John
The long whip. New York: David McKay Company, Inc. (c1969)

Hill, Roscoe, comp.
Affirmative school integration; efforts to overcome de facto segregation in urban schools. Beverly Hills, Calif.: Sage Publishing (1969)

Hill, Roy L
Carrie J. Carroll, and other poems. Philadelphia: Dorrance, 1962
Precat A29712

Himes, Chester
Blind man with a pistol. New York: Morrow, 1969

Hoover, Dwight W, comp.
Understanding Negro history. Chicago: Quadrangle Books (c1968)

Howard University. Graduate School
The new Negro, thirty years afterward. Washington: Howard University Press, 1955
Precat A29364

Hughes, Langston
La poesie negro-américaine. Paris: Seghers, 1966
Precat A29266

Montage of a dream deferred. New York: Holt, 1951
Precat A30919

Hurston, Zora Neale
Seraph on the Suwanee. New York: Charles Scribner's Sons, 1948
Precat AO9530

Their eyes were watching God, a novel. Philadelphia, London: J. B. Lippincott, c1937
Precat AO4498

Jackson, Booker T
God looks down.... Fort Smith, Ark.: South & West, Inc., 1968

Jackson, Mahalia
Movin' on up: the Mahalia Jackson story. New York: Hawthorn, 1966
Precat A28722

Jacobs, Mrs. Harriet
Incidents in the life of a slave girl. Boston: author, 1861
(Apply Rare Book Collection)

Jay, William
Inquiry into the character and tendency of the American colonization, and American Anti-Slavery societies. 6th edition. New York: Negro University Press, 1969 (1838)
Precat A30573

Kalven, Harry
The Negro and the first amendment. Chicago: University of Chicago Press (1966, c1965)
Precat A28622

Keech, William R
The impact of Negro voting; the role of the vote in the quest for equality. New York: Rand McNally, 1968

King, Martin Luther
The measure of a man. Boston: Pilgrim Press, 1968

The trumpet of conscience. New York: Harper & Row (c1967, 1968)

Lakos, Lionel
A house divided: the life and legacy of Martin Luther King. New Rochelle, N. Y.: Arlington House, 1968

Larkins, John Rudman
Alcohol and the Negro: explosive issue. North Carolina: Record Publishing Company, 1965
Precat A30826

Levitan, S A
Youth employment act. Kalamazoo, Michigan: Upjohn Institute for Employment Research, 1963
Precat X409 (Commerce)

Logan, Rayford Whittingham
The Negro in the United States: a brief review. Princeton, New Jersey: Van Nostrand, 1957
Precat A29926

Lomas, Charles
The agitator in American society. Englewood Cliffs, New Jersey: Prentice Hall, 1968

McCall, Dan
The example of Richard Wright. New York: Harcourt, Brace & World (1969)

Macy Conference on Negroes for Medicine, Fort Lauderdale, Florida, 1968
Negroes for medicine (by) Lee Cogan. Report of a conference. Published for Josiah Macy Foundation by Johns Hopkins Press, Baltimore, Maryland (1968)
Precat A31028

Mahoney, William
Black Jacob. New York: Macmillan, 1969

Mahood, H R, comp.
Urban politics and problems: a reader. New York: Charles Scribner's Sons (1969)

Major, Clarence, ed.
The new black poetry. (1st edition) New York: International Publishers (c1969)

Malvin, John
North into freedom; the autobiography of John Malvin. Cleveland: Press of Case Western, 1966
Precat A28714

Margolies, Edward
The art of Richard Wright. Carbondale, Illinois: Southern Illinois University Press, 1969

Masotti, Louis H, comp.
Riots and rebellion; civil violence in the urban community. New York: Sage Publications, 1968

Maston, Thomas Bufford
Segregation and desegregation: a christian approach. New York: Macmillan, 1959
Precat A30169

Meir, August, comp.
The making of Black America; essays in Negro life and history. New York: Atheneum, 1969

Mellon, Matthew T
Early American views on Negro slavery; from the letters and papers of the founders of the republic. New York: Bergman (c1969)

Moore, Jenny
The people on second street. New York: William Morrow & Company, Inc., 1968

Nathan, Richard P
Jobs and civil rights; the role of the Federal Government in promoting equal opportunity in employment and training. Washington, D. C.: Brookings Institute, 1969

Nelson, Bernard Hamilton
The fourteenth amendment and the Negro since 1920. New York: Russell & Russell, 1946
Precat A29859

One year later; an assessment of the nation's response to the crisis described by the National Advisory Commission on Civil Disorders, Urban America, Inc., and The Urban Coalition .... New York: Praeger Publishers (1969)

Oppenheimer, Martin
The urban guerrilla. Chicago: Quadrangle Books (1969)

Orfield, Gary
The reconstruction of southern education: the schools and the 1964 Civil
Rights Act. New York: Wiley-Inter-
science (1969)

Parks, Gordon
Gordon Parks: a poet and his camera.
New York: Viking Press, 1968

Pease, William Henry
Black Utopia: Negro communal exper-
iments in America. Madison: State
Historical Society of Wisconsin, 1963
Precat A28748

Pinkney, Alphonso
Black Americans. Englewood Cliffs,
New Jersey: Prentice-Hall, 1968

Pool, Rosey E, comp.
Beyond the blues. Kent, England: Hand
& Flower Press, 1962
Precat A2915

Porter, Gladys L
Three Negro pioneers in beauty culture.
New York: Vantage, 1966
Precat A29728

Powell, Adam Clayton
Marching blacks. New York: Dial Press,
1945
Precat A25500

Preston, Edward
Martin Luther King: fighter for freedom.
New York: Doubleday & Company, Inc.
(1968)

Pride, Armistead S
The Black press: a bibliography ...
Prepared for Association for Education
in Journalism Ad Hoc Committee on
Minority Education, Jefferson City,
Missouri: Lincoln University, 1968

Quarles, Benjamin
Black abolitionists. New York: Oxford
University Press, 1969

Race and science: the race question in
modern science. New York: Columbia
University Press, 1961

Rogers, Joel Augustus
Nature knows no color line. 3rd edition
New York: Helga M. Rogers, 1952
Precat A303418

Sex and race. New York: J. A. Rogers,
1942-44. 3 vols.
Precat A30141

Rosenbloom, Richard S, comp.
Social innovation in the city; new enterprises for community development.
Cambridge: Harvard University Press,
1969

Russell, Jean
God's lost cause: a study of the church
and the racial problem. (London) SCM
Press, Ltd. (1968)

Savage, Henry
Seeds of time, the background of
Southern thinking. 1st edition New
York: Holt, 1959
Precat A27002

Schlesinger, Arthur M
The crisis of confidence: ideas, power
and violence in America. Boston:
Houghton Mifflin, 1969

Nothing stands still: essays.... Cambridge: Harvard University Press, 1969

Schoener, Allon, comp.
Harlem on my mind: cultural capital of
Black America 1900-1968. New York:
Random House (c1968)

Schoenfeld, Seymour J
The Negro in the Armed Forces: his
value and status - past, present, and
potential. Washington: Associated
Publishers, 1945
Precat A25114

Schulz, David A
Coming up Black: patterns of ghetto
socialization. Englewood Cliffs, New
Jersey: Prentice-Hall, Inc. (c1969)

Scott, Benjamin
The coming of the Black man. Boston:
Beacon Press (c1969)

Segal, Ronald
The Americans: a conflict of creed and
reality. New York: The Viking Press
(1969)

Shapiro, Fred C
  Race riots. New York: Crowell, 1964
  Precat A28750

Whitmore. Indianapolis and New York:
  The Bobbs-Merrill Company (1969)

Shuman, R Baird
  Nine black poets: edited and with an
  introduction by R. B. Shuman. Durham
  North Carolina: Moore Publishing Company, 1968

Silvera, John D
  The Negro in World War II. (n.p.)
  (Apply Circulation Desk)

Sleeper, C Freeman
  Black power and Christian responsibility; some Biblical foundations for
  social ethics. Nashville, Tennessee:
  Abingdon Press, 1969

The social implications of early Negro
  music in the United States. New York:
  Arno Press & the New York Times,
  1969

Spangler, Earl
  The Negro in Minnesota. Minneapolis:
  Denison, 1961
  Precat A28699

Spence, Raymond
  Nothing black but a cadillac. New York:
  G. P. Putnam's Sons, 1969

Stampp, Kenneth M, comp.
  Reconstruction: an anthology of revis-
  ionist writings. Baton Rouge: Louisiana State University Press (1969)

Stearns, Marshall
  Jazz dance; the story of American
  vernacular dance. New York: Macmillan, 1968

Strother, Horatio T
  The Underground Railroad in Connecti-
  cut. Middletown: Wesleyan University
  Press, 1962
  Precat A28721

Thornbrough, Emma Lou, comp.
  Booker T. Washington. Englewood
  Cliffs, N.J.: Prentice-Hall, 1969

Tucker, Sterling
  Beyond the burning: life and death of
  the ghetto. New York: Association
  Press, 1968

Tuckman, Bruce W
  Preparing to teach the disadvantaged;
  approaches to teacher education. New
  York: Free Press, 1969

Turner, Darwin
  Black literature; essays.... Columbus,
  Ohio: Charles E. Merrill Publishing
  Company (1969)

Turpin, Waters Edward
  These low grounds. New York, London:
  Harper & Brothers, 1937
  Precat A25692

Ullman, Victor
  Look to the North star: a life of William
  King. Boston: Beacon Press (c1969)

The urban crisis: a symposium on the
  racial problem in the inner city. Edited
  by David McKenna. Grand Rapids,
  Michigan: Zondervan Publishing House
  (c1969)

Van Vechten, Carl
  Nigger heaven. New York: Alfred Knopf,
  1926
  Precat AO4751

Von Hoffman, Nicholas
  Two, three, many more. Chicago:
  Quadrangle Books (1969)

Wassing, René S
  African art; its background and tradi-
  tions. New York: Abrams, 1968

Weatherford, Willis Duke
  American churches and the Negro.
  North Quincy, Mass.: Christopher Pub-
  lishing House, 1957
  Precat A29366 (Main, Social Work)

Weaver, Richard M
  The southern tradition a bay.... New
  Rochelle, New York: Arlington House
  (1969)

White, Newman Ivey
  An anthology of verse by American
  Negroes: edited with a critical introduction, biographical sketches of the
  authors and bibliographical notes....
  Durham, North Carolina: Moore Publishing Company, 1968

Wipple, Charles King
  Relation of the American Board of Commissioners for Foreign Missions to slavery. New York: Negro University Press, 1969
  Precat A30575

Wirt, Frederick M, comp.
  New dimensions of freedom in America. San Francisco, California: Chandler Publishing Company (1969)

Wish, Harvey, ed.
  Slavery in the south: first-hand accounts of the Antebellum American Southland. New York: Farrar-Straus, 1964
  Precat A30461

Wood, Forest G
  Black scare; the racist response to emancipation and reconstruction. Berkeley: University of California Press, 1968

Wright, Sarah E
  The child's gonna live. (New York) Delacorte Press (c1969)

Yerby, Frank
  The treasure of pleasant valley. New York: Dial Press, 1955
  Precat A28768

  The vixens, a novel. New York: Dial Press, 1947
  Precat AO5245

  A woman called Fancy. New York: Dial Press, 1951
  Precat AO5556

Young, Whitney Moore
  Beyond racism: building an society. New York :McGraw-Hill, 1969

AUTHOR AND PERSONAL NAME INDEX

Franklin, Charles Lionel 113
Franklin, John Hope 25, 60, 75, 79
Frazier, Edward Franklin 5, 25, 79, 100
Fredrickson, George M. 60
Freed, Leonard 170
Freedom of Information Conference 26
Freeman, Frederick 60
French, Mrs. A. M. 60
Freuchen, Peter 150
Friedman, Leon 26, 113
Friends, Society of.... 26, 60
Friese, Philip C. 113
Fromm, Erich 5
Frontiers of America. Columbus Chapter, 79
Frost, Joe L. 123
Fuchs, Estelle 123
Fuller, John L. 161
Furnas, Joseph Chamberlain 60

-G-

Gaines, Ernest J. 150
Gaines, Francis Pendleton 79
Gallagher, Buell Gordon 26
Galloway, Oscar Fitzgerald 123
Gannett, Henry 26
Gara, Larry 61
Garfinkel, Herbert 26
Garn, Stanley M. 88
Garner, James Wilford 79
Garraty, John A. 113
Garrison, William Lloyd 60, 61, 62, 64, 66, 71
Garvey, Amy Jacques 26
Garvey, Marcus 26
Gates, Reginald Ruggles 161
Gates, Robbins L. 123
Genovese, Eugene D. 61
George, James Zachariah 61
George, Wesley Critz 26
Georgia. Governor, 1917-1921 (Hugh M. Dorsey) 79
Gibbs, Mifflin Wistar 27
Gibson, Althea 89
Gibson, John William 27
Giddings, Joshua Reed 61
Gilbert, Douglas 137
Gilbert, Olive 61
Gilbertson, Catherine (Peebles) 150
Giles, Hermann Harry 123
Gill, John 61
Gillard, Rev. John Thomas 5, 170
Gillette, William 113
Gilligan, Francis James 27
Gilmore, Harlan Welch 100
Gilmore, James Roberts 151
Ginzberg, Eli 27, 92
Ginzburg, Ralph 100
Gist, Noel Pitts 100
Gittell, Marilyn 123, 170
Gittings, James A. 170
Gladden, Edward Erwin 113
Gladden, Washington 79
Glazer, Nathan 51, 80
Gleason, Eliza Valeria (Atkins) 166
Glick, Paul C. 108

Glock, Charles Y. 170
Gloster, Hugh Morris 151
Glueck, Sheldon 108
Goff, Kenneth 27
Goff, Regina Mary 51
Goffin, Robert 137
Gold, Robert S. 137
Goldberg, Isaac 137
Golden, Harry Lewis 27
Goldman, Freda H. 123
Goldner, William 92
Goldstein, Naomi 27
Golsten, Robert C. 27
Goldwin, Robert Allen 27, 123
Goode, Kenneth G. 170
Goodell, Walter 137
Goodell, William 61
Goodlett, Carlton Benjamin 3
Goodloe, Daniel Reaves 61
Goodman, Mary Ellen 3
Goodwin, Daniel Raynes 61
Gordon, Armistead Churchill 151
Gordon, Asa H. 27
Gordon, Edmund W. 123
Gordon, Milton Myron 100
Gordon, Mitchell 100
Gore, George William 123
Gosnell, Harold Foote 113
Gossett, Thomas F. 12
Gowan, John Curtis 124
Grabill, Wilson H. 108
Graham, Hugh Davis 27
Graham, Lorenz 151
Graham, Shirley 61, 137, 164, 170
Grambs, Jean Dresden 124
Grant, Joanne 27
Gray, Susan Walton 124
Gray, William Herbert 124
Grayson, William John 61, 80, 151
Greeley, Horace 61
Green, Constance (McLaughlin) 27, 80, 100
Green, Mrs. Elizabeth Atkinson (Lay) 151
Green, Paul 151
Green, Robert Lee 124
Greenberg, Jack 113
Greene, Harry Washington 27, 124
Greene, Lorenzo Johnston 27, 113
Greene, Mary Francis 124
Greenhut, Melvin Leonard 92
Greer, Scott 92
Gregoire, Henri 100
Gregory, Dick 27, 151
Gregory, James Monroe 61
Gregory, John Walter 100
Grier, Eunice 28
Grier, William H. 28
Griffin, John Howard 28
Griffin, John N. 151
Griffiths, Julia 61
Grimes, Alan Pendleton 114
Grimke, Archibald Henry 62
Grisson, Mary Allen 138
Griswold, Erwin Nathaniel 114
Grodzius, Morton 51
Gross, Bella 28
Gross, Seymour 151
Grossack, Martin M. 28

Magidoff, Robert 155
Mahoney, William 172
Mahood, Harry Richard 172
Maier, Henry William 115
Mailer, Norman 102
Major, Clarence 172
Malvin, John 172
Malzberg, Benjamin 162
Manas, John Helen 35
Mandel, Bernard 65
Mandelbaum, David Goodman 35
Mangum, Charles Staples 35
Maningault, G. 13
Mannix, Daniel Pratt 102
Marcus, Lloyd 13
Marden, Charles Frederick 13
Margolies, Edward 155, 172
Mark, Mary Louise 35
Marrow, Alfred Jay 102
Marzh, J. B. T. 139
Marshall, Burke 35
Marshall, F. Ray 35
Marshall, Herbert 155
Martin, Asa Earl 78
Martin, Fletcher 35
Martin, John Bartlow 35
Martin, Oscar Baker 162
Martin, Roscoe Coleman 115, 164
Martyn, Carlos 65
Marx, Gary Trade 35, 102
Maryland. Morgan State College,
  Baltimore 128
Maslow, Will 128
Mason, Philip 102
Masotti, Louis H. 172
Massachusetts. Commission Against
  Discrimination 103
Massie, James William 65
Maston, Thomas Bufford 172
Masuoka, Jitsuichi 103
Mathews, Basil Joseph 35
Mathews, Donald G. 65
Matlack, Lucius 66
Matthews, Donald R. 35
Matthews, Joseph Brown 35
May, Edgar 109
May, Sammuel Joseph 66
Mayer, Edith H. 35
Mayerson, Charlotte Leon 51
Mayhew, Leon H. 93
Mayo, Amory Dwight 128
Mayo, Marion Jacob 4
Mayor's Conference on Race Relations,
  Chicago 35
Mays, Benjamin Elijah 6, 155
Mays, Willie 89
Mazyck, Walter H. 13
Means, Eldred Jurtz 155
Mecklin, John Moffat 35
Meece, Leonard Ephraim 128
Meier, August 35, 172
Meldon, Charles Manly 35
Mellen, George W. F. 66
Mellon, Matthew Taylor 66, 172
Melone, Thomas 155
Meltzer, Milton 36, 66
Mendelson, Wallace 36
Mercier, William Benjamin 164

Meredith, James Howard 128
Merkel, Benjamin 66
Merriam, Alan P. 166
Merrick, John 15
Merrill, Walter McIntosh 66
Merriman, George Spring 66
Merton, Robert King 109
Merton, Thomas 6
Mes, G. M. 9
Metcalf, George R. 36
Metfessel, Milton Franklin 139
Meyerson, Martin 93
Mezzrow, Milton 139
Michael, Donald N. 93
Michael, W. E. 128
Michigan Employment Security
  Commission 43
Mid-Century White House Conference on
  Children and Youth 109
Millea, Thomas V. 51
Miller, Abie 36
Miller, Arthur Selwyn 128
Miller, Elizabeth 166
Miller, Harry L. 128
Miller, Herman Phillip 93
Miller, Kelly 36, 82, 128
Miller, Loren 115
Miller, Robert Moats 109
Miller, Warren 155
Miller, William Robert 36, 103
Millspaugh, Martin 93
Minor, Richard Clyde 82
Mira de Amescua, Antonio 155
Missouri. Negro Industrial Commission 93
Mitchell, Glenford E. 36
Mitchell, James B. 93
Mitchell, Loften 155
Moellering, Ralph Luther 6
Moffat, Adelene 103
Montgomery, Harry Earl 109,
Moon, Bucklin 36
Moon, Henry Lee 115
Mooney, Chase Curran 9, 36
Moore, George Henry 66
Moore, Jenny 172
Moore, Truman E. 94
Morais, Herbert Montfort 162
Moran Lopez, Fernando 156
Morand, Paul 88, 156
Morgan, Alun 139
Morrow, Everett Frederic 75
Morris, Willie 36
Morse, Jedidiah 66
Morton, Lena Beatrice 156
Morton, Richard Lee 75
Mose, Ashriel L. 128
Mossell, Sadie Tanner 162
Motley, Willard 156
Morton, Robert Russa 9, 36
Mott, Lucretia 58
Mphahlele, Ezekiel 88
Muelder, Hermann Richard 66
Mundy, Paul William 109
Murchison, Carl 109
Murphy, Beatrice M. 156
Murphy, Edgar Gardner 109
Murphy, John C. 109
Murphy, Raymond John 36

Murray, Pauli 36
Muse, Benjamin 36, 128
Myers, Gustavus 6
Myrdal, Gunnar 37, 94

-N-

Nathan, George Jean 156
Nathan, Hans 39
Nathan, Richard P 172
Nathans, Elizabeth 115
National Advisory Commission on
Civil Disorders 103
National Association for the Advance-
ment of Colored People 37, 42, 89,
103, 115, 166
National Association of Intergroup
Relations Officials. Commission on
School Integration 128
National Association of Manufacturers of
the United States of America 94
National Committee on Segregation in
the Nation's Capital 37
National Community Relations Advisory
Council 94
National Conference of Social Work 109
National Conference on Equal Employ-
ment Opportunity 115
National Conference on Fundamental
Problems in the Education of
Negroes 37, 128
National Conference on Small
Business 37
National Conference on the Christian
Way of Life 37
National Conference on the Problems of
the Negro and Negro Youth 37
National Council of Teachers of English.
Task Force on Teaching English to
the Disadvantaged 129
National Council of the Churches of
Christ in the United States of
America Div. of Christian Ed. 167
National Council of Women of the United
States. Human Relations Committee 13
National cyclopedia of the colored
race 37
National Education Association, Com-
mission on Professional Rights and
Responsibilities 129
National Industrial Conference Board 37
National Manpower Council 94, 164
National NEA-PR&R Conference on Civil
and Human Rights in Education 129
National Negro Health News 37
National Opinion Research Center 94
National Scholarship Service and Fund
for Negro Students 129
National Urban League 37, 94, 109, 167
Nearing, Scott 103
Neely, Alvin J. 129
Neff, Lawrence Wilson 37
Nell, William Cooper 73
Nelson, Bernard Hamilton 172
Nelson, Dennis Denmark 38
Nelson, John Herbert 156
Nelson, Rose K. 139

Nelson, Truman John 38, 82, 156
Nelson, William Stuart 7
New England Education Commission
For Freedmen 66
New Jersey Conference of Social Work.
Interracial Committee 103
New Jersey Library Association
Bibliography Committee 167
New York Association for Improving the
Conditions of the Poor 162
New York (City) City Commission on
Human Rights 94
New York (City) Interdepartmental
Neighborhood Service Center 109
New York (City) New School for
Social Research 94
New York (City) Public Library
Schomburg Collection of Negro
Literature 167
New York (State) States Commission
Against Discrimination 38
New York (State) University. Bureau of
Guidance 129
New York (State) University. Commis-
sioner's Advisory Committee on
Human Relations and Community
Tensions 129
New York Herald Tribune 103
Newark, New Jersey, Mayor's Commis-
sion on Group Relations 103
Newbold, Nathan, Carter 129
Newby, Idus A. 38
Newcomb, Harvey 38
Newman, Dorothy (Krall) 38
Newsome, Albert Ray 38
Nicol, Helen (Osterrieth) 94
Nicholls, William H. 82
Nichols, Charles Harold 66
Nichols, Lee 38
Nichols, Roy Franklin 66
Niebuhr, Helmut Richard 7
Niles, John Jacob 140
Nilson, Charles H. 156
Nilsson, Tore 89
Noar, Gertrude 129
Noble, Jeanne L. 129
Noble, Stuart Grayson 129
Nolan, William A. 38
Nolen, Claude H. 38
Norfleet, Marvin Brooks 129
Norgren, Paul Herbert 39, 94
Norman, Loyal Vernon 129
Norris, Hoke 39
North Carolina. Governor's Commission
for the Study of Problems in the Edu-
cation of Negroes in North Carolina
129
North Carolina. State Board of Public
Welfare 39
North Carolina. University Institute of
Government 129
Northrup, Herbert Roof 39
Northrup, Solomon 66
Northwood, Lawrence King 51
Nowlin, William Felbert 115
Nye, Russel Blaine 66

Tyler, Leona E.   4
Tyson, Elisa   71
Tyson, John Shoemaker   71

-U-

Ulanov, Barry   141
Ullman, Victor   174
United Nations Educational Scientific
 and Cultural Organization   89
United States Bureau of Education   133
United States Bureau of Public
 Assistance   111
United States Bureau of the Census   111
United States Business and Defense
 Service Administration   45
United States Census Office   111
United States Civil Service Commission
 116
United States Civil War Centennial
 Commission   71
United States Commission on Civil
 Rights   45, 52, 85, 105, 116, 133
United States Commission on Civil
 Rights. Louisiana State Advisory
 Committee   96, 133
United States Commission on Civil
 Rights. Maryland Advisory Committee
 96
United States Commission on Civil
 Rights. Massachusetts Advisory
 Committee   52, 134
United States Commission on Civil
 Rights. Michigan States Advisory
 Committee   46
United States Commission on Civil
 Rights. Mississippi Advisory
 Committee   116
United States Commission on Civil
 Rights. North Carolina Advisory
 Committee   116
United States Commission on Civil
 Rights. South Dakota Advisory
 Committee   85
United States Commission on Civil
 Rights. State Advisory Committees
 Division   46
United States Committee for the First
 World Festival of Negro Arts   143
United States Committee on Fair
 Employment Practice   96
United States Community Relations
 Service   14
United States Congress. House.
 Committee on Education and
 Labor   134
United States Congress. Joint
 Committee on Economic Report   105
United States Congress. Senate.
 Committee on Education and
 Labor   96
United States Department of Justice   116
United States Department of Labor.
 Division of Negro Economics   76
United States Department of Labor.
 Office of Planning and Research   46

United States District Court. Mississippi
 (Sourthern District, Jackson Division)
 116
United States Equal Employment
 Opportunity Commission   96
United States Federal Board for
 Vocational Education   164
United States Government Contract
 Committee   96
United States Housing and Home
 Finance Agency   52, 96
United States Housing and Home
 Finance Agency. Intergroup
 Relations Service   52, 96
United States Housing and Home
 Finance Agency. Office of
 Program Policy   52, 96
United States Library of Congress   46
United States Library of Congress.
 Division of Bibliography   168
United States Library of Congress.
 Gertrude Clarke Whittall Poetry and
 Literature Fund   158
United States National Student
 Association   134
United States. National Youth
 Administration. Ohio   96
United States Office of Advisor on
 Negro Affairs   46
United States Office of Education   134
United States Office of Education. Equal
 Educational Opportunities Program   134
United States President's Committee on
 Civil Rights   116
United States President's Committee on
 Equal Employment Opportunity   96
United States President's Committee on
 Equality of Treatment and Opportunity
 in the Armed Forces   165
United States President's Committee on
 Government Employment Policy   116
United States Public Health Service   163
United States Public Housing
 Administration   52
United States Securities and Exchange
 Commission   105
United States Supreme Court   71, 76
United States Treasury Department   46
The United States Unmasked   13
United States Women's Bureau   46, 96
United States Works Progress Admini-
 stration. Georgia   96
United States Works Progress Admini-
 stration. Illinois   85
University Commission on Southern Race
 Questions   46

-V-

Valien, Preston
see (Masuoka, Jitsuichi)
Van Deusen, John George   46, 76
Van Dyke, Henry Jackson   71
Van Eurie, John H.   71
Van Rensselaer, Cortland   71
Van Vechten, Carl   174
Vance, Rupert Bayless   105

—194—

over. ———⟶

-W- Continued

Vander, Harry Joseph   117
Vander Zanden, James Wilfrid   14
Vandiver, Frank Everson   85
Vahanen, Kosti   141
Villard, Oswald Garrison   71
Vincent, Clark E.   111
Virginia. Commission on Constitutional
   Government   117
Visscher, William Lightfoot   158
Visser't Hoogt, William Adolph   7
Vogeli, V. Jacque   46
Von Hoffman, Nicholas   46, 174
Voorhees, Daniel W.   71
Voorhoeve, Jan   168
Vose, Clement E.   117

-W-

Wade, Richard C.   72
Wagandt, Charles Lewis   73
Wagley, Charles   14
Wakefield, Dan   46
Walker, Anne Kendrick   46
Walker, David   72
Walker, Helen Edith   46
Walker, Maggie L.   22
Walker, Margaret   158
Wallace, Mike   47
Ward, Samuel Ringgold   72
Waring, Robert   158
Warner, Robert Austin   85
Warner, Sam Bass   105
Warner, William Lloyd   85, 105, 117
Warren, Robert Penn   47
Warsoff, Louis A.   117
Washington, Booker Taliaferro   12, 35,
   43, 47, 72, 84, 85, 104, 121, 134, 170,
   173
Washington, Ella Mae (Barnett)   164
Washington, George   13
Washington, Joseph R.   7
Washington Afro-America   96
Washington (State) University. Institute
   of Labor Economics   96
Waskow, Arthur I.   47
Wassing, Rene S.   174
Waterman, Julian Seesel   90
Waters, Ethel   141
Watkins, Ann   158
Watkins, Sylvestre C.   159
Watson, Homer K.   111
Wattenberg, Ben   105
Wattenberg, William W.   105
Watters, Pat   117
Watts, Frederick Payne   47
Watts Writers' Workshop   159
Waynick, Capus M.   47
Weatherby, William J.   159
Weatherford, Willis Duke   47, 105, 174
Weaver, Richard Mervin   52, 174
Weaver, Robert Clifton   20, 47, 106
Webb, Richard Davis   72
Webster, Noah   72
Webster, Staten W.   134
Wedlock, Lunabelle   9
Weeden, Miss Howard   159
Weinberg, Kenneth G.   85

Weinberg, Meyer   134, 168
Weinstein, Allen   72
Weld, Theodore Dwight   71, 72
Welfare and Health Council of New York
   City. Research Department   111
Wells, Tom Henderson   72
Welsch, Erwin K.   168
Weltner, Charles Longstreet   47
Wesley, Charles Harris   7, 47, 74, 76,
   97, 135
West Virginia. Bureau of Negro Welfare
   and Statistics   97
West Virginia. Department of Education
   135
Westin, Alan F.   48
Weston, George M.   72

-X-

Xavier University, New Orleans, La.   50

-Y-

Yarbrough, William Henry   73
Yates, Elizabeth   50
Yates, William   106
Year   50
Yerby, Frank   160, 175
Young, Andrew Sturgeon Nash   90
Young, Donald Ramsey   14
Young, Marechal Neil Ellison   106
Young, Whitney Moore   50, 175
Young Women's Christian Associations.
   United States National Board. Depart-
   ment of Data and Trends   50

-Z-

Zakharova, Maria Nikolaevna   73
Ziegler, Benj(in Munn   14
Zilversmit, Arthur   73
Zimmermann, Arnold Albert   161
Zinn, Howard   50

TITLE INDEX

—211—